AROUND THE WORLD
IN A DUGOUT CANOE

AROUND THE WORLD IN A DUGOUT CANOE

THE UNTOLD STORY OF CAPTAIN
JOHN VOSS AND THE *TILIKUM*

JOHN M. MACFARLANE
AND LYNN J. SALMON

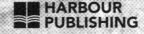

HARBOUR
PUBLISHING

Harbour Publishing Co. Ltd.
P.O. Box 219, Madeira Park, BC, V0N 2H0
www.harbourpublishing.com

Edited by Arlene Prunkl
Indexed by Rebecca Pruitt MacKenney
Dust jacket design by Anna Comfort O'Keeffe
Text design by Roger Handling
Printed and bound in Canada
Jacket credits: front bottom—Maritime Museum of British Columbia;
   back—Archives of the Canadian Rockies item lux_i_b1_13_17

Harbour Publishing acknowledges the support of the Canada Council for the Arts, which last year invested $153 million to bring the arts to Canadians throughout the country.

Nous remercions le Conseil des arts du Canada de son soutien. L'an dernier, le Conseil a investi 153 millions de dollars pour mettre de l'art dans la vie des Canadiennes et des Canadiens de tout le pays.

We also gratefully acknowledge financial support from the Government of Canada and from the Province of British Columbia through the BC Arts Council and the Book Publishing Tax Credit.

Library and Archives Canada Cataloguing in Publication

Title: Around the world in a dugout canoe : the untold story of Captain John Voss and the Tilikum / John M. MacFarlane and Lynn J. Salmon.
Names: MacFarlane, John M., author. | Salmon, Lynn J., 1965- author.
Description: Includes bibliographical references and index.
Identifiers: Canadiana (print) 20190146745 | Canadiana (ebook) 20190146796 | ISBN 9781550178791 (hardcover) | ISBN 9781550178807 (HTML)
Subjects: LCSH: Voss, John Claus, 1858-1922—Travel. | LCSH: Tilikum (Canoe) | LCSH: Voyages and travels. | LCSH: Canoes and canoeing. | LCSH: Adventure and adventurers.
Classification: LCC G420.V67 M33 2019 | DDC 910.4/5—dc23

Frontispiece: The *Tilikum* at Margate, England, at the end of her voyage.
John MacFarlane collection.

TABLE OF CONTENTS

PREFACE

I received an invitation to write an article on Captain John Voss from a Paris publishing house for a book they were preparing on the one hundred greatest seamen in world history. I was surprised to see Captain John Voss listed with the likes of Vasco da Gama, Captain James Cook and other familiar names. The publishers suggested that Voss was one of the greatest small craft sailors of all time. The four pages allocated to my section barely touched the topic, though. Trying to tell the story more fully initiated this book project. In reflection I thought I knew the story very well: departing in 1901 from Victoria, British Columbia, the ethnic German, Danish-born Canadian mariner Captain John C. Voss and his newspaperman friend Norman Kenny Luxton began their voyage across the Pacific in a converted First Nations cedar canoe called the *Tilikum*.

Their story is amazing and every bit as remarkable today as it was in 1901. It is a timeless story of conquering fear and doubt and facing enormous challenges with pluck, ingenuity and roll-up-your-sleeves determination.

But as I began to delve into the story, it quickly became apparent that it wasn't going to be possible to give a proper account of the voyage in just a few pages. To my great surprise, I found the actual story to be far different from the published accounts written by both Captain Voss and Norman Luxton. They not only contradict each other on many important points but both contain inaccurate information.

Much misinformation about Captain Voss and the voyage persists to this day, and is repeated and further distorted by writers on the Internet. With this in mind, I decided I was not willing to accept the "facts" passed from writer to writer without applying a more critical review to these sources. I embarked on a worldwide search for original archival material and accounts of the *Tilikum*'s voyage from contemporary press reports of the day and uncovered a wealth of new and fascinating information.

I have found Voss to be a complex personality. In his element as a sea captain, he handled drunken crew members and waterfront bullies with unreserved authority. When ashore, he charmed prime ministers, bishops, mayors and leading citizens while they feted him and awarded him honorary memberships in their yacht clubs. He was invited to lecture to academics at the meetings of geographical societies through the efforts of the explorer Ernest Shackleton. He was a popular orator and able to hold his own in sophisticated social settings. However, it had become standard practice to characterize him as a drunken boor and subsequent writers have unkindly and unfairly perpetuated this myth.

There is no doubt that Voss was a tough man, a master mariner who commanded a sailing ship and was mate in many others. He came from a working tradition that demanded immediate, unquestioning obedience. He was exactly the sort of man required for successful travel around the world in a dugout canoe—decisive, logical and a fearless, natural leader. But he would have been an unlikely friend—full of interesting and fascinating stories but not inclined to be anyone's chum.

The positive aspects of Voss's character are likely those that Norman Luxton saw as the most useful in a future partner. Considerably younger and seeking unbridled thrill from adventure, Luxton instead discovered there was little excitement to be had from the endless monotony of days at sea, and he suffered greatly from the strain of the terrible living conditions in the vessel. He was removed from anything familiar and completely reliant on Voss to navigate them to their destination.

Having produced the seed money for the project, Luxton no doubt felt he had equal ownership of both the boat and the voyage. But there can be only one captain and Luxton, unfamiliar with the concept of command, likely harboured resentment—and possibly fear—over what he considered to be the hostile and intolerable behaviour Voss demonstrated toward him.

Trapped aboard for fifty-eight days at sea with no landfall to provide some much-needed space, Luxton resigned from the voyage at the first opportunity. There appeared to be no animosity in their parting at the time; only years later did Luxton craft a narrative that was unkind to Voss and largely unsupported by the evidence left behind.

Over his three-and-a-half years in the *Tilikum*, Voss grew to have complete confidence in the vessel. He never seemed to doubt his sailing ability or the sturdiness of the craft to achieve his goal. In fact, he appears to have relished the many hardships and enjoyed most of the challenges thoroughly. It was only when faced with a life-threatening illness or losing the second of his mates overboard that he admitted to feeling defeated—but only briefly.

After he arrived in England, in 1904, Voss parted from the *Tilikum* to seek out new adventures. She was sold after a lengthy exhibit in London, her fame making her a desirable possession for a series of new owners. Her uniqueness as a West Coast Canadian dugout canoe was also what made her ill-suited for cruising in the Thames Estuary, and after several unsuccessful attempts to sail her as a yacht, she was eventually beached and forgotten. In 1930 the people of Victoria, BC, arranged to bring her home, where she was placed on continuous public display until 2015. Generations of Victorians, as well as mariners around the world, know the name *Tilikum*.

As I compared Voss's and Luxton's books, the discrepancies between fact and fiction regarding many aspects of the voyage became obvious. The two accounts simply do not correlate. Numerous unanswered questions remained after more than a hundred years of telling and retelling the story, fiction warped into fact in the minds of both men.

For example, why didn't Luxton publish his book? He owned a newspaper and the means to publish anything he wanted. Instead, years after his death in 1962, his daughter published a book, *Luxton's Pacific Crossing*, a version that contains accusations of drunkenness and murder against Voss that have been poisonously repeated by bloggers over the years without any substantiation.

As for Voss's published efforts, who was the mystery editor who really wrote the text of his book, *The Venturesome Voyages of Captain Voss*? Voss handwrote an original unpublished account in the salty language of a ship's captain but there is little evidence to support the idea that he wrote the polished words in the book that carries his name. It must have been crafted by a ghost writer or editor. Why did the long succession of editors and publishers never correct the glaring factual and spelling errors in the text? Why didn't Voss insist on having the true story published? It is much more interesting than the events recorded. Is it possible he never read the published version? What happened to the royalties from the book?

Voss died in 1922, broke and in obscurity. Yet over the years following the publication of the account of the voyage, he should have accumulated a small fortune generated from his many activities. Curiously, Voss was elected on two separate occasions as a Fellow of the Royal Geographical Society in London. Twice he didn't follow through by paying the fee to complete his appointment. Why would he have passed up an opportunity he had been seeking?

The enduring fact is that Captain John C. Voss is one of the greatest small-craft sailors of all time and established himself as an early pioneer of adventure cruising. This was truly the start of challenge-based, long-distance recreational sailing; Voss developed this activity for those who followed their own thirst for adventure on the sea. His simple charm, courage and showmanship have combined to create a character for the ages.

Today the *Tilikum*'s fate is uncertain—she is much loved but unwanted. In spite of people travelling long distances to see her, she is no longer on display but kept in a waterfront warehouse. In 1965 the Maritime Museum of British Columbia in Victoria became her steward, but as of 2019 the museum itself is now without a permanent venue to properly care for and display her. This situation could and should change in the future. My hope for a happy outcome on this issue is unbounded.

Captain Voss and his peculiar little vessel are symbols for our time, examples of what can be achieved by individuals or small groups of people with focus and determination. The *Tilikum* is a valuable treasure spanning almost two hundred years of BC history and culture and now owned by the people of British Columbia. As much as the Parliament buildings and the arctic ship *St. Roch*, she is an important part of our province's history and cultural heritage. The fact that the little vessel still exists in the collection of the Maritime Museum of British Columbia is a testimony to her endurance and the fascination her story still holds, also evidenced in the continuing publication of Voss's book.

The story of the man and the voyage is worth keeping alive for present and future generations of mariners of British Columbia—and the world.

—John M. MacFarlane

The writing of the story of this remarkable vessel and the many people associated with her over the years—those who sailed in her, wrote about her, transported her and saved her for future generations—was made possible by the preservation efforts of archives, museums and libraries found around the world. By pulling these scattered fragments together into one book, we were able to assemble a more complete picture of the *Tilikum* and her human companions. That the *Tilikum* story endures makes her journey from the rainforests of Vancouver Island to ports of the Southern Hemisphere and home again a truly outstanding universal achievement.

—Lynn J. Salmon

1

JOHN CLAUS VOSS

Johannes (John or Jack) Claus Voss was born on August 6, 1858, in Moordiek near Elmshorn, Schleswig-Holstein. He remained in Europe during his formative years but left home around the age of sixteen. Eventually he landed in Canada and made his way to the West Coast, settling on Vancouver Island. Once arrived, he always considered himself thoroughly Canadian though his background has caused historians no end of confusion.

At the time of his birth, Moordiek was part of Denmark. After 1866 the area fell under Prussian control and in 1871 a number of countries unified to become Germany. This accounts, in some measure, for the oft-repeated confusion as to Voss's birth nationality—in fact he was able to claim Danish, Prussian and German birthrights.[1] His parents were Heinrich and Abel Voss (née Gerdt).

His father, also born in Moordiek, ran a tavern in his home and later in life became the administrator of the estate at Horst that belonged to the Monastery Itzehoe.

Voss had three brothers and a sister—Heinrich, Hermann, Anna and Peter. Peter died in 1864 at the age of nine. On October 12, 1876, John's mother died. His father remarried on November 21, 1879, but had no other children.[2]

In all the photographs and existing portraits of Voss, the captain appears well dressed and is carrying himself in a confident and commanding fashion, usually wearing a traditional master's uniform, sporting gold braid and naval-style cap of the time. He was roughly five-foot-four in height, a heavy-set man yet quick in his actions. His face was benignly stern and businesslike, featuring a large bushy moustache.

**Captain John Claus Voss in the uniform of a merchant
service mate serving in sailing ships.**
Maritime Museum of British Columbia.

Norman Luxton described Captain Voss as "Taciturn, almost surly, he did not make a very favorable impression in some ways. But he had something about him, an aura of power and confidence that the man who is particularly good at a job demanding action usually develops. I felt sure that the Voss reputation for seamanship was not exaggerated."[3]

Voss's maritime career began in 1877, when he undertook seamanship training at Hamburg. He worked his way through the ranks and positions of the merchant service under sail. In 1884 he served as master in the Nova Scotia barque *C.W. Palmer* carrying nitrate from the west coast of South America. In April 1887 he served as second mate in the American ship *Top Gallant* (under a Captain Wickberg). In 1892, he sailed across the Pacific as chief mate in the ship *Prussia* (this was not the same vessel as the *Preussen*, a German steel-hulled, five-masted, ship-rigged windjammer built in 1902 often seen in marine history books).[4] Subsequent to that he held command of several vessels as a master, which entitled him to be called by the courtesy title of captain, though in all likelihood he had qualified as a master prior to this appointment.

In 1894 Voss was the master of a small schooner, the *Emerald*, with a mate named Svenson. Together they smuggled a cargo of opium into the United States, landing at Point Reyes, California. Their us connection included corrupt, senior, United States Customs officials who were arrested red-handed in San Francisco's Golden Gate Park. Voss and Svenson sailed back to Victoria, BC, apparently having been paid off. Victoria's *Daily Colonist*[5] reported that they then purchased a small restaurant called the Empire, on Johnson Street, to "launder" their money in a respectable business.

Voss was a man of many talents and not afraid to take calculated risks. In addition to his *Tilikum* voyage and other maritime pursuits, he engaged in numerous ventures, including running hotels, bars and stores, speculating in mines, and engaging with a German, George Haffner, on the *Xora* expedition to treasure hunt at Costa Rica's Cocos Island. A man who thirsted for fortune and excitement, Voss never shied away from a deliberate gamble. Things did not always end in his favour but that never kept him from embarking on the next great adventure.

In 1895 Voss was in partnership with John B. Perry as a hotel

The Queen's Hotel at the time of Voss's ownership.
Part of a letterhead in the collection of the Archives of the Canadian Rockies.

and restaurant keeper in the Queen's Hotel on Store Street, under the business name of Voss and Perry. In 1895 Voss took over Perry's interest.[6] In 1899 Voss also became proprietor of the Victoria Hotel, which was later renamed the Windsor Hotel.

Voss also owned the Chemainus Hotel—a fancy name for what was really just a boarding house—located next to a company store. Voss operated a butcher shop there (noted for its black sausage), which he was still running as late as March 22, 1901.[7]

Captain Voss was a tough character on the waterfront. It was rumoured that he took advantage of his bar's patrons to render clients senseless with drink and knockout drops to "crimp" (sell) them to shipmasters needing a crew. Also known as "shanghaiing," this disreputable practice would find the victims the next morning in the forecastle of a ship as unwilling crew members at sea on their way to some foreign port.[8]

Aside from all his ventures and adventures, Voss was also a family man, married to Dora, with whom he had a daughter (Caroline, or Carrie) and two sons (Harry and John). Mrs. Voss worked in the hotel business as the housekeeper of the Osborne Hotel in Crofton, BC, for some months in 1902. That same year she moved to Victoria to assume similar duties at the Dominion Hotel (now the Dominion Rocket condominiums on Yates Street).[9]

By all accounts, Captain Voss's wife and children adored him.

Their letters to him while he was away from home on his voyages
are filled with loving emotion and expressions of longing to see
him again.[10] Despite this, Dora hints at the lack of an income to
support the family, inferring she was left completely on her own
to cope financially. They did eventually separate sometime after
the voyage, but as late as 1903 Voss was still writing to Dora.
During the years of the *Tilikum* voyage, between 1901 and 1904,
Voss was unable or unwilling to send suitable funds, and it was
around this time that Dora moved to Portland, Oregon, with
their two sons, eventually joined by Caroline, who was attending St. Ann's Academy for schooling. The family later dispersed
throughout Washington, Oregon and Colorado.[11]

After the end of the *Tilikum* voyage in London in September of 1904, and throughout the rest of his life, Voss's business
affairs did not proceed smoothly. Rather, he battled with constant financial shortfalls. In October 1905 he announced plans
to host educational sea tours:

Capt. Voss' Cruise. Former Victorian of *Tilikum* Fame Organizing Cruise

Captain J.C. Voss FRGS is organizing through the agency of Law,
Youl & Co. a cruise in a schooner-rigged yacht of 50 tons, 52
feet long, to points in the Mediterranean, "off the beaten track".
Six passengers will be carried each being charged 150 pounds,
approximately $750, for the passage. The vessel will start from
Southampton this month and will proceed to the Azores or
Western Islands, thence to a Spanish port, and then will make an
itinerary of the unfrequented ports of the Mediterranean Sea,
especially those of the Grecian archipelago, Adriatic Sea, Asia
Minor, Egypt and North Africa. An endeavour will be made to
arrive at such places as Nice, Mentone, Monte Carlo, etc. during
the regatta season in this neighbourhood. Having exhausted the
interest of the Mediterranean it is then proposed to proceed to
Madeira and cruise among the beautiful islands of the Canary
Group. If time permits a visit to the Cape Verde Islands might be
planned and thence once more to the Azores, homeward bound
arriving at Southampton the beginning of May 1906. The actual

cruise however will be altered from time to time to suit the ideas
of the passengers provided that Captain Voss deemed such
alterations advisable. Should any or all of the passengers desire
to learn practical navigation and seamanship Capt. Voss under-
takes their tuition in these subjects, the passengers to provide
their own books and instruments.[12]

There is no indication that this cruise actually took place. It
may have simply been a marketing scheme that did not result in
any bookings.

In 1906 Voss joined the doomed Talbot Clifton Expedition
to Ecuador. John Talbot Clifton was an English landowner and
a compulsive traveller who explored many countries, including
Peru, where he joined Voss. Voss later recounted his activities for
the Victoria papers:

Leaving his now famous *Tilikum* at London where it was exhibited at Earl's Court, Capt. Voss and a companion went to Ecuador
on a mining venture but found a revolution in progress and fever
rampant, making it impossible for them to carry out their plans.
Speaking to a *Colonist* reporter Capt. Voss said "On January 18
I saw the battle in which the revolutionists overthrew the government. The revolutionary party, which had been planning the
outbreak, went to the police station in Guayaquil, where I was
staying. They rushed the place and grabbed the rifles from the
guardsmen, broke open the doors, looting a large amount of
rifles and ammunition. With the stolen arms they began shooting at random, up in the air and up and down the streets making
it unsafe for anyone to stay in the vicinity. Then when the revolutionists began to gather, led by a man named O'Farrell (he's not
an Irishman but a Native) they marched up to the government
barracks about eight or nine blocks away where they attacked
the troops. The troops met them and they had a fiercely fought
battle in the streets. They fought for two hours all being packed
pretty solid in the big street. The streets of Guayaquil are fairly
wide. It was bad fighting, for in the two hours that they fought no
less than 253 people were killed and over 300 were wounded.

Top: Members of the Talbot Clifton Expedition at Quito,
Ecuador, 1906 (from left): G.C. McKenzie, Mr. Plumley, George
Chance (expedition photographer), Captain J.C. Voss.
John MacFarlane collection.

Bottom: A baggage tag from the Talbot Clifton Expedition
of 1906 that was saved as a memento by George Chance
who pasted it in a first edition copy of Voss's book.
John MacFarlane collection.

The battle ended the revolution, for after the two hours fighting the government troops gave in and surrendered to the revolutionists. Next morning the government at Quito surrendered and the revolutionists were victorious."[13]

"I lectured a great deal and wrote various accounts of my voyage, appearing at the request of the Royal Geographical Society. The *Tilikum* was also exhibited at various places in England and at Earl's Court. The boat is now in London. I went from there to Ecuador on a mining venture, and have now returned home, having had a very long and adventurous voyage."[14]

Voss returned to Victoria via New York City about eighteen months later. He had struck up a friendship with optometrist George Chance of Dunedin, South Africa, who was the photographer on the Talbot Clifton Expedition. In testimony to that friendship formed fourteen years earlier, Chance purchased a first edition of Voss's book in Yokohama in 1920.

THE VOSS AWARD

The Voss Award, named in honour of Captain John Voss, was first awarded by the Joshua Slocum Society in 1904 or 1905 for "the most notable two-man transoceanic passage made during the past year." According to the society's website, "The first Voss Award was presented to Ian Major and Gordon Sillars for their crossing of the Atlantic in *Buttercup*, a unique yacht with a streamlined cockpit cover, servo rudder and wind vane self-steering gear, unstayed cantilever mast, and square sail."[15] The Joshua Slocum Society International was disbanded in July 2011. The society's mission was to honour all solo long-distance sailors who accomplished epic voyages.

After his return to Victoria, Voss married Mary Anna Croth of St. Louis, Missouri, on April 17, 1906. Little is known of her—perhaps Voss met her during his journey from New York back to Victoria—and tragically she died in Victoria later that year on August 30 at age forty-three.

Voss retained ownership of the St. Francis Hotel (also known as the Oriental Hotel) on lower Yates Street in Victoria, which he reopened in 1906 and then sold in 1907.

In November 1906 he purchased the *Ella G.*, a small wooden-hulled sealing schooner of 49 feet, with the participation of two Japanese partners.[16] From 1905 to 1907 Voss was the master of the *Jessie*, a 75-foot schooner-rigged freight vessel built to a yacht design that was operating in the North Pacific Ocean. In 1907 he took her from Victoria to the Columbia River. Voss recalled that she was a very fast sailor.

This was clearly a time of upheaval in Voss's life. In 1906 he was appointed "captain" of the first Dominion lifeboat. She was stationed initially in a navy boat shed at Esquimalt[17] near Victoria and outfitted with a Lyle gun (for shooting rescue lines) with funds raised by both the Life Boat and the Lifesaving Association of British Columbia.[18]

The lifeboat was intended to assist vessels that ran into difficulty at the entrance to Juan de Fuca Strait or found themselves off course and in peril along the harrowing western coastline of Vancouver Island. Propelled by oars, the lifeboat was to be towed to scenes of disaster requiring assistance by "any steamship that happens to be available." The federal department of Marine and Fisheries was responsible for installing the lifeboat, which was originally meant to be in service only during winter months.[19]

To garner public support while no doubt also appealing to his instructional nature Voss went to considerable effort to stage a "shipwreck" using a derelict in the Gorge waterway to demonstrate the skill required of the boat crew when attending a vessel in distress. The crowd was treated to a simulated rescue complete with sound signals, blue lights, the firing of the Lyle gun and deployment of a breeches buoy.[20]

Voss's tenure as coxswain did not last long. He was not happy with the rate of pay offered—between five and eight dollars a month while oarsmen received a mere three dollars a month—based on thirty cents an hour for two five-hour practise sessions a month.[21]

Ultimately the dispute over the pay rate forced Voss to resign less than five months after his appointment to the lifeboat. The unsuitable location of the lifeboat was also in question and the decision was made to move it to Bamfield Creek to be closer to where vessels might require its services.[22] Before she was relocated Voss oversaw the installation of spars at the Point Ellice Bridge.[23]

The *Quadra*, the new Victoria lifeboat, making its maiden
voyage in the harbour, under oars as it was originally intended.
Captain Voss is probably the coxswain at the tiller.
Image F-02889 courtesy of the Royal BC Museum and Archives.

Navigator of *Tilikum* Fame Will Have Charge of Lifeboat Crew—Captain Voss Appointed

Capt. J.C. Voss, who recently made application for the position of head of the life-saving crew to man the life-boat built
at Vancouver for the Department of Marine and Fisheries has
been given the appointment and will begin at once the selec-
tion of a crew subject to the ratification of the local agent of the
Department of Marine and Fisheries. Captain Voss' experience
at sea in all kinds of weather in small craft of less displacement
than the new boat with air tight compartments at either end
has well fitted him to take charge of the life-boat crew. Captain
Voss was at the head of two daring ventures, in one of which he
"out-Slocumed" Slocum. Seven years ago today, Captain Voss
and a local newspaperman, Percy McCord with Captain Haan of
the sealing schooner Jessie, left Victoria in the little sloop Xora

and voyaged to Cocos Island and Callao and thence returned to San Diego where they sold the craft. In May 1901, Capt. Voss and N.K. Luxton set out on a more daring enterprise, no less a venture, than to circumnavigate the world in a war-canoe. Capt. Voss bought an Indian canoe cut from a cedar tree in 1861, fitted the craft with a deck and rigged her with three masts carrying 35 yards of sails, and in this frail and tiny craft he navigated across the Pacific Ocean in all weathers from Victoria, to Fiji and thence to Australia making part of the voyage without comrade. After circumnavigating the coast of Australia he visited New Zealand, and then went across the Indian Ocean to South Africa, cruised on the African coast, visited St. Helena and the Azores and navigated by way of the Atlantic to London. Since his return to Victoria he engaged again for a time in the hotel business, being lessee of the St. Francis Hotel until he recently sold his interests in that hotel. Training exercises will be commenced as soon as Capt. Voss selects a life-saving crew.[24]

In 1908 Voss is reputed to have sailed the *Milton Stuart* from The Lizard, a peninsula in Cornwall, England, to Santa Rosalía, Mexico—a voyage of 125 days.[25] (The *Milton Stuart* was renamed as the *Thekla* in 1892, so there is inconsistency in this report.)

Voss left Victoria around 1908, moving to Japan where he operated for several years out of contact with his Canadian friends and associates. From 1909 to 1911 Voss was the owner and master of the Japanese sealing vessel *Chichijima Maru*,[26] a 75-foot sealing schooner based at Yokohama and operating along the coast of Siberia. In 1910 he sealed in company with Captain Victor Jacobsen (also in a Japanese-flagged vessel), a well-known sealer from Victoria. Voss recalled that the *Chichijima Maru* laid to excellently under a three-reefed foresail sheet well in and a close-reefed trysail, the sheet flat amidships, making seven points leeway.

In 1911 the new North Pacific Fur Sealing Convention, an international treaty that ended the decimating overhunt of fur seals that had occurred unchecked over previous decades, put Voss, along with every other sealer, out of business. A fund was established as a provision of the treaty to compensate the owners of sealing vessels. Voss used the money he received to finance his

A letter from Captain John Voss while at the Royal Queensland Yacht Club (Brisbane) to the Royal Geographical Society, July 25, 1914, explaining why he had not been able to pay the required dues to complete his fellowship in the society.

Tilikum *Fonds of the collection of the Maritime Museum of British Columbia.*

1912 voyage on the *Sea Queen* with two Yokohama yachtsmen, F. Stone and S.A. Vincent, as partners.[27]

After the voyage of the *Sea Queen*, Voss became a nautical celebrity in Japan. His book, *The Venturesome Voyages of Captain*

Voss, was published privately at Yokohama in 1913. In reviewing Voss's notes for the text, the first editor of his manuscript apparently undertook a rewrite so extensive that it changed the complexion of the story. Many details are omitted, distorting Voss's ordeals and accomplishments.

While he was sailing out of Japan, Voss was elected as a Fellow of the Royal Geographical Society in 1914, but he failed to pay the necessary fee to complete his election. The letter informing him of his election arrived in Japan while he was at sea and experiencing the devastating effects of a typhoon in the *Sea Queen*. He was renominated for a fellowship but again did not pay the fee after his election—perhaps this time he was voyaging in the *Tilikum II* and the First World War was starting. In any case, he was never officially registered on the list of members as a Fellow.[28]

Voss seemed to have given up the sea when in 1918 he moved to the town of Tracy, California, losing touch with many of his colleagues and spawning the popular but inaccurate story that he was lost at sea during his brief voyage in the *Sea Queen*.

His last years, from 1918 onward, were spent in Tracy, where he had relatives. He drove a Ford motorcar as a jitney and died, penniless, from pneumonia on February 27, 1922.[29]

An accurate though melancholy tribute describes Captain Voss: "Yet a mighty seaman he was, born hundreds of years after his time, delayed for some unaccountable reason in the Unknown."[30]

WAS CAPTAIN VOSS MAD?

Norman Luxton and other modern writers have made the assertion, without any evidence of support, that Voss was "mad." Obviously his goals were very unusual for the time. He was not part of the mainstream of society but rather an individualist—a survivor. All this tended to set him apart from the social norms of the day.

He was pragmatic, peculiar and human. He endured sleep deprivation, fear, hunger, thirst, sickness and inexperienced mates. These pressures no doubt accentuated any quirks in his personality and character. He bore these pressures yet was still able, at numerous ports of call, to be gregarious, extroverted, practical and supremely confident in his skill as a mariner, and he grew into the role of storyteller and showman.

Although Voss did not live by the norms of turn-of-the-

Left: The portrait of Captain J.C. Voss taken in Sydney, Australia, 1900, after his arrival from the trans-Pacific portion of the voyage.
Archives of the Canadian Rockies, Luxton Fonds Lux /I/B-4.

Right: The tombstone of Captain Voss in Tracy, California. He is buried in Section A, Row 3, Lot 19 of the Tracy Public Cemetery.
Tilikum *Fonds of the collection of the Maritime Museum of British Columbia courtesy of the Tracy Area Genealogical Society.*

twentieth-century society, he was not unlike a significant number of other mariners in the world with whom he would have easily related. He was popular with the press, the yachting community and the leaders of the day. He addressed the issue obliquely himself: "The cruises which I have made in small vessels not infrequently have been denounced as foolhardy undertakings. However, when I had given a short explanation such doubters would become silent. They soon understood that there is still much to be learned about breaking waves, and that there is no better way to study the safety of ocean travel than these solitary cruises on which all kinds of weather and sea dangers are met with and fought."[31]

2

TREASURE HUNTING IN THE *XORA*

DREAMS OF BURIED TREASURE

Voss's first recorded experience with small-craft sailing came in 1897. Seated in the lobby of the Queen's Hotel, he was approached by an American acquaintance, George Haffner, who brought him a letter from Jim Dempster, an old friend of Voss's. The letter recommended Haffner to Voss and asked him to consider a proposal. Haffner told Voss that he believed he knew the location of buried treasure on Cocos Island off the west coast of Central America. A hunt for this treasure—millions of dollars in gold—was to be the objective of a new expedition. Haffner wove a complex web involving the Royal Navy, the government of Costa Rica and Voss, with the hope of recovering the fortune reportedly buried on the shores of the island.

Sometime earlier, Dempster had chartered the *Aurora*, a sealing schooner, sailing her from Victoria to Cocos Island, located 325 miles from the Pacific coastline of Costa Rica. The *Aurora* expedition's crew had made several unsuccessful excavations searching for an alleged treasure. They became discouraged and ran short of provisions so they returned to Victoria, giving Haffner passage with them. Shortly after their departure, Dempster fell ill and Haffner volunteered to nurse him. On his deathbed, Dempster confided in Haffner about the treasure. Haffner then asked Dempster for the name of someone in Victoria who could be trusted to obtain a useful vessel and crew to return to Cocos. Dempster volunteered Voss's name and wrote the letter that Haffner presented two weeks later at the Queen's Hotel.

Voss was skeptical, asking why Haffner had not removed the treasure for himself while serving in the *Aurora*. Haffner indicated that he had known little of the intentions of the expedition and had taken a dislike to the master of the vessel, who revealed nothing to him. But Haffner possessed an official permit from the Costa Rican government to secure the treasure should it be found. He confided to Voss that he'd already been on the island for nine months before the arrival of the *Aurora* and thought he had located the treasure's position. (This should have been a clue to Voss that there was something amiss with the whole affair—why were they still searching for the treasure if Haffner knew where it was?)

Voss was offered one-third interest in whatever treasure was found on the island; the other two shares would be divided between the Costa Rican government and Haffner. Voss became intoxicated with the fantasy of becoming a millionaire, wholeheartedly becoming an active member of the syndicate.

A ROYAL NAVY CONNECTION

In preparation for the excursion, Voss secured a 100-ton schooner for the voyage. However, after all Voss's preparations, Haffner advised him that the large schooner was no longer necessary, explaining he had undertaken discussions with Admiral Henry St. Leger Bury Palliser of the Royal Navy. Palliser was the commander-in-chief of H.M. Ships and Vessels on the Pacific Station (carrying his flag in HMS *Imperieuse*) and had agreed to make the voyage to Cocos Island with Haffner to recover the treasure.

Initially it seemed unlikely to Voss that HMS *Imperieuse* would be assigned to such a scheme. However, the Royal Navy committed the ship to the search and a crestfallen Voss, who was no longer needed, resigned from the expedition. Voss then made a compact with himself to become more realistic in his goals. "I solemnly vowed that I would never again build castles in the air or have a good time and spend money in advance on the strength of a promise of good prospects, but would wait until I actually had the cash in hand."[32]

About three months later, Voss received a letter from Haffner:

Dear friend Voss,—I have to admit that I feel very sorry indeed at not having accepted your advice with regard to the hundred-ton schooner, and the advantage of your company for a trip to Cocos Island, but you know that at one time I felt confident that it was to my advantage to avail myself of the man-of-war.

Sorry to say the trip turned out a complete failure inasmuch as I should never have been able to make use of the treasure after having placed it aboard the *Imperieuse*.

During the voyage down, an officer one day questioned me about the treasure and asked me whether I knew what would be done with it after it was on board, and when I said, "It will be taken to Victoria," he replied that a treasure such as that, when shipped on a British man-of-war, would have to be handed over by the Admiral to the British Government, who would in turn hand it back to the rightful owner ...

After carefully considering the officer's statement I made up my mind that the treasure should not be shipped on board this vessel, in fact, that it should not be found with my help.

On our arrival at the island work was at once commenced under my leadership, and I kept the men at a safe distance from the correct spot.

Of course great excitement prevailed the whole time, and everybody expected to see gold bricks and diamonds flying about by the shovelful. But gradually disappointment set in when nothing came to light after all the hard labour.

The officer then told me that I must have made a mistake in

the location, which I reluctantly admitted remarking at the same time that I really did not know of any other place it might be. The good-natured officer looked at me with a smile and said that he would have to report my statement to the commander.

That night, when I went on board, I expected a severe calling down, but nothing happened.

However, the next morning we put to sea again and made for Acapulco, where I was put on shore, and where I am staying at the present time.

I certainly must give the British credit for being good-natured people, as they took it all in good part. If I had played that trick on Americans I am certain they would have first keelhauled me, then hanged me on the main yard and put twelve bullets through me, after which they would finally have drowned me to make sure that I was dead.

Now, dear friend, I herewith repeat the offer made a short while ago in Victoria. Come down here as quickly as possible with any kind of vessel you consider fit, and we will then sail to Cocos Island, secure the treasure, and put on board as much of it as the vessel will safely carry. If we cannot bring off the whole at once we will leave the rest on the island for a second voyage, as it will be quite safe where it lies now.

Kindly let me hear from you as soon as possible, c/o the G.P.O., Acapulco, Mexico. —Yours very truly, G. Haffner.[33]

Again Voss was gripped with excitement, though it was tempered by his earlier disappointment. But the prospect of becoming rich was again very alluring. His thin finances permitted consideration of a smaller craft and allowed him to make a purchase with fewer members of the syndicate.

PURCHASE OF THE *XORA*

Voss found the *Xora,* a us-built 10-ton sloop constructed of Oregon pine with a heavy wood centreboard. The *Xora* was built as an A-class sailing yacht for Commodore Hensall of the Elliott Bay Yacht Club in Seattle, Washington. In 1895 she was sold to a Victoria Yacht Club syndicate, which deemed her to be one of

The *Xora* "lying to the sea anchor and under riding sail."
Captain J.C. Voss, in the first edition (1913) of The Venturesome Voyages of Captain Voss.

the best-equipped and most handsomely fitted yachts in local waters. Her length was 35 feet with a beam of just 12 feet. The *Xora* wore a mainsail, gaff topsail and a jib. She could carry two hundred gallons of fresh water and food for three people for four months. She had a straight stem and overhanging counter stern. The *Xora* was named for a river (also spelled as *Xhora*) located in the Eastern Cape area of South Africa in what is now known as Transkei.

Voss admitted that at that time he would not have thought such a small craft could stand up to the stresses produced by a heavy gale at sea. His experience in the *Xora* was critical to the balance of his life afterward.

OFF TO A TREASURE ISLAND
The *Xora* departed from Victoria on July 6, 1898, bound for Cocos Island with a crew consisting of Captain Percy McCord (the master, known as Mac) from Alberta, Harry Voss (who may have been a brother to John Voss), Captain Voss and Captain Jack

Haan. They sailed from the James Bay Boathouse and cleared
the harbour as a yacht—to conceal their intentions. Haan and
Harry Voss found the conditions in the small vessel quite unlike
a larger ship and were uncomfortably close to being seasick. Mac
had a terrible time, so they anchored in Sooke Harbour until the
weather became more favourable.[34] They used this opportunity
to take on additional stores and rearrange their stowage.

On July 13 they set sail again and soon cleared Cape Flattery.
The heavy seas reminded Voss of several close calls he had had at
sea earlier in his career. Taking heavy seas on deck, either over
the bow or over the stern, is a serious business for a sailing craft.
It can prove fatal to a vessel and is to be avoided at all cost. Voss
considered the situation and decided that in such a small craft
they should heave to (meaning to slow or stop a boat by turning
sideways) and wait for better conditions.

He experimented with different courses to find one that
would allow them to lie comfortably in the large seas. He also
experimented with the aspect of the boat to the running seas, the
amount of canvas she was carrying, and then finally to deployment of a sea anchor that he fashioned—something he had never
used before. They did not have an anchor on board so he had to
make one himself.

He made the crude sea anchor by lashing together the main
boom crutch, some boards from the bunks (about six feet long)
and some canvas into a bundle. He fastened a forty-pound
anchor to the bundle and then attached a three-inch rope. All
this was dropped over the weather bow. They took in the staysail
and when the sea anchor was fifty yards away, they secured the
end of the line to the mast.

With the mainsheet hauled in flat he expected the boat to
swing head to wind, but this was not what happened. The vessel
swung almost broadside against the wind and sea, nearly causing
them to turn turtle. They lowered the mainsail, which helped, but
they were still shipping water. Voss then tried something more
radical and hoisted a small sail aft—but without a mizzen-mast
he bent on the tack of the storm staysail to the end of the main
boom, unhooked the main peak halyard, bent on the head of the
staysail to it and hauled the sheet forward instead of aft. The *Xora*
responded immediately, swinging head to wind and now riding

comfortably on the sea anchor. Under this rig the *Xora* drifted between one knot and three-quarters of a knot per hour. This continued for two days, with the little vessel handling the seas easily until the gale abated.

Sailing again, they passed Guadalupe Island on July 25. Guadalupe Island, or Isla Guadalupe, is a volcanic island located 150 miles off the west coast of Mexico's Baja California peninsula. The coastline is rugged and inhospitable. They were able to shoot a goat on shore, providing the crew with fresh meat for several days. They also harvested sea turtles for food. Arriving at San Blas, they were boarded by port authorities who warned them the weather was dangerous and they should take their boat up the San Blas River for safety.

While there they learned that George Haffner had died of fever in Acapulco. In spite of this, they decided to press on; Voss was sure he could visualize from memory the location of the treasure, marked with an *X* on Haffner's chart. They arrived at Cocos Island on September 7, 1898. The next day they anchored in Chatham Bay.

COCOS ISLAND

Voss and Mac rowed the dinghy into Wafer Bay to be closer to the treasure site. There they saw a small house from which a tall, thin man with a two-foot-long beard emerged with a small, pleasant-looking woman. When they got close enough the man introduced himself as August Gissler, the governor.

Gissler was a German-born adventurer and treasure hunter. The Costa Rican government had appointed him as governor to act as a caretaker of Cocos Island. In over twenty years there, Gissler is said to have never found more than six gold coins, despite diligent searching. When Voss and Mac explained that they were treasure hunters, Mrs. Gissler told them gold bricks were scarce on the island. The Gisslers proved to be fine hosts and the crew of the *Xora* were pleasant guests.

Gissler persuaded Voss to move the *Xora* around to Wafer Bay and to moor to the trees near the shore, but on crossing the bar they hit a rock and the boat filled rapidly with water. They pulled their stores, ballast and gear onto shore. Despite her lightened load, the *Xora* remained stuck on the rock and full of water.

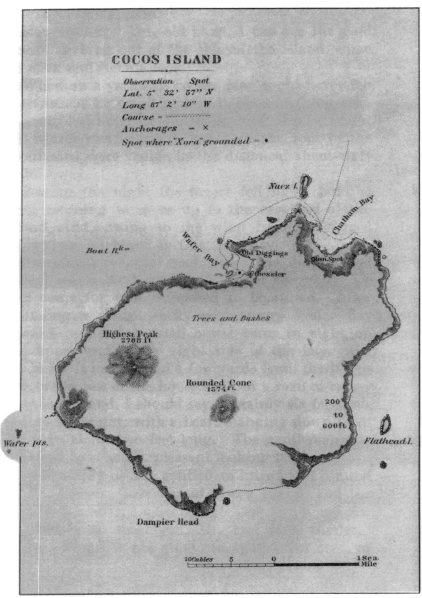

Designed by W.G.Vied, Tôkyô

A contemporary sketch map of Cocos Island.

W.G. Vied, in the first edition (1913) of The Venturesome Voyages of Captain Voss.

The situation was serious but Voss was determined to solve the problem.

They cut trees to use as levers at low tide when the shore would be dry. It took two hours to heave her off the rock. They then set about repairing the bottom. She was once again afloat and moored beside Gissler's house. Gissler promised to help them provision from the natural bounty of the island.

Their main goal, however, was to locate the treasure. Voss theorized that the treasure, which must be of massive weight, had been carried near to shore in a ship's boat and then dumped overboard on the sandspit at high tide. At low tide the sandspit was exposed, which would have allowed the crew to bury it deep in the sand. Gissler had indicated that the spit had never been searched—after all, it was underwater for six hours a day.

Haan and Voss took the dinghy toward shore, but a boiling surf and inexperience landing a boat on a beach caused the dinghy to capsize, dumping both men into the water. Voss made for the beach while Haan, a strong swimmer, pulled the dinghy back to the *Xora*.

That night Mac did not return from an exploration into the centre of the island. He did not respond to shots fired, leading Gissler to speculate he had been attacked by wild boars. Gissler set out in a search the next morning. He shortly returned with Mac, who announced he had shot several wild boars.

Several weeks passed with no sign of treasure, and the crew grew tired of fishing and hunting. The time had come to put to sea. They sailed the *Xora* light over the bar and placed the ballast and stores on board once she was anchored in deep water. Many of their stores had been spoiled by the accident on their arrival, and they did not have enough to take them home. They decided to sail down to Guayaquil, Ecuador, to pick up enough provisions for the journey back to Victoria. They left Cocos Island on September 22 without so much as a single piece of gold. In fact, of the over three hundred treasure expeditions that have searched Cocos Island over the years, none are known to have ever found any treasure.

Arriving in Guayaquil harbour five days later, they dropped anchor but were advised to avoid the city of Guayaquil due to an outbreak of fever there. They pressed on to Callao, Peru, which they entered on October 11. At Callao, Voss departed for Panama.

There was no canal at that time so he travelled by rail across the Isthmus of Panama. At Panama, he took a steamer for New York and carried on to Victoria by CPR train.

The *Xora* travelled north under Percy McCord as master. He departed at Mexico and left the others to make their own way to Victoria. The story and fate of the *Xora* grows cold at this point, and it is presumed that she was sold—but there was a rumour she sailed again in 1900 from Victoria for Paris with Captain Jack Haan and Harry Voss.[35]

This treasure-hunting cruise in the small *Xora* set the stage for Voss to accept the challenge of sailing around the world in a 38-foot dugout canoe. The Cocos Island experience inspired the confidence he had to possess to embark on such a journey. The lessons he learned about sailing small craft over great distances, in heavy-weather conditions, would later prove invaluable for Voss as he ventured out over the great oceans in the *Tilikum*.

3

NORMAN KENNY LUXTON

Voss's mate for the start of the voyage in the *Tilikum* was Norman Kenny Luxton. Luxton was born at Upper Fort Garry, Manitoba, in 1876. His father, W.F. Luxton, along with John A. Kenny (a close family friend and the source of Norman's middle name), founded the *Manitoba Free Press* (later the *Winnipeg Free Press*) in 1872,[36] just two years before Manitoba joined Confederation.

Norman Luxton grew up with distaste for the structured learning that school provided but was by no means lacking in curiosity about the natural world around him. He liked the outdoors and spent many summers fishing and canoeing, especially enjoying the time he spent with naturalist George Grieve, who was very influential in Luxton's life, introducing him to taxidermy

Portrait of Norman Kenny Luxton after his arrival in Sydney, Australia.
Adelaide Photo Co., Sydney, Australia, in the collection of the Archives of the Canadian Rockies, Luxton Fonds Lux/I/B-4.

and his "love of nature."[37] (George Grieve was a noted Winnipeg taxidermist with a shop on Main Street along with many other taxidermists. Winnipeggers eagerly attended these shops and exhibitions because, until 1932, the city had no permanent public museum to exhibit natural history specimens.) In 1892, at the age of sixteen, Luxton embarked on a series of travels to satisfy his love of adventure. By his own admission he found life unfulfilling, always trying to quell a hunger by seeking out new, exciting endeavours. He took a post as an apprentice clerk for the Indian Agency at Rat Portage (now Kenora), Ontario, but did not find the work to his liking despite some exploits with canoes and guarding money shipments.[38] It was mostly dull with little in the way of future prospects. By seventeen, he had made up his mind to head west.

Luxton was described by his daughter as "a slight man, five-foot-seven, both wiry and resilient. His step was springy, his reactions quick, his temper uncertain, his blue eyes piercing yet always with laughter in them. His two-inch-brimmed round Stetson hats, specially made for him, were so much a part of him they became symbolic."[39] Luxton staked his future on tales of wealth that he heard. "All my life I had been hearing about the Cariboo gold fields and thought I might be one of the lucky ones. I was not so."[40] Although British Columbia's Cariboo Gold Rush had begun in 1860 and reached its peak by 1865, subsequent "rushes" were eagerly reported. In 1886 the discovery of gold at Fortymile River in the Yukon triggered an influx of miners, and in 1897 Dawson City became ground zero for the largest invasion of gold-seekers from all over the world. In 1898 gold was discovered at Nome, Alaska, taking many of the hard-luck cases away from the Yukon, and by 1899 the Dawson City dream had ended. But the stories of instant wealth and easy money had lured tens of thousands of prospectors to the gold fields.[41] Young and fit, Luxton headed west with big ideas of "striking it rich," only to find harsh work in even harsher conditions. He did not spend much time in his pursuit of gold, retreating to Calgary and finding work with the *Calgary Herald* newspaper.

His first job for the paper was to collect overdue payments, testing his mettle to outwit tough characters owing substantial debts to the paper. Over the next eight years, he filled a variety of newspaper jobs as needed: reporter, typesetter, manager, delivery boy and book salesman.

By 1900 Norman had left Calgary for Vancouver, where he briefly published a weekly gossip sheet called *Town Topic*,[42] a joint venture with Frank Burd. The two men wrote, edited and printed the editions for sale, cranked out on an old hand press. Although marginally successful, the paper eventually failed and Luxton joined the ranks of reporters at the *Vancouver News Advertiser*.

Luxton's early timeline in the west becomes murky. He was in Vancouver and also spent time in Victoria. He also claims to have spent (at least partially) two seasons with seal hunters in the Bering Sea. He makes a bold assertion about this, referencing a certification of first mate, having qualified under "Captain Anderson of the sealing fleet to Bering Sea during the 1898–1899 and 1900 [seasons]."[43]

This perceived lack of seagoing credentials was always a thorn in Luxton's side; he was often dismissed as having no prior experience at sea. And in fact no proof of this certificate exists. There is little doubt, had he gone to the sealing grounds to work, that he would have had countless vivid stories to share. The absence of such recorded adventures is telling. In his handwritten notes he contrarily indicates that he had done one voyage: "My experience at sea was of course limited … a time or two around Vancouver Island, with many short trips, and two trips into Bering Sea, were all I had ever had in sailing boats."[44] It's more likely that Luxton, through his association with friends who were sealers, hopped a ride to the grounds for the purpose of reporting on the hunt and years later would warp this into a full qualification.[45]

In Victoria, Luxton worked with the editorial staff of the newspaper *In Black and White*, self-described as "one of Victoria's most newsy publications." He found this work as uninspiring as any of his newspaper jobs before, still searching for that elusive "something" to take him out of his boring existence and into a life of meaning. His association and friendship with Voss and the subsequent planning of their world voyage looked like a hopeful solution to his restlessness.

Luxton did not directly take part in preparing the *Tilikum*. But once the dugout canoe was fitted out and brought around to Oak Bay, from where the voyage was to launch, he and his brother George took the *Tilikum* on a brief sail into Juan de Fuca Strait. George was mightily impressed with the craft, writing to their mother to praise the canoe's seaworthiness: "Norm's *Tilikum*, she sails like a fish … She stands rough weather fine … It was just … exhilarating!"[46]

Departure the next day, May 21, 1901, signalled the beginning of Luxton and Voss's extraordinary odyssey in the sturdy canoe. For the next two months they endured storms, unvaried rations

and the ever-present threats of thirst, hallucinations and, perhaps most challenging, each other. That Luxton did not enjoy his
time at sea is apparent. Confined to a small space in constantly
changing weather conditions without enough experience for him
to make his own evaluations of how safe he was, he became worn
down by the grind of the ceaselessly boring routine until he had
privately decided that once they reached a proper landing place
he would take a break from the *Tilikum* and head to Sydney, Australia, via steamer.[47]

Luxton originally intended to find a mate to temporarily
replace him while keeping his share in the voyage. But he began
to have doubts of ever returning to the *Tilikum* after he took a
room in a private hotel in Manly, near Sydney, suffering from
coral poisoning in his feet.

Luxton sought medical treatment from a hospital in Sydney
when he arrived by steamer. In letters he wrote home he stated,
"I have made up my mind that when I get to Sydney that will
be the last time I get into that canoe. If we can push through
to England I [will] go by a liner and ship a man in my place. But
no more small boats for me."[48] Having firmly decided to leave
the venture all together, Luxton implored Voss to do the same.
It likely rankled Luxton that Voss was determined to keep going.
But Luxton's thirst for this kind of excitement had waned. He
never boarded the *Tilikum* again.

After he parted with Voss in Australia, Luxton joined the
Canadian Australian Steamship Company as an able seaman.
He served in the *Aorangi*, working his passage home on a voyage
from Wellington to Suva, Honolulu and Vancouver. He arrived
back in Victoria on March 21, 1902.[49]

Being a newspaperman and eager to make some money for his
efforts, Luxton reported immediately to the local *Daily Colonist*,
which stated vaguely that, "he [Luxton] has many strange incidents to tell of the *Tilikum*'s daring voyage." A longer narrative
was published four days later: "The Voyage of the *Tilikum*: Mr.
Luxton Tells of the Unique Voyage of the Novel Craft."[50]

Following the voyage, Luxton went to Banff to recuperate.
He was exhausted and needed to heal from the stresses of the
voyage and the coral poisoning. In 1904 he married Georgina
McDougall; incidentally, she is reputed to have been the first

non-Indigenous child born in what became Alberta. Her family background included traders and ranchers; she fit well with Luxton and his dreams for their life in Banff.

Banff was full of opportunities for a man who loved the outdoors, and Luxton put great effort into promoting Banff as "Fifty Switzerlands in One" as well as "the Playground of the Canadian Rockies."[51] He collected, traded and sold First Nations artifacts. He opened a trading post called The Sign of the Goat and shipped taxidermy specimens to museums and private buyers around the world.

He was a shrewd businessman and journalist and a relentless self-promoter. Among his many business ventures, he operated the Lux Theatre, the King Edward Hotel, several restaurants and a wood-burning, steam-powered tour boat on Lake Minnewanka in Banff National Park. He owned several houses, some of which he operated as rooming houses. His love of journalism inspired his purchase of the *Crag and Canyon* newspaper in 1902; he ran this paper until 1951, contributing editorials whenever he had something on his mind. Passionate about nature and conservation, he suggested the purchase of bison from Montana to restore the herds to Canada. Near the end of his life, he was able to open the Luxton Museum to feature his sizeable collection of artifacts.[52]

In the midst of the stupendous beauty of the Rockies, over the winter months of 1927 and into 1928, Luxton finally found time to write a manuscript covering his portion of the *Tilikum*'s journey. Those fifty-eight days at sea with Voss had played a major role in his life, seemingly striking the wanderlust from his soul and allowing him to settle in Banff, marry and build his empire of tourist businesses. He had read Voss's account and made numerous "corrections" and notes in his personal copy, but, as for his own account, he stated clearly, "It won't be published. I wrote this for my daughter. I wanted her to have this record."[53]

With this in mind, Luxton's manuscript opens as follows: "Those who read must remember that more than a quarter of a century had passed before I commenced to put my thoughts in writing ... and also it is an answer to a published book called *The Venturesome Voyages of Captain Voss*."[54]

Over the years, despite being familiar with the workings of a press and able to publish his own newspaper, Luxton did not publish his own typed and bound account. Voss, in contrast, began preparations to publish his account as early as 1904, corresponding with Luxton about his plan, telling Luxton in a letter that he "... got a first class man wrighting [sic] it up."[55] It took until 1913 for Voss to get his story printed.

After Luxton's death in 1962, it was another nine years before a publisher approached Luxton's daughter Eleanor about publishing her father's manuscript. This man, unnamed in the publication, recalled an encounter with Luxton from the 1930s while serving as an RCMP constable in Banff. He never forgot that Luxton had written his account of the voyage. Persuading Eleanor to edit the manuscript, it was published in answer to Voss's popular account.

Eleanor, a graduate in mechanical engineering with a fulfilling career working on locomotive designs for the CPR in Montreal, had a keen interest in Canadian history. She correctly identified her father as having made a curious contribution to the early years of a burgeoning country. That the manuscript is mired with unsubstantiated claims can only be the fault of a man who openly declared that his story was never to be published and that his "notes are more like half-forgotten dreams than actual happenings."

A century later, out of context, with the principal players in the *Tilikum* story long gone, it is best to leave the last word with Luxton regarding his feelings about Voss and the perilous voyage they undertook: "'Would you repeat the trip again?' I am often asked. Quite candidly and truly no, but not for anything would I have missed it. Under different circumstances, with a larger boat, the voyage would have been divine, and in such a boat if Voss were master, I would not have hesitated to go where the winds and storms might drive."[56]

Norman Luxton was buried in his beloved town of Banff, Alberta, in October 1962.

4

"OUT-SLOCUMING" JOSHUA SLOCUM

ORIGINS OF THE VOYAGE

In late 1900 Norman Luxton felt much like Herman Melville's Ishmael with "a damp drizzly November" in his soul as he sat in the dingy second-floor office of the struggling gossip sheet *In Black and White* on lower Johnson Street in Victoria. The winter days were grey and short, and Luxton's chilly walk home left him plenty of time to evaluate his life and daydream of exotic adventure. Adding to his depression, his was not at all what he had imagined the life of a young journalist would be, and he felt a great need for change. He recalled, "I was looking for what I did not know, but it was a great something that I knew I was without."[57]

A few blocks away, Captain John Voss, the seasoned master mariner from the age of sailing ships, sat in the lobby of the Oriental Hotel, one of a number of hotels and restaurants that he owned and ran. But he was foremost a deep-sea sailor at heart and he missed the adventure of life under sail. His latest hotel venture was not thriving and he was considering closing it and going back to sea.

In a perfect collision of two people desiring big-thrill adventure, Luxton and Voss, who had known each other through the small Victoria business scene for two years and had shared a drink on occasion, devised a plan to tackle a round-the-world voyage, mirroring the then-popular American adventurist Joshua Slocum and his successful—and hugely profitable—exploits on board a small oyster boat. Slocum had taken three years to circumnavigate the world single-handed in his boat, *Spray*, a 36-foot, 9-inch oyster sloop that he had rebuilt. It was the first voyage of its kind. The *Spray* was lost with Captain Slocum aboard sometime on or after November 14, 1909, after he had sailed from Vineyard Haven, Massachusetts, bound for South America.

Luxton recalled the inception of the idea this way: "Captain Voss and I had been friends for two years. I heard many yarns from him." He added, "Of course I realized that the venture would need more than an idea and ambition for success. It required experience at the helm, and Voss seemed the very man."[58] Voss recalled that, "I had been acquainted with Mr. Luxton for some time, and knew him to be a temperate man, full of ambition, and his word as good as his bond. I accepted his proposal."[59]

Luxton considered buying an 80-ton sealing schooner for $10 per ton for their massive undertaking, but Voss talked him out of it. A sealer was much too commonplace and lacking in challenge for Voss. If he was going to sail around the world, he was going to do it in something that no one else had thought of before. "A sealer?" he exclaimed disgustedly. "Pshaw, tat's too easy."[60]

Together they hatched the idea of a novel voyage that would make a circumnavigation in a vessel smaller than the *Spray*. Luxton wrote later that Voss "accosted me with 'Say, Luxton, I have something to submit to you for your consideration.' We met in the Garrick's Head Inn, in Victoria, over a steaming bowl of soup. He suggested we set sail in a dugout canoe and sail to islands around the world. An Indian canoe, tat's what."[61]

Luxton accepted the offer the next day and proposed that they could recreate Joshua Slocum's voyage, write about it and outdo it—making them famous and perhaps also rich. Later Luxton repeatedly stated that rumours of a $5,000 wager as the motivation for the voyage were inaccurate and were, in fact, fabricated. He wrote, "The bet is a story of Captain Voss, as he says it gives some reason for our trip and perhaps it will help us in business. Though honestly I am not much struck with it myself."[62]

In an interview in Sydney, Australia, Luxton and Voss offered a different version:

How the venture came about is a matter of interest. At a dinner one evening in Minnesota, U.S.A., at which the company was composed largely of Canadians and Americans, the triumph of the Yankees in having sailed the smallest vessel around the globe (the *Spray*, which came here with Captain Slocum) was referred to with pride. "A Canadian could go one better," was remarked by someone, and Mr. Luxton, a Canadian journalist, who happened to be present, was mentioned as the man to demonstrate the belief. A wager of 5,000 dollars a side resulted between the Americans and Canadians, the stipulations being that the boat was to be smaller than Captain Slocum's *Spray*, and that after, once leaving Vancouver the voyagers were not to draw on home for further supplies, but were to make their own way during the voyage. Mr. Luxton was joined in the venture by Captain J.C. Voss.[63]

SLOCUM'S INFLUENCES ON LUXTON AND VOSS

Joshua Slocum, though born in Nova Scotia, moved to the United States as a young man and fully embraced being an American. He rebuilt a derelict sloop, the *Spray*, in a field at Fairhaven, Massachusetts, over thirteen months between early 1893 and 1894. Between April 24, 1895, and June 27, 1898, Slocum, alone aboard the *Spray*, crossed the Atlantic twice (to Gibraltar and back to South America), negotiated the Strait of Magellan, and crossed the Pacific. He called at ports in Australia and South Africa before crossing the Atlantic for the third time to return to Massachusetts after an incredible solo journey of forty-six thousand miles.

On his return, the popular and articulate Slocum gave lectures and lantern slide shows to well-filled halls. His journal was first published in instalments in *The Century Magazine* before being issued in book form in 1900. The book was lavishly illustrated. He wrote a number of subsequent books, though none approached the popularity of *Sailing Alone Around the World*.

The significance of this achievement cannot be overstated. Slocum accomplished what no one had ever done before—all who came after him must stand on his shoulders, having benefited from his experiences. It is natural that his achievements would motivate others in an effort to best him—or to capitalize on the intense interest from the public, whose bonfire he had lit. Throughout the voyage of the *Tilikum*, the popular press continually drew comparisons to the *Spray*.[64]

Slocum was a pioneer in the realm of circumnavigation in an age before the development and production of accurate charts, electronic navigation aids or a uniform system of identifying marine hazards. For instance, as a solo navigator, there was no relief for him at the helm when he needed rest. As a result, he devised a system of lashing the wheel into what a later era might call a kind of mechanical autopilot. He took pride in the fact that the *Spray* had sailed two thousand miles west across the Pacific without his once touching the helm. Any improvements and innovations aboard the *Spray* were an inspiration born of necessity.

Voss and Luxton would learn the hard way what their vessel's limitations would be and how to overcome them. They each spent a considerable time apart and alone while on duty in the cockpit. Although there were two of them in the crew of the boat, the duty routine had one man on watch while the other rested. These conditions closely resembled those experienced by a solo navigator.

EARLY OCEANIC YACHT CRUISING

In addition to Joshua Slocum, two other early oceanic yacht voyagers were Alfred Johnson, in an 1876 trans-Atlantic solo crossing, and Bernard Gilboy, in an 1882–83 solo Pacific voyage from San Francisco most of the way to Australia. Beyond those precedents, there was very little transoceanic yacht cruising before the voyage of the *Tilikum*. Small-boat voyages across the Pacific were unheard of—and Voss certainly had little outside information to which to refer. He had to translate his bigger sailing ship experiences and scale them down to a small yacht.

After the voyage of the *Tilikum*, there was an increase in "competitive"

circumnavigation. The publication of books and newspaper articles undoubtedly
inspired others to pick up where the *Tilikum* had left off. The most noteworthy of this
group include:

- Harry Pidgeon's (American) 1921–25 solo circumnavigation via the Panama Canal
  in the 34-foot yawl *Islander* and again, with a part-time crew, in 1932–37
- Alain Gerbault's (French) 1923–29 solo circumnavigation via the Panama Canal in
  Firecrest
- Edward Miles's (American) 1928–32 solo circumnavigation in two different schooners
- Louis Bernicot's (French) 1936–38 circumnavigation via the Strait of Magellan in
  the 41-foot *Anahita*
- Vito Dumas's (Argentine) 1942–43 single-handed circumnavigation of the south-
  ern oceans, including the first single-handed passage of all three great capes in
  the ketch *Lehg II*
- John Guzzwell's (British) 1955–59 Victoria-to-Victoria solo circumnavigation in
  the *Trekka*
- John Hughes's (Canadian) 1986–87 voyage aboard the *Joseph Young*, which was
  the first Canadian solo circumnavigation

THE *TILIKUM*, A FIRST NATIONS DUGOUT CANOE

The ocean-going canoes of the Nuu-chah-nulth people on the
west coast of Vancouver Island represent one of the most significant developments in First Nations culture. These large vessels
not only transported people and trade goods over long distances
and through all sea conditions but also enabled the pelagic pursuit of whales, sea lions, seals and sharks.

The *Tilikum* likely began life as a whaling canoe. Her dimensions of 38 feet place her near the typical 40-foot lengths of these
ocean-going craft. Larger canoes, built for transporting families and
trade goods, sometimes reached lengths of an astounding 60 feet.

These large canoes were carved from single cedar trees, either
deliberately felled or found on the ground after storms in the
temperate rainforests that crowd the coastline of Vancouver
Island. The massive tree trunks—some more than six feet in
diameter—were carved and hollowed without the use of written
plans or instructions. Canoe carvers were highly respected in
Nuu-chah-nulth culture and learned how to gouge canoes from

solid tree trunks with knowledge acquired and passed down through generations.

Typically, a canoe-length log was cut from the tree trunk. A suitable log for a large canoe required a butt end of at least six feet. Trees were selected for their straight grain, with no twists in the trunk, and their proximity to water for launching.

The massive logs were hollowed and shaped using adzes, mallets and wedges. To start, the basic shape of the canoe was cut out with adzes, chopping the excess wood away to roughly form the bow and stern. The interior wood was excavated using all three tools, splitting large chunks of wood from the solid log. In the refinement stages, carving tools replaced the heavier, less accurate adzes and mallets, scraping out the body of the canoe to an exact thickness. Some canoe hulls show evidence of the use of a clever system to determine the thickness of the sides of the canoe. Small holes were drilled in the wood, which gave accurate indications of whether more wood needed to be removed. When carvers were finished, they simply knocked in small wooden plugs to fill the holes.

The carving process for large canoes took two summers to complete. The initial blank of the canoe would be left to cure over the winter and the following spring the build would continue.

An unfinished canoe blank as seen in 1995, in the bush on Haida Gwaii, reported to have lain untouched since it was started about thirty years earlier.

Lynn J. Salmon photograph.

The final job, after attaching the extended bow and stern pieces, was to widen the canoe. This was not easily achieved but vital to maintaining the seaworthiness of the canoe.

Canoes of forty feet were generally six feet wide, a ratio roughly of one foot of beam for every eight feet of length. To achieve this beam, the canoe was filled with water and fire-heated rocks were placed inside with a cover of cedar mats to capture the steam generated. This method pushed the sides of the canoe outward as well as lifting the prow and aft sections, lending longitudinal strength to the hull. The functional and decorative fore and aft pieces were carved separately and added last along with the thwarts and seating. As a final hardening measure, and to draw the naturally protective oils to the surface, the outer hull was exposed to fire to char the exterior.[65]

The resulting vessel was an ocean-capable paddling craft with a flattish bottom and flaring sides, high in the ends for lift and lower amidships for paddling, and with a deeply immersed forefoot to minimize pounding. Some of these canoes carried a one- or two-masted spritsail rig.[66]

HOW VOSS AND LUXTON OBTAINED THE CANOE

The origin of the dugout canoe from which the *Tilikum* is fashioned is now shrouded in mystery and contradictions. No one knows, with any certainty, which of the numerous plausible versions is correct. Voss presents a straightforward account in the published version of his book:

> ... while I was looking round about the east coast of Vancouver Island, where there are boats of all sizes and build, I came across an Indian village where I saw a fairly good looking canoe lying on the beach. It struck me at once that if we could make our proposed voyage in an Indian canoe we would not alone make a world's record for the smallest vessel but also the only canoe that had ever circumnavigated the globe. I at once proceeded to examine and take dimensions of the canoe, and soon satisfied myself that she was solid, and also large enough to hold the provisions and other articles we would have to carry on our cruise. While I was looking over the canoe an old Indian came along and

gave me to understand, in very broken English, that he was the owner of the vessel and was willing to sell her. He presented me with a human skull, which he claimed was that of his father, who had built the canoe fifty years earlier.[67]

Norman Luxton corroborated this account with some interesting variations:

Only by hard talking and the display of eighty silver dollars was Captain Voss able to secure the relic. Why? Because it was in this hundred-year-old cedar tree that Captain John Voss and Norman Kenny Luxton, newspaperman (myself), had decided by cold reasoning and sea-knowledge that we would cross the Pacific Ocean.[68]

Interestingly, there is no mention by either Voss or Luxton that the *Tilikum* was decorated in any way. In fact, Luxton claims to have carved the figurehead himself.

Naval architect Tad Roberts observes:

It is not too surprising that Captain John C. Voss, when looking for a small vessel able of making ocean voyages, was attracted to the type. Voss had doubtlessly seen the West Coast canoes in action during his travels. The hunters engaged by him sometimes brought their dugout canoes with them for use in the pelagic operations in the north. He would also have seen them at the ports of embarkation on the BC coast. He had an eye for a good boat.

First Nations people have been developing the designs of their canoes for centuries. By trial and error they found a design that could cope with beach launching, breaking waves and all types of West Coast weather. Some were capable of going beyond the horizon, and long voyages. They were also able to innovate, adapting subtle changes influenced by early explorers and traders.

The flare in the topsides of the hull sheds water, lifts the hull and the very light materials make it very buoyant. The whaling

canoe is a good sea boat and very safe for a crew working off
beaches with big surf.

It was a very good choice for the challenge facing Captain
Voss and he found these qualities early in the voyage. After she
had been tested he never lost complete faith in the capabilities
of the hull design and materials.[69]

In the archives of the Maritime Museum of British Columbia there are other equally logical yet unproven versions of the
canoe's origin. One account, written by a man named Jack Fleetwood in 1926, gives some enticing clues, but the details of its
origin are poorly documented:

(August Bazil) Paul related to me [Fleetwood] how a huge
canoe had been beached in the brush in a salina (tidal salt
bayou) a bit south of Kil-Pah-Lats village, near Deep Dene,
which was at that time abandoned and the old house unoccu-
pied. It was thirty-thirty-five feet long maybe eight-nine feet
wide and had been beached maybe twenty-five-thirty years as
the three West Coast [Vancouver Island] men had got sick and
died of smallpox. The local Indians wouldn't go near the canoe,
presumably because of the disease. I asked if they were Mah-
Thayla-Moochk (Port Alberni) men, but he [August Bazil Paul]
said "No they came from near Ahousat."

I asked what had happened to the canoe and was told that
"about twenty-five years before a man came from Victoria, not a
King George man (English), maybe German, I think, and he looks
for that boat somebody tells him about, and that she is lying, lying
long time in the bush." He's got some whiskey, good whiskey and
he's giving two, three mans some whiskey. He's talking, talking,
lots, lots and he's making big talk for himself (boasting.) Then
Dick Friday said he owned the land so he owned the canoe. This
man pays Dick Friday, and two other mans for the canoe. She's
not very good now, but he's talking big like he wants this canoe
to go some other place, long, long way. He buyed it, maybe thirty
dollars, maybe thirty-five dollars. Then he comes back and he
gets old man Tinkley (John Tinkley, who lived at Deep Cove) to

take that canoe on some logs to Galiano. I guess he's going to fix it there. No, I never see him again.[70]

Wilson Duff, a curator at the British Columbia Provincial Museum in Victoria (now the Royal British Columbia Museum), provided additional anecdotal information to the Maritime Museum of British Columbia told to him by three Ahousat First Nations men who claimed they knew the builder of the canoe:

> Tilikum was built by an old Indian called Old Moses of Kelsemat, near Ahousat about 1895. Old Moses, it was said, sold the canoe to another Indian for $200. This Indian sold it to Voss. The canoe was classed as a whaling canoe, Oo-Oo-Ta-Hats.[71]

Victoria shipping agent Henry King (a partner in shipping agents King Brothers in Victoria), in an article by Ainslie J. Helmcken, the archivist of the City of Victoria, recalled the vessel and stated that, "In Voss' lecture at the Oriental Hotel ... in 1904, he said he purchased the canoe at Clayoquot for $50.00 (Cowichan Indians did not have sealing or whaling canoes)."[72]

Later Henry King corrected himself by claiming he purchased the canoe at Cowichan Bay, but that it had been built at Clayoquot because it had to be built somewhere near the rainforest in order to get a cedar tree large enough from which the canoe could be carved.

As the years passed, other people began to participate in the story after the fact. As with any great saga, some improbable versions of the story began to surface when they could no longer be investigated or corroborated by the original participants, adding to the mystery and confusion of the Tilikum's origins.

An account from Mayne Island suggested that the Aitken and DeRousie families were both involved with the Tilikum—claiming to having built and used the canoe prior to Voss purchasing it from the family. Nellie Aitken Georgeson, daughter of John Aitken, related:

> [John Aitken] and Bill de Rousie [sic] beachcombed from Victoria to the Gulf Islands. They owned the Tillicum [sic] at one time; and in her sailed up the West Coast. Tillicum was to be

sailed round the world by Captain Voss, and take her final place of honour in Thunderbird Park, Victoria.[74]

In 1908 John Aitken owned a store at Miners Bay on Mayne Island where he was postmaster from 1912 to 1916. It is possible he and DeRousie worked on the *Tilikum* in Vollmers Boat Yard, and the telling and retelling of that experience grew into a story of full-scale ownership.

Mrs. DeRousie says that the big canoe her husband built was later sold to Capt. John Voss for his famous ocean voyages and that it is the one now on display in Thunderbird Park.[75]

Photographs taken of the *Tilikum* shortly after her conversion were located in an album belonging to Archie Georgeson of Galiano Island, kept by his niece for many years. Georgeson was the nephew of John Aitken, further deepening the mystery of their connection to the *Tilikum's* origins.[76]

When the *Tilikum* was initially acquired by the Maritime Museum of British Columbia in 1965, great effort was put into tracking down the origin of the canoe. Much investigative work was done and through correspondence with Lottie Vollmers, the daughter of boat-builder Harry Vollmers, she related the story that her father was hired by Voss to do the conversion work, collect the *Tilikum* from Cowichan Bay on Vancouver Island and tow the canoe to his boat works on Galiano Island. This is supported by similar claims from the City of Vancouver archivist Major J.S. Matthews who recorded the *Tilikum* sold for seventy-five dollars at Cowichan Bay. Experts contacted at the time the *Tilikum* was brought indoors to the museum credit the style of canoe to the Nuu-chah-nulth and its origins from the 1880s.[77]

In the original versions of both Voss's and Luxton's accounts of where or how the canoe was acquired, Voss makes no acknowledgment of anyone assisting with the work on the *Tilikum* and Luxton makes only brief mention: "For the best part of a month this old hull was worked on with the assistance of a carpenter."[78]

In reality, however, work to make the *Tilikum* ready for ocean voyaging was a combined effort by Voss, Vollmers and Vollmers's carpenter-assistant John Shaw.

MODELS

Model makers have had fun capturing the *Tilikum*'s legacy. Mr. H. Hartrick reported that his father made a model of the *Tilikum* and donated it for display at the Mechanics Institute in Walhalla, Australia. There is also a fine model of the *Tilikum* in the collection of the Maritime Museum of British Columbia in Victoria, built by Commander Nicholas Beketov.

Norman K. Luxton built a large-scale model of the *Tilikum* for display in the Museum of the Canadian Rockies in Banff. (The Luxton House Museum also has a replica of the figurehead, in storage, that was used as part of this model.)

There is also a miniature model of the *Tilikum* in a whisky bottle in the collection of the Maritime Museum of British Columbia.

Model maker Kelvin Dodson of Vancouver built a motorized pond model in 1980.[73]

Left: A model of the *Tilikum* in the collection of the Maritime Museum of British Columbia, built by Commander Nicholas Beketov, who had served in the Imperial Russian Navy at the time of the Russian Revolution.
Lynn J. Salmon photograph.

Right: A model of the *Tilikum* built by Norman K. Luxton about 1923 in the collection of the Luxton House Museum, Banff, AB.
John MacFarlane photograph.

5

PREPARING TO VOYAGE

THE VESSEL CONVERSION

After the *Tilikum* was purchased, the canoe was towed to Shaw's Landing at Spotlight Cove on Galiano Island. John Shaw lived at Shaw's Landing, which was a post office on the island. Voss hired the Vollmers Boat Yard to undertake the work on the conversion of the *Tilikum* to a seagoing yacht. Harry Vollmers was German-born and a former shipwright who had transited twice around the world during his career in sailing ships. His son Henry, who was eight at the time of the *Tilikum*'s arrival at Spotlight Cove, recalled that it was his father who towed it there.[79] (After their yard burned in 1908 the Vollmers moved to Nanaimo, BC, where they established Vollmers's Shipyard.) Voss built a log grid skidway on the shore of a nearby small islet and covered the craft with a temporary shelter structure to protect against the weather during construction, carried out during April and May 1901.

Voss, Vollmers and Shaw worked on the conversion of the vessel, creating the hold spaces, raising the gunwales fourteen inches off the water, building the tiny cabin and decking over the entire top of the canoe.[80]

Three masts were erected to carry thirty-eight yards of sail (Luxton recounts it as 225 square feet). They carried at least two suits of sails, which were replaced periodically throughout the voyage. Mrs. Vollmers sewed the first set of sails from canvas on a foot-powered sewing machine that was donated decades later to the Maritime Museum of British Columbia along with many of Harry Vollmers's original shipwright tools.[81]

Voss divided up the sail area onto the three masts, an unusual rig configuration for a small boat. Technically she was a three-masted schooner. But she was very narrow and unstable so they

The *Tilikum* under sail at Spotlight Cove, Galiano Island, BC, in 1901, crewed by Captain Voss and shipwright Harry Vollmers. (This image hung on the Vollmers' living room wall for fifty years.[82])

Image E-04094 courtesy of the Royal BC Museum and Archives.

needed a sail plan that had a low centre of effort.[83] Also, when Voss streamed a sea anchor from her bow, he needed a riding sail that could be set on an after-mast. The *Tilikum* carried no self-steering gear so the three masts allowed different sail plans that allowed the boat to be balanced.

Luxton describes the vessel conversion in detail, which is remarkable because he had not attended to the work himself.

> The sides were built up seven and [a] half inches, and held in place by one inch square oak ribs, bent to run from bow to stern twenty-four inches apart from top to bottom inside the canoe. Inside, two-by-four joists or floor timbers were fastened, over which was laid a kelson of the same dimensions. A keel of oak three by eight inches on the outside bottom of the canoe was bolted to the kelson, then three hundred and eighty pounds of lead were fastened to the bottom of the keel. All this was to prevent the canoe from breaking or splitting, the keel and kelson sandwiched the bottom of the canoe, and the ribs crossed the natural grain of the long sides and bottom. The keel was some twenty-eight feet, the overall some thirty-two feet, about a five-foot beam and the depth of thirty-six inches.
>
> Ten feet from the bow a water-tight bulkhead was built with a floor hatch on the deck. Directly after this came the cabin of about eight feet in length. About fourteen feet from the bow bulkhead came an aft bulkhead, also water-tight. Immediately in front of this aft bulkhead there were two galvanized water tanks under the cockpit or well, and their fore ends were flush with the hatch that led into the cabin from the cockpit so that they formed part of the aft end of the cabin well. These tanks were built to the shape of the sides of the canoe and were held in place by two inch square pieces of wood resting on the floor joists. These tanks each held about eighty gallons of water. Immediately aft and behind the wash board of the cockpit came the aft hatch just in front of which was the mizzen mast, and through the centre of the cabin came the mainmast. The foremast was just fore of the cabin wall and fore of the mast came the fore hatch.
>
> The bow of the canoe to the end of the bowhead reached

some seven feet. With a jib sail, foresail, mainsail and spanker, all her canvas would hardly measure two hundred twenty-five square feet. Peak and throat halliards [sic] all trailed back to the starboard outside of the wash board of the cockpit, snubbed over small wooden cleats; the sheets down the port side of the canoe were held in the same way. Thus a man sitting in the cockpit at the helm could in a moment let every running gear on the canoe loose. The masts were all secured by small thin steel wires. Ballast was put beneath the floor boards, to the extent of six-hundred pounds, and effectively held in place by the floor. Four small sacks of sand were usually kept in the cockpit to trim ship.[84]

The exterior of the boat was painted white with red trim. The interior was not painted prior to departure.

Voss was happy with the modifications. In a letter to a friend in San Francisco, he stated, "Having finished her, and having stood on my head, lain on my back and looked down on her from the nearest tree, I am forced to the conclusion that I have never seen anything of her size so molded and proportioned."[85]

Voss's confidence in the *Tilikum* grew over the months but was not initially shared by anyone who was aware of their undertaking. The *Tilikum* was variously described as "ridiculous," "queer looking" and a "dainty looking little lady ... but a very frail craft to have buffeted the gales of three oceans." If opinions on her appearance were mixed, opinions on her chances of survival were not. Armchair sailors and mariners alike were certain the boat would not weather a heavy sea.

Naval architect Tad Roberts[86] stated recently:

In my opinion, technically the rig would be called a "tern" schooner. I believe this term originated in Nova Scotia. In a true schooner the furthest aft sail is also the largest. In *Tilikum* the aft sail is smaller than those [gaff headed] forward of it. The designer L. Francis Herreshoff popularized this rig in the 1940s–1950s, but never called it anything specific that I've read. One of his drawings in *The Common Sense of Yacht Design* is titled, *Tilikum II?*

I would not say that *Tilikum* was unstable. We don't have the information to make that statement yet. Like a Banks Dory, her bottom is narrow and relatively flat, and her sides have considerable flare. This shape is tender [tippy] when lightly loaded but gains stability with increased load. So as she was loaded and freeboard decreased, stability increased dramatically. There is one mention in Voss's book of a 300-pound customs officer stepping on the rail and putting the deck under.

We could draw one of two conclusions from that: 1) The boat was heavily loaded and freeboard rather low, or 2) The boat was lightly loaded, floating high, and thus very tender.

Self-steering gear was not yet invented when Voss made his voyage. Self-steering using a wind vane did not appear until Frenchman Marin-Marie used it [on a powerboat] on Arielle's trans-Atlantic voyage of 1937. With four small sails well spread over the length of the ship, coupled with her long shallow canoe body, the boat could be easily balanced in varying wind strengths and course directions by raising or lowering sails as needed.

PROVISIONING FOR SEA

Once her conversion was complete, the *Tilikum* was provisioned and furnished with the gear needed for the voyage.[87] All the provisions, clothing, wood for the fire and other gear weighed a total of four tons. The furniture in the cabin was a bunk and locker on each side. All this weight added to the stability ballast calculation in addition to the weight of the freshwater supply.

It cost Voss and Luxton $1,000 to equip and victual the *Tilikum*. These supplies included:

- water (the two galvanized metal tanks each carried eighty-seven gallons)
- apparatus for capturing rainfall to refill the tanks
- canned goods (enough for six months)
- hard tack
- fresh vegetables
- cooking utensils
- medicine chest
- "wee" wood stove
- .30-30 rifle
- .44 Winchester rifle

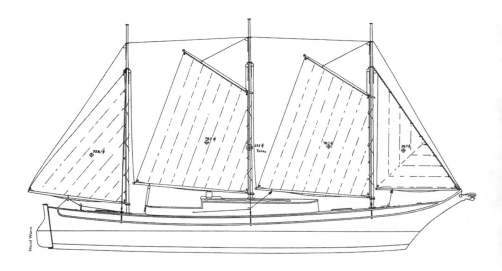

Nicol Warn

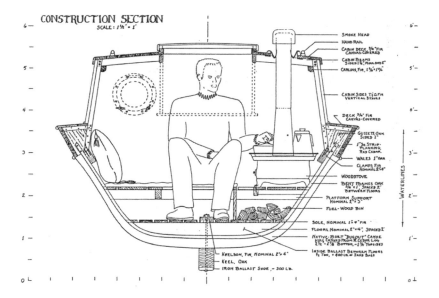

CONSTRUCTION SECTION
SCALE : 1½" = 1'

SMOKE HEAD
HAND RAIL
CABIN DECK, ¾" FIR
CANVAS-COVERED
CABIN BEAMS
SIDED 1½", MOULDED 2"
CARLINS, FIR, 1⅜"×1⅞"

CABIN SIDES T&G FIR
VERTICAL STAVES

DECK ¾" FIR
CANVAS-COVERED
GUSSETS, OAK
SIDED 1"
1¼" STRIP-
PLANKING,
RED CEDAR
WALES 1" OAK
CLAMPS, FIR
NOMINAL 2×4"
WOODSTOVE
BENT FRAMES OAK
⅝"×1", SPACED 2"
BETWEEN FLOORS
PLATFORM
SUPPORT
NOMINAL 2"×5"
FUEL-WOOD BIN
SOLE, NOMINAL 1½×4" FIR
FLOORS NOMINAL 2"×4", SPACED 2"
NATIVE-BUILT "DUGOUT" CANOE
HULL CARVED FROM R. CEDAR LOG
2¾" – 2⅝ BOTTOM, – 1⅜ TOPSIDES
INSIDE BALLAST BETWEEN FLOORS
½ TIN, ± 400 LB. IN SAND BAGS

KEELSON, FIR, NOMINAL 2"× 4"
KEEL, OAK
IRON BALLAST SHOE, – 300 LB.

WATERLINES

Top: The *Tilikum*'s sail plan.

Nicol Warn in The Resolution: The Journal of the Maritime Museum of British Columbia *by permission of the author.*

Bottom: Cross-section of the interior of the *Tilikum* showing the tight fit for occupants (only one crew member was comfortably accommodated inside at a time).

Nicol Warn in The Resolution: The Journal of the Maritime Museum of British Columbia *by permission of the author.*

- 16-bore shotgun (and another shotgun unspecified)
- .22 long-barrelled Stevens pistol (and another revolver unspecified)
- camera and two gross of photographic plates
- "Horis" quadrant [sic] (second-hand; cost: fifty cents). Luxton called it a sextant, noting that it had a cracked mirror and that some of the mirror was missing.
- small spirit compass
- Waltham P.S. Bartlett watch #2850606 (which lost $\frac{1}{5}$ of a second each day). Luxton says that the watch was his, extracted from the gold case in which it was normally set. He had Victoria jeweller William L. Challoner calibrate and set it in a new case. It is thought that he left the watch with Voss after leaving the voyage.
- two metal anchors
- a copy of the South Pacific Directory for 1884 and one marine chart of the South Pacific purchased from a second-hand store

The "wee" stove was about fourteen inches square with a four-inch grate. They carried resinous kindling that allowed them to boil water for coffee quickly and easily. (Luxton stated that they burned blocks of well-seasoned resin that had been scavenged from inside old-growth tree stumps, where it had been extruded from exposure to the warm sun and hardened into pure lumps that were highly flammable.) It was vented to the outside by a metal smoke chimney through the cabin roof. The stove was probably purchased second-hand.

PREPARATIONS FOR THE VOYAGE

Luxton revealed his intention to participate in the voyage in letters to his parents and friends in St. Paul, Minnesota. They naturally tried to persuade him to abandon the scheme. In one letter a friend stated,

> It occurs to me that there is no money in it, and that the primary objective of the expedition is a love of adventure. Why then, risk your life on so perilous a trip? There is one chance in a million of your coming out of it alive, and that one is not worth playing for.[88]

Despite the warning, Luxton was already calculating ways that revenue might be generated by the voyage. Luxton had the newspaperman's eye for a good story and what could be more

The *Tilikum* just launched in Spotlight Cove at Galiano Island, BC.
Maritime Museum of British Columbia.

thrilling than to sail around the world in an Indian canoe? Years
later, in his unpublished account, Luxton never fully forgave Voss
for going "back on his word and drafting an account ... under the
title *Adventurous Voyages* [*sic*] ... that was not wholly accurate."[89]

Voss declared in his manuscript that his intention was to circumnavigate the globe to establish a world record, to visit numerous out-of-the-way islands and to experience the sea in a small
boat. He considered the *Tilikum* to be smaller than an ordinary
ship's lifeboat. He further wrote that,

> ... my proposition was even jeered at not only by lands men but
> experienced sea faring men and after inspection of my boat it
> was the general expression that I would never return. They were
> thinking that it was an utterly impossibility for so small a boat to
> live on the Ocean in heavy weather.

With my past experience I was thoroughly convinced that any ordinary boat can live at sea, if properly handled. Of this fact I have certainly convinced the whole world and I have also lectured before the principal geographical societies in many countries and also the scientific societies on this subject. They were thoroughly convinced of my achievement. I may state that my achievement will not only be interesting but of great value from a life-saving standpoint and also of great value to the scientific world.[90]

ARMAMENT

Norman Luxton mentioned that,

Digging in the sand one day for iron gravel to ballast the canoe I came across a most wonderful brass cannon with very old markings which proved its Spanish origin. Hardly twenty inches long with a bore for muzzle loading two inches in diameter; it was quite as good as the day some venturesome landing party had lost it. Proudly this was mounted to the bottom of the hatch of the *Tilikum*, so that with the release of a catch and a flip of the fore hatch the cannon came up to a position ready for firing.[91]

Luxton reported that on one occasion,

I could see about two hundred and fifty yards distant some twenty catamarans, all empty. Jack [Voss] told me when he came aft that the Natives had been lowering their catamarans all night over the cliff. The Native people apparently had carried them two miles across the island for only one reason Jack could see. He waited for them to get in mass formation and close enough. Then he trained the cannon on them and fired. Every one of the Natives went overboard and out of sight, like so many Hell-diving ducks. Jack had not known that I had unshipped the cannon at Apia and had neglected to make it fast again. The result was that the recoil of the black powder kicked the gun from the block and, before Jack realized it, rolled overboard and was lost forever.[92]

Curiously, Voss makes no mention of this cannon anywhere in his book. Filling a muzzle-loading cannon with black powder would have been an awkward affair as described by Luxton. It also would have required carrying black powder in the equipment stores. It does not ring entirely true that such a cannon was ever carried aboard the *Tilikum*.

AT LAST, READY TO GO

From Spotlight Cove the positioning cruise to Oak Bay took seven hours, after which Voss and Luxton anchored off the old Mount Baker Hotel. While briefly there, Henry H. King (later a partner in the Victoria-based shipping agency King Brothers) helped to install canvas on the decks before the departure.

Astonishingly, Voss and Luxton showed little interest in doing a proper "shakedown cruise" prior to sailing the boat to Oak Bay or even later when they sailed out onto the vast Pacific Ocean. Luxton and his brother George took the *Tilikum* for a day sail and were satisfied the dugout canoe was seaworthy and sound.[93]

Voss and Luxton gave no indication of how they managed

**The *Tilikum* at Oak Bay in 1901. This is one of the few
images that shows an anchor at the bow.**

*Originally from the collection of Major F.V. Longstaff; now in the collection of the Maritime Museum of
British Columbia.*

personal hygiene. No doubt they used a bucket to relieve themselves while they were on watch in the cockpit, dumping the contents over the side. Washing themselves and their clothes would have been more problematic; fresh water was in such short supply that it would be used only for cooking and drinking. Infrequent rain would be captured using the sails and poured into their containers on board. Salty seawater would be used for brushing teeth, shaving and bathing as well as washing their cooking utensils, dishes and bedding.

Both Voss and Luxton noted very few of the mundane details of their routine. Those glimmers of domestic duties tend to stand out when included. Luxton cut Voss's hair and trimmed his beard at Penrhyn Island to make him look more presentable. More than likely one of the first tasks ashore would be a visit to a barber. In photographs taken in South Africa, Voss looks positively dapper. The bulk of clothing that Voss possessed (including the uniform he is frequently photographed in) was shipped ahead to his next port of call. This made sense as most items on board the *Tilikum* succumbed quickly to mould and a permanent dampness that no amount of bailing could counteract.

There is no record of whether they wore shoes or went barefoot, or whether they carried any foul-weather gear while on board. Unfortunately for historians, neither left many clues about these practical aspects of their life at sea.

6

ACROSS THE PACIFIC

THE CONTRACT BETWEEN LUXTON AND VOSS

L uxton and Voss engaged the Victoria legal firm of Langley and Martin to draw up a contract of partnership to formalize their relationship: Captain Voss was the master and Luxton was the mate.

Luxton stated in his book that he had "reserved the literary rights of the adventure." The *Tilikum* was

> ... to be used in any manner whatsoever, to make money, show purposes, particularly in civilized ports. If either partner quit, through sickness or otherwise, he sacrificed one-third of his half interest. It was a simple, cut and dried agreement. Captain Voss could not order the canoe to wherever he wished though senior officer. I really was the business manager, and in like manner had to consult Voss as he had to consult me as to places to sail.[94]

Top: The *Tilikum* leaving Oak Bay, Victoria, for the Pacific islands. Captain Voss is in the white shirt. Norman Luxton is to Voss's right, O.B. Ormond next, then Mrs. Dora Voss (and family group of three). George E. Luxton took the photo on May 21, 1901.

Image A-66929 courtesy of the Royal BC Museum and Archives.

Bottom: A monument to the *Tilikum* at Oak Bay, placed by the Thermopylae Club in 2001 to mark the centennial of her departure.

Jamie Webb photograph, Thermopylae Club.

The *Tilikum* left Victoria from Oak Bay on May 21, 1901. Voss and Luxton tell two different versions of the departure. Voss claimed that flags were flying and hundreds of people crowded the waterfront. Hats and handkerchiefs were waved by friends who never expected to see either of the men again. He said that such a send-off was never before witnessed in Victoria and that even guns were fired in salute. Voss undoubtedly was enjoying a moment of exaggeration with his readers.

It's more likely that Luxton's account is closer to the truth. He states that the departure was actually just a small number of friends and relatives, including his friend O.B. Ormond, his brother George Luxton and Mrs. Voss and her three children. Luxton wrote that Voss's leave-taking was very emotional while Luxton allowed himself only handshakes and words of encouragement from his friends. The photographic evidence on their departure day lends credibility to Luxton's quieter description.

After departing from Oak Bay, the *Tilikum* had many miles to cover to reach the entrance of Juan de Fuca Strait. The width of the strait is as much as eighteen miles and in a small craft with sail as her only propulsion, the voyage was off to an unexpectedly slow start. Voss reported at this time that the *Tilikum*, under full sails, could make five to seven knots per hour at best (one knot equals approximately 1.15 miles per hour). However, in the following chapters, Voss's reports on his daily progress at sea almost always indicate a faster speed than what is likely to have been accurate. Perhaps the *Tilikum* actually made better hull speed than five to seven knots, but even so, his summaries of ocean legs do not seem accurate when analyzed.

Voss determined the route for their epic voyage should first take them across the Pacific to take advantage of winds that would be favourable to their worldwide adventure. With only a handheld watch for a chronometer and a small compass in gimbals in a box, the two men departed in a light breeze, ready to tackle the immensity of the Pacific Ocean in a small dugout canoe.

On their first day of sailing, they made it only as far as Sooke, a small settlement overlooking a naturally protected harbour to the west of Victoria. They anchored at 1700 that evening to await a more favourable wind. Because the *Tilikum* had not had a proper trial run, the men were no doubt discovering how best to trim the boat, set the sails and shape a course.

Early the next morning they weighed anchor to take advantage of an east wind, heading toward Cape Flattery, which is situated at the northwestern edge of Washington State. This tip of land is at the "hook" of the strait; in order to sail southwest to the open sea, they first had to sail northwest to round the hook. This would be their jumping-off point and the last land they would see until arriving in the distant Pacific islands. However, they were once again foiled in their attempt as later in the day the wind blew from the west, forcing them to anchor back at Sooke Harbour, where they were laid up for three days.

Unusual for mariners, Voss seemed determined to avoid us waters, where they could have taken advantage of the winds and currents along the coast and would have found good anchorages for respite from storms before heading into the Pacific.

Luxton was regaled during the voyage with Voss's tales of people-smuggling activities but may not have known that in 1894 Voss had been a "person of interest" in an opium-smuggling case in San Francisco.[95] He and his mate in the schooner *Emerald* had landed drugs from Victoria at Point Reyes, California. The American connections were corrupt senior customs officials who were subsequently arrested. us court officials tried to lure Voss back to testify against his confederates, which he declined to do, fearing arrest. This likely explains why he did not shelter on the us shore of Juan de Fuca Strait or call at San Francisco or Hawaii, as most mariners would have done.

According to Luxton, from a story told him later by his brother (who wrote it in a letter initially to their mother), the us revenue cutter *Grant* had been keeping a watch on the departure of the *Tilikum*. Their intent, presumably, would have been to capture Voss when he entered us waters. Their departure from Victoria within hours of the *Tilikum* leaving Oak Bay was an unlikely coincidence. The cutter was out four days until forced to return to Victoria after running into a rock, suffering grave damage. George wrote: "The plain facts were the *Grant* had an eye on Voss and wasted two or three weeks running up and down the coast waiting for the *Tilikum* to leave and when she was in United States waters ... they would search her."[96]

After their forced layover they made another attempt to sail into the Pacific, but the wind drove them to seek shelter in Port San Juan, another ideal, sheltered anchorage north of Sooke.[97] A local farmer and some First Nations people met them on their arrival.

Luxton's unlikely recollection of the struggle to reach this anchorage is the first of many inconsistencies in his account of the voyage. He refers to Voss being incapacitated with seasickness, a condition that is never mentioned by the captain himself or by any who subsequently sailed with him. The voyage had gotten off to a rather lame start, perhaps prompting Luxton to embellish his story with his heroics, attempting to frame himself as a credible mariner for his potential readers. "To make matters worse," he wrote, "Voss got his usual sea-sick spell that came with every gale, and I took the tiller. Fortunately, I did because inside of half an hour when it was almost dark I recognized the entrance into San Juan Inlet [Port San Juan] otherwise it would have been a case of fight the storm all night or blow back to Race Rocks."[98]

At Port San Juan, John Joseph Baird, a local settler and old friend of Luxton's from Winnipeg, invited Voss and Luxton to have dinner with his family, an offer that was gladly accepted. The farmer and his wife and child presented a table covered with a sumptuous feast. Voss asked whether they might take a snapshot of the family and the large turkey that was waiting to be carved. Before taking the photo, Voss inquired whether the flash apparatus would frighten the child. The mother assured him it would not, but to the contrary the little girl fell to the floor in fear. The mother rushed to pick her up, and in the process she upset the table, smashing the photographic apparatus and knocking the turkey to the floor. The dog, standing nearby, seized the turkey and made for the door, much to the chagrin of the farmer. They sat down instead to the typical farmer's bill of fare consisting of ham, bread and cheese.[99]

Voss and Luxton remained at Port San Juan for eight days, waiting for a change in the wind and weather. Eventually the wind began to blow from the northeast and appeared favourable for departure. At last the journey was about to begin! Within minutes the anchor was hauled on deck, and they set the sails and shaped a course down the harbour toward Cape Flattery.

The trading post of Mr. McKenzie at Dodger Cove, in Barkley Sound.
Norman Luxton photograph in the collection of the Archives of the Canadian Rockies.

The wind picked up and by mid-morning the *Tilikum* was sailing under storm canvas.

The *Tilikum* shipped quite a bit of water, initially not proving to be very seaworthy. She was perpetually wet, leaking through cracks in the hull and requiring constant bailing. They ran along the Vancouver Island coastline up under the lee of Cape Beale and anchored in a small cove at nightfall. After changing their wet clothes and having a cup of tea, the two of them turned in for the night.

Awakened by heavy tossing and rolling of the boat in the middle of the night, the crew was forced to sail to find a safer anchorage. They headed for Dodger Cove, on Diana Island, five miles northwest of Cape Beale. Entering the cove, the *Tilikum* encountered heavy beds of seaweed, choking the rudder. After cutting the canoe free from the seaweed, they found anchorage in front of Ohiat, a First Nations village.

Voss and Luxton seemed content to remain near this friendly

village for several weeks. While at Dodger Cove, they had several interesting experiences with the First Nations people. On one occasion Voss encountered a party of eighteen men fitting out three canoes for a whaling expedition. The headman agreed to take Voss along, on the understanding that he should provide his own food. Each canoe was about 24 feet long and crewed by six men each. In the canoe were long lines, harpoons and some inflated sea lion bladders. The weather was calm and the water was smooth. Whales were spouting and throwing their tails up in the air in all directions. Later, when a monster of a whale surfaced within five feet of the canoe, the action began.

> The harpooneer threw his lance but missed and the whale threw up its tail and swam off. The old head-man, who was steering the canoe, cursed the harpooner for missing and at the whale for not being a little closer to the canoe. Later in the afternoon a whale surfaced close to a canoe and the harpoon found its mark, buried deep in the flesh of the whale. In the next second, the whale flipped the canoe into the air with its tail breaking the canoe in two pieces. The head-man ordered the other two canoes to go to their assistance retrieving floating gear and crew members. The broken canoe was towed back to the village to be replaced by another. The next morning they made another start and one of the harpooneers found his mark. The whale started to run [and] a long line fastened to the harpoon was let out.
>
> On the end of the line were tied three inflated sea lion bladders. When the whale ran deep at times all three bladders would disappear under water. The canoes followed paddling with all their might to catch up with the line. In about half an hour the whale had stopped running and the canoes caught up to the line. [The] crews pulled in the line until very close to the whale [and] they drove in three more harpoons. With a canoe on each side of the dying whale [they] began to guide it to the shore. The whale was put up on a sandy beach at high water which left it high and dry at low tide. The whole village appeared to participate in cutting up the whale and the pieces placed in equal piles for allocation to the different families.[100]

The *Viva*, a sealing schooner, recruiting First Nations hunters for the Bering Sea seal hunt on the west coast of Vancouver Island.
Norman Luxton photograph in the collection of the Archives of the Canadian Rockies.

After this two-week distraction, Voss and Luxton moved the *Tilikum* on July 5 to an anchorage close to a natural spring, where they washed their clothes and took on fresh water. Anchored in the vicinity was the sealing schooner *Viva* from Victoria, busily recruiting Indigenous hunters for the Bering Sea seal hunt. Voss and Luxton spent their last night before departure on the *Viva* in the company of Henry Copeland, an old friend of Luxton's from Winnipeg who was among the crew on board.

According to Luxton, the dinner was an attempt to "shanghai" him for the sealing grounds and prevent him from embarking on his voyage with Voss. All was thwarted when he escaped being locked in a passenger cabin aboard the *Viva* and swam to the *Tilikum* in readiness for their departure the next morning.[101]

The *Tilikum* underway at sea rounding Cape Flattery into the open Pacific
Ocean. Luxton took one of the very few images from the deck of the vessel.

Norman Luxton photograph in the collection of the Archives of the Canadian Rockies.

THE TRANS-PACIFIC CROSSING

On July 6, 1901, the *Tilikum* weighed anchor and the crew planned
a course to the west.[102] At 1800, while the two men drank a cup
of tea and ate bread and butter, Cape Flattery was finally rounded
and their last sight of North America dropped behind the horizon. In his account of the voyage, Voss noted that it would be five
years before he would set eyes on the same beautiful shore again.

With their voyage now firmly under way, Luxton and Voss
worked out the watch routine for the sea. They agreed that the
watches would be six hours long, and would be executed as "one-
on and one-off." Voss considered that Luxton, although inexperienced, was competent enough to steer the vessel unsupervised.
It was agreed, however, that if the sails needed trimming Voss
would be called from resting to undertake the work. They would

alternate in the cooking of meals: the man coming on watch would cook the meal for the one coming off. Their small cast-iron stove was fuelled by firewood that sometimes burned well and at other times smoked them out of the cabin. They each received half a gallon of water per day.

Luxton recalled that the menu at sea was simple:

> It was Sunday and we always had pancakes. Jack was pretty strong on pancakes so he cooked them that day. Our bill of fare so far did not require a great deal of cooking; it was astonishing how well our wood was lasting. A few pieces the size of a lead pencil boiled the water for coffee or porridge, or heated the canned meat and vegetables. Our menu ran like this: breakfast, oatmeal or corn meal, bread or coffee. Lunch and dinner, canned tomatoes, peas or beans, ham or bacon, also canned meats and currie [sic], bread and tea at 10 PM, canned preserves, bread and tea or coffee. The bread, of course, was sea biscuits and everything that was not canned had green mould on it and it tasted accordingly.[103]

They ate well while the fresh provisions lasted. When conditions permitted, Luxton cooked ham and eggs and prepared coffee as well as bread and butter for breakfast at 0600. For lunch Voss opened a one-pound tin of meat, boiled some potatoes and vegetables and made an Irish stew with a cup of coffee and some bread and butter. Dessert was tinned plum pudding. For supper they ate leftovers—bread with butter and cheese and tea. This was their regular diet until the fresh food ran out, after which they relied on tinned meats and dry goods.

Voss never commented on the integrity of the hull, but Luxton recounted a number of instances when there were significant ingresses of water. This had a devastating effect on both provisions and gear. Everything became mouldy and caused the labels on canned food to fall off.

Even their shared plug of T&B tobacco (a Canadian-made product manufactured as T&B Myrtle Cut Tobacco by George E. Tuckett and Son, Hamilton, Ontario) had absorbed water so that it swelled up. Before use it had to be cut up and dried in the sun on deck. Luxton was disappointed to find that its flavour was lost in the process.

BIG SEAS, SMALL ANCHOR

Voss and Luxton quickly gained experience in handling the little vessel in heavy seas, particularly when running before breaking waves. Their first attempt to deploy a sea anchor was to tow a blanket on a rope to act as a drogue (this creates drag and holds the vessel in line with the direction of the running sea). The *Tilikum*'s deck was barely fourteen inches above the water in smooth seas; any waves from rough and confused seas were a constant threat to the integrity of the small craft. In these conditions, Luxton would tie a lifeline around his waist and go forward to launch the sea anchor.

VOSS'S PATENTED SEA ANCHORS

In 1901 the use of sea anchors was not widespread. Some mariners employed warps—long loops of rope towed from the stern—to slow the forward progress of a vessel in heavy winds and seas. Some masters towed drogues—often bundles of blankets, canvas or heavy gear—to function similarly to a warp. Captain Voss also employed oil bags in an attempt to calm seas immediately adjacent to his vessel.

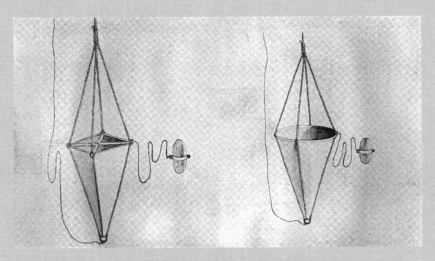

Voss's designs for his sea anchors (square and round versions).
From the first edition (1913) of The Venturesome Voyages of Captain Voss.

Voss developed a design for a sea anchor based on the ones he had built for himself as previous versions wore out or broke. He wrote:

> The sea anchor which I had in the Tilikum measured 22 inches in the ring and has taken Tilikum successfully through 16 violent gales and used the same in crossing the famous Sumner and Wanganui Bars in New Zealand. A perfect sea anchor which will act on a boat for both keeping boats head on to the sea and also to run before it.[104]

This documentation is an example of how he envisioned bringing a "scientific" approach to describing principles of small-boat handling.

> A sea anchor should be light and strong and is constructed by taking a hard wooden ring which is not too heavy. Sew on a heavy canvas bag around the ring, and sew the canvas in a gather so that it comes nearly to a point leaving an opening in the bottom. After the canvas is sewn together to the ring it will look like a clown's cap or the shape of a funnel. Put in four eyelets at an equal distance just below the ring so that (for example) if the ring is two feet in diameter take two pieces of 1 ¾ inch rope four feet long and splice one end in every eyelet. Let the two bits come together and leave an eye for the anchor line to fasten to the lower part of the sea anchor ... where there is an opening put in a becket for the tripping line fastening. Fasten a trip-line on one side and fasten a small weight to one side of the ring. This enables the anchor to be quickly dumped so that it can either be retrieved or emptied. It will also stop it from twisting around and fouling the lines.
>
> In a larger size sea anchor it is better to make the mouth square as it will slow better. Instead of a ring use 1–2 inch wood for the square and 3 feet pieces of hard wood or if soft wood then larger dimensions. Bore hole in the center and bolt together. Bore a hole one inch from the ends and open it up. Sew on the canvas so that the mouth will have four corners. Put a rope around the edge and one eyelet in each corner. Take the same kind of rope as would be used on a round anchor and reef four ends through the four holes with a stop knot to fasten to the eyelets. Put a weight on one side as with the round anchor. To stow it away take off two of the stops, bring the two sticks together and wind the canvas round the sticks. Put in a bag made for that purpose.[105]

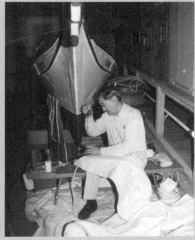

Left: Captain Voss with his patented sea anchor, probably taken near London, England, at the conclusion of his voyage. He is still credited today as a pioneer in the use of this gear in small vessels.
World Wide Magazine, 1904.

Right: Master sailmaker Ron Mack sewing a traditional suit of canvas sails for the *Tilikum* restoration display at the former Maritime Museum location at Bastion Square in Victoria.
Maritime Museum of British Columbia.

Voss's second publisher, Weston Martyr, included anecdotal material on sea anchors in the first edition of *Venturesome Voyages* that he garnered from Voss in their conversations in Yokohama. Voss was very proud of his design. At first he experimented with towing an old blanket on the end of a rope and then trailing a traditional canvas sea anchor from the bow while heaved to in a storm.

Captain Voss's design obviously predates modern technological advances. His design is of historical interest, but modern designs and materials have addressed technical issues that were unforeseen by Voss.

Importantly, Richard Henderson, in his treatise on single-handed sailing, states that Voss provides "much good advice on how to handle a small boat in heavy weather, but one should not be misled into thinking a modern yacht will behave as did the *Tilikum* when lying to a sea anchor."[106] Modern yachts are much different in all respects from the *Tilikum*. They are so light for their size that they can make forward progress in heavy winds on the masts, rigging and superstructure—without sails.

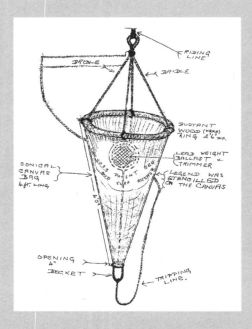

Captain Voss's patented sea anchor (this rendering was created in 1995 as part of early research undertaken by the MMBC curatorial staff).
Maritime Museum of British Columbia.

The function of the "drag" impressed Luxton:

> The drag is most important ... [the sea anchor] is tied by its own line to the bow of the boat and floats to the crest of the oncoming wave that would sweep the deck of the boat. Meeting this small resistance of the drag the crest of the wave is broken, thus making a canyon for the boat to pass through. The line of the drag should be played out far enough so that when the boat is on the crest of the wave the drag would be on the crest of the next oncoming wave, while the sea anchor line is only out half the distance. The sea anchor keeps the boat head on, and the drag breaks the white water or top of the wave which otherwise would sweep the boat and break it into kindling wood ... For this advice he gives to the world, if for nothing else, I could readily forgive Voss for breaking his agreement with me by stealing the Tilikum's story across the Pacific, for he has given to the seafaring men fool-proof advice which if followed out will save many ships and more lives.[107]

Voss understood the terror such conditions could evoke. When a gale was running at its height the wind was whistling through the rigging and the large monster seas with snow-white caps came through at tremendous speed and overpowering noise. It was very uncomfortable for an inexperienced man. Still the *Tilikum* rode the seas head on in perfect safety. On one such occasion, Voss told his mate to have a good look at the running of the waves and the way the boat behaved. Luxton thought that it was impossible to write it up, and if he could his readers would never believe it.

The next morning at 0600 they got up and made breakfast. Voss reflected that it no doubt sounded odd that they were cooking breakfast on board that little boat in a heavy gale, whereas he had served in 2,000-ton ships where a sea had broken the galley weather door and washed the pots and pans and everything else in the galley out the lee door. But on the *Tilikum* they managed to cook regardless.

The use of the sea anchor kept the boat drier than during their passage to the open sea, and the *Tilikum* began to reveal her abilities as a sea boat when handled properly.

On a good day under sail they managed 100 to 125 miles per day. The weather grew warmer as they headed south. Every noon, Voss shot a sun sight with the sextant. When they were 350 miles

The barquentine *Mary Winkelman* passing at sea.

Norman Luxton photograph in the collection of the Archives of the Canadian Rockies.

southwest of San Francisco, they sighted a sail off the starboard bow. They changed course to intercept her and when they drew alongside they found her to be the us barquentine *Mary Winkelman*. The captain's wife sent over some fresh loaves of bread and she and the captain invited the *Tilikum*'s crew aboard for dinner. But a heavy sea was running, causing Voss to fear that something might happen to the *Tilikum* if they came too close. Just as Voss swung the tiller around to resume his course, the captain shouted out that he would report their position when he reached San Francisco—which he did.

Luxton recalled the encounter differently from Voss's version, saying that they passed under her stern with only a very short time to exchange information. The master of the *Mary Winkelman* gave Voss his position, which had been taken the day before. Voss asked the captain to report them when he reached San Francisco. Luxton imagined millions of readers of newspapers carrying their story and the resulting publicity.[108]

The 522-ton *Mary Winkelman* was built at Seabeck, Washington, by Hiram Doncaster in 1881. In the 1890s she was owned by A.H. Paul of San Francisco, who worked in the Hawaiian Islands trade. The *Mary Winkelman* made the voyage from Honolulu to San Francisco in eleven days in 1893. Later she was acquired by the Charles Nelson Company, which retained ownership until November 13, 1923.[109]

The sea became more placid as they sailed south. Luxton was slowly gaining experience and developing skills at sea, but he continued to harbour doubts about the capabilities of the *Tilikum*. He declared that she should be in a glass case instead of being at sea. In fact the two men often felt as if *they* were in a glass case. The heat in the cabin gradually became unbearable, and in the cockpit they found it difficult to avoid falling asleep. Voss reported that on one occasion, Luxton did drift to sleep while at the tiller. The *Tilikum* shifted her course and the wind fell from her sails. The flapping caused Voss to wake, and he rushed up on deck to find Luxton fast asleep.

The next morning, Luxton remarked that Voss must have slept well because during the night he had made enough noise "to wake the dead" after the *Tilikum* had unexpectedly shipped a sea (taken water on board) in almost calm weather. Voss pointed out that it was almost impossible that the boat should ship a sea in such smooth water and asked Luxton if he had been possibly asleep and dreaming that the sea had broken over the vessel. "Dream be hanged," Luxton responded. "Feel my clothes." His clothes were indeed wet, but not because of a phantom breaking sea. Rather, Voss had taken a bucket of water and thrown it on Luxton to wake him. He had then merely returned to his bunk, satisfied that Luxton would never again fall asleep on watch just as the *Tilikum* never again "shipped a sea in that kind of weather."[110]

Luxton refuted this story. "No one threw any water … and if you dozed off, the boom of the mainsail soon woke you up when the *Tilikum* came up into the wind."[111] This was just another example of two vastly different accounts told by Voss and Luxton of the same events during the voyage.

IN THE DOLDRUMS

In the northeast trade winds they averaged one hundred miles per day. When they reached the ten-degree latitude, they were becalmed in what Voss called "the dull room." He had misconstrued the term *doldrums* as "dull room"; he tended to spell English words phonetically. The weather is very changeable in this area—one minute it may be a heavy rain, which is sometimes accompanied by heavy winds, and the next it might be dead calm with the hot sun burning down.

Conditions on the open cockpit were brutal. Luxton got badly sunburned on his neck and the back of Voss's hands broke out in water blisters. Luxton's bare feet reacted badly to the salt water, which caused the skin to crack.

Food—especially fresh food—was always of interest to the men. Flying fish were plentiful, crossing the deck day and night. A number of them struck the sails and spars before dropping onto the deck. This helped to vary an otherwise plain diet. At one point, the sea anchor trapped a good-sized sea turtle, and the men were delighted to think they would enjoy a turtle soup. But when they had it nearly up to the rail it slipped through the ring of the sea anchor, made a few heavy kicks that tore the canvas and escaped through the hole to gain its liberty. It was a great disappointment for the two men, and in the excitement Voss forgot to take his daily observation of the noon sun. When Luxton went

" THE MONOTONY WAS BROKEN BY CATCHING A SEA TURTLE."

Voss and Luxton unexpectedly snare a sea turtle in the *Tilikum*'s sea anchor.
World Wide Magazine, *1904.*

back into the cabin he found the pea soup he had been preparing burned to the bottom of the pot.

By August 14 the wind was coming from the southeast and they picked up the trade winds. Originally they had intended to make for the Marquesas Islands, but because of their position and the prevailing winds they changed their minds and headed for Penrhyn Island. The trade winds were blowing fresh and the *Tilikum* was sailing well. One day she made 177 miles; it was her best mileage day of the whole voyage.

The tedium of the doldrums and the close living conditions were having an adverse effect on Luxton. He began to experience depression and to despair that it would only be a matter of time before they would meet their end in a watery grave. The doldrums contributed to other problems—Luxton began to hallucinate. The first was what he described as a huge animal floating on the top of the water, as long as a sailing ship. It was unfamiliar in shape and was unlike any whale they had previously seen. It was dark grey and showed no fins or flukes. The second was an apparition of his friend George Grieve of Winnipeg, sitting on the cabin roof. (When Luxton arrived in Australia he learned that Grieve had died shortly before his apparition appeared on the *Tilikum*.)

The routine at sea can be very tedious for an inexperienced sailor such as Luxton, unaccustomed as he was to such idleness. The monotonous view never changes, and this can continue for days at a time. In the doldrums there is hardly any wind, so there are few seamanship duties to break the routine.

On September 1 they took in the sails and heaved to under storm sails for the night. Voss reckoned their position to be thirty miles east of Penrhyn Island. He had been told that the island was small and low, so he wanted to make landfall in daylight when it might be seen as far away as eight miles from a low vessel like the *Tilikum*. Disappointingly, at daylight there was no sight of land, so they set all the sails and steered to the west.

After breakfast Voss took a sun sight, which put him ten miles east of the island. Luxton was down below in the cabin washing the dishes and despairing about ever seeing land again. An hour later Voss thought he had glimpsed land, calling the good news to Luxton. But for his mate, there was still no land to be seen. It would be easy to miss landfall with an atoll only a couple of yards above sea level. Luxton was very disappointed and went down into the cabin "almost broken-hearted." When the atoll finally came into clear sight, Luxton felt "like a newborn baby."

It had been almost two months to the minute at sea since they had departed.

7

PENRHYN ISLAND AND BEYOND

O n September 4, when they were about four miles from Penrhyn Island in the northern group of the Cook Islands, Voss took stock of their situation. They heaved to and began to formulate a landing plan: how they would prepare and how they would act.

Voss reread the entry in the South Pacific Directory, published in 1877:

> In the narrative of the United States Exploring Expedition it states that the Island was by estimate 50 feet high and was found to be 9 miles long NNE and SSW and about 5 miles wide with an extensive lagoon having in it many coral patches. There is a boat entrance into it on the Northwest side. There appears

to be continuous villages with cocoanut groves throughout its whole extent and the island is evidently very thickly peopled. The ferocity of the savages precluded possibility of attempting a landing.[112]

The United States Exploring Expedition of 1838–42 was undertaken to explore and survey the Pacific Ocean and beyond. Its description of the "savages" worried Voss, who seemed to have had inordinate fears of cannibals reputed to inhabit the South Pacific islands. Despite having spent nearly two months at sea, Voss suggested to Luxton that since they still had provisions and water they should give the island a pass and sail for Samoa. Voss remarked, "Where will we be if a crew of a large vessel could not make a landing?"

Luxton, restless, seeking adventure and probably desiring to get off the boat for some beach time, strongly objected. Voss retorted the cannibal inhabitants might "have us for supper."[113]

The ship's officers of HMS *Torch* at Penrhyn preparing to convene a court.
Norman Luxton photograph in the collection of the Archives of the Canadian Rockies.

Luxton reminded him that they were armed with plenty of ammunition and could protect themselves if necessary. He remained adamant they must go in to the shore.

Voss conceded defeat. He noted, from the log of HMS *Falcon*, a seventeen-gun Royal Navy *Cruizer*-class sloop launched in 1854, that there was a good entry for a small vessel on the northeast end, and as the wind blew from the east-southeast it would be possible for the *Tilikum* to sail in through this entrance. If the Indigenous people proved hostile, Voss and Luxton could sail on the same wind through the lagoon and out the western end.

In preparation they loaded the rifles, shotguns and revolvers. They put some of the sand and gravel ballast around the cockpit for fortification. Voss was jumpy and definitely expected an attack as they sailed into the lagoon. The land was low but covered from one end to another with coconut trees. Two wrecked vessels lay on the beach, pounded by the surf.

Sighting two men in the trees, Voss told Luxton to shoot them so there would be two less to deal with later. Luxton refused the order, reminding his mate that they were not there to look for trouble, but they would certainly find it if they caused it. They continued on, steering for a village on the shore.

To their surprise they came up beside a 150-ton schooner, the *Children of Tahiti* (Indigenous name, *Tamari Tahiti*), anchored in the bay. Voss hoisted "our little Canadian flag," which was answered by the schooner hoisting the French flag. As they came alongside the schooner the Captain called out in plain English, "Where are you from?" After they had secured the *Tilikum* alongside, Voss and Luxton were asked to come on board.[114]

The men introduced themselves as Captain George Dexter, his partner Captain Joe Winchester[115,116] and their sailing master, Captain Te Pau, who was a son of the former king of Tahiti. After offering a short explanation of the voyage of the *Tilikum*, Luxton and Voss were invited into the cabin for some refreshment and a good square meal.

Winchester was an Englishman who had arrived in Tahiti as a young man, married there and become a French citizen. He became Dexter's business partner in the two-masted native trading schooner *Children of Tahiti*. Winchester's daughter, Sarah Teraireia Winchester, would marry James Norman Hall, co-author

The schooner *Children of Tahiti* (Indigenous name, *Tamari Tahiti*).
Norman Luxton photograph in the collection of the Archives of the Canadian Rockies.

with Charles Nordhoff of *The Bounty Trilogy—Mutiny on the Bounty, Men Against the Sea* and *Pitcairn's Island*. Hall was a prolific writer, both in collaboration with Nordhoff (twelve books) and on his own (seventeen books, countless essays and poems, and at least one play).

Later, the village chief came aboard and the sailing master introduced him to Voss and Luxton. Te Pau interpreted, saying the chief welcomed them to their harbour and asked them to come ashore to dine with him and his people, an invitation Voss readily accepted.

Afterward they walked through the village, noting the houses were built of Oregon pine lumber but roofed with coconut fronds. When Voss asked how they got the lumber, he was told that it had washed ashore from the vessels they had seen wrecked on the outer reef. One of the wrecked vessels had come from Puget Sound in Washington State with a cargo of lumber for Australia.

After waiting more than three months for rescue, the crew sighted a second vessel entering the lagoon. The Indigenous people and the shipwrecked sailors got in boats to welcome the new ship. But mistaking the approaching boats as hostile, the ship's crew began to fire shots at the welcoming fleet before turning back to sea. Instead, the castaways sailed to Samoa, where they took passage on a steamer to Australia. After reporting the accidental loss of the ship and cargo, they cabled to Puget Sound to duplicate the order. The lumber was put on another vessel bound for Australia but ran onto the beach right beside the first ship.[117]

The *Children of Tahiti* moved across the lagoon the next day with the *Tilikum* in tow. On the other side they met Royal Navy Commander Norman G. Macalister of HMS *Torch*, which was anchored outside of the lagoon. HMS *Torch* was an *Alert*-class sloop of the Royal Navy, built at Sheerness Dockyard and launched in 1894. She was based in Australia but undertook extensive cruises through the Pacific islands. Macalister advised them to look after the Indigenous people—it would earn them much respect.[118] Macalister was very interested in the *Tilikum* and gave Voss some navigation charts, telling him he would see them again in Australia.

The Indigenous people put the *Tilikum* ashore among the trees and cleaned and painted the hull. Captain Dexter sailed on to another village, taking Luxton along to photograph different parts of the island. Voss was left alone and unable to communicate with the workers as he watched them refurbish his boat.

On Voss's second day alone one of the villagers approached him and introduced himself in English, surprising Voss. He introduced himself as Dick Brown, born in Jamaica. He had arrived in the South Pacific as the result of a shipwreck years before. He built a bake oven, got some flour from a trader and began baking bread. Although it was not high quality, it was a novelty much sought after by the Indigenous people. In a short time he worked up a very good business. He stayed on the island and became good friends with the chief as he continued to run his baking business.

Luxton, needing a break, stayed with Captain Dexter for more than a week. He was probably glad of the chance to be away from Voss and to be ashore. The locals worked about three hours each day on the *Tilikum* and for the rest of the time played a game

Captain Te Pau of the schooner *Children of Tahiti*.
Norman Luxton photograph in the collection of the Archives of the Canadian Rockies.

resembling cricket. Voss slept in the hammock on the veranda of an Indigenous hut.

One morning, as the locals prepared for their day's work and sport, Voss took a walk around the beach of the lagoon. He had travelled for some miles when he thought he heard voices. Thinking there might be another village nearby, he passed through the underbrush of the coconut trees. It was so thick that he had to crawl on his hands and knees. Pushing through, he came upon a freshwater pond in a clearing in which women of all ages, some of them unclothed, were bathing. As soon as they saw him they all let out a war cry and began a direct run for him. Later, Dick Brown told Voss he was lucky the women had not caught him; they would have administered rough justice because the area was forbidden to all men.

The schooner with Luxton on board returned on September 17. He had taken many photographs from all over the island. Unfortunately, a large number were spoiled by exposure to salt water.

By this time the *Tilikum* was once more afloat after her refit and in excellent condition. On September 18 all the ballast, stores and water were on board, ready for an ocean voyage. Supplied with an abundance of fresh coconuts from the chief and his people, they said farewell and the *Tilikum* sailed out of the lagoon. To make the vessel comfortable they had to throw most of the coconuts overboard. They then shaped a course for Manihiki Island.

MANIHIKI ISLAND (ISLAND OF PEARLS)

Located in the northern group of the Cook Islands, Manihiki is also known as the "Island of Pearls." On Voss and Luxton's arrival, inhabitants of villages urged them to anchor nearby. However, the two men were mistrustful, preferring to search along the coast of the island for a good, safe anchorage. They found nothing suitable; Manihiki's geography was much like that of Penrhyn. There was a lagoon but apparently no entrance even for a small boat, so they stood off the shore at sea.

The next morning a small boat came off the beach paddled by two men and carrying an older gentleman in the stern. Voss and Luxton drew alongside carefully, trying not to scratch the new paint on their hull. The old gentleman looked at them, stating, "I king!" Voss responded rather rudely, saying he didn't much look like a king. One of the crew announced in English that the old gentleman was Apollo, the king of Arika.

Voss recalled:

This was the first time in my life that I spoke and shook hands with a King. I invited Mr. King on board which he accepted with a little bow. He was a man of about 50 years old, fairly heavy set and stood about 5 feet 6 inches without his boots (he said he never wore boots in his life). The man who introduced him was the trader, also a Native, but who had come on board with the king as an interpreter. His name was Williams, a very nice gentleman.

Mr. Williams was a great assistance to me during our stay on the island. He first asked all the particulars with regard to our trip. After I gave him full information where we were from and what we were going to do and in such a little vessel, he interpreted it to the King who opened his eyes wider and wider as

Mr. Williams told him the story. When he was through telling him all he asked dozens of different questions which we all had to answer. He then gave us a hearty handshake and invited us to come ashore to dine with him at one o'clock. The King then gave us a handshake, stepped on board his canoe, and went back to shore. Mr. Williams stopped on board for a while and gave us some details and suggested that we stay a few days.

At 12 o'clock my mate and I went on shore along with Mr. Williams. By the time we arrived the King, Queen and two princesses with all the tribe men and women and children were lined up along the beach. The first one we met was the King and after he gave my mate and myself a hearty handshake he addressed his people and spoke for about 20 minutes. Afterwards Mr. Williams interpreted some of the speech to us—the King said that we were not the first white men to come there. They had seen many white men in large vessels but they could not understand how we got there in that small vessel. He told the people that they should do all they could possible to prove to us that they appreciated our visit to their tiny island.

The impressive Council House on Manihiki Island.
Norman Luxton photograph in the collection of the Archives of the Canadian Rockies.

We were taken to a very large hall about 75 feet long and 40 feet wide. The walls of the building was [*sic*] a kind of limestone and the roof was made out of a wood frame and coconut leaves. There was a large table in one corner of the building about 20 feet long and about 6 feet wide. In the middle of this table was a whole roasted pig and the rest of the table was covered with all kinds of dishes—whatever they were I do not know. Most of the dishes were made out of coconut. What they could not get on the table they put underneath as there was as much food there under the table as there was on top.

Behind the table was a wooden bench roughly put together, in the same way as the table. We were asked to sit on this bench and the King and his family sat on another like it. Mr. Williams sat on the bench with us and then all the inhabitants of the village came in and squatted all over the building. The King then said a few words to his people and us.

What about the King and his family and his people? Are they not going to eat with us I asked? Mr. Williams told us that all the food was for us. I said that there was enough for 400 people. I asked Mr. Williams about knives and forks. He told us that they have no such things—he told us to "just take hold of the hind leg of the pig. See how nice it comes apart." Mr. Williams spoke the truth. My mate took hold of one leg and I the other. It came apart without any difficulty and we pitched into it.

About two minutes later two young ladies came along each one with a beautiful Panama hat nicely decorated up with different coloured ribbons made out leaves. They put one on each of us. A few minutes later two more ladies came along, took the two hats off, and placed two others on our heads and put the first set on the floor. This was more than my newspaperman mate could stand. He told the trader Mr. Williams "Will you please tell those women that the first one of them that puts another hat on me that I am going to kiss her." Mr. Williams at once translated this to the people who then all had a general conversation and a good laugh. We of course could not understand a word when all at once an old lady who must have been 90 to 100 years old

The islanders decorate the *Tilikum* at Manihiki with pandanus leaves.
Norman Luxton photograph in the collection of the Archives of the Canadian Rockies.

came hobbling along with one of the beautiful hats to put on my mate's head. It was the first and only time that my young mate took backwater.

We spent some time eating from the pig and the other things [and] the ladies brought more hats that they piled up alongside. After we had done all possible to the pig we left the large hall. As we stepped out of the door the King asked us through Mr. Williams if we would be good enough to come with him to his palace. We of course accepted and accompanied him to a building nearby built on the same principles as the large hall. The palace had a wooden floor and had two sleeping places.

On a rough table there were all sorts of things to eat but instead of a pig there were 12 chickens. The two princesses waited on us but as Mr. Williams was not present we could not understand a word. They wore calico dresses with white flowers in their black hair.

The pig had spoiled our appetite and therefore we were not able to do much to the chickens. We got up and said good-bye to the Royal Family. Outside we were met by some of the Natives who led us down to the water. They all wore fancy hats and Mr. Williams told us that they were all going aboard the *Tilikum* with us. I told them that they would turn the boat over if they did but they all said they were strong swimmers. I watched from the shore and three boatloads of them went out and completely covered her in mats and ribbons. Then three ladies went out and took everything down, rolled it up nicely and put it in the cabin. Later all the young people went to Mr. Williams' home where he had a large hall. The men sat on one side and the women on the other. A singing master stood between them and at about 2100 the singing started and kept up until one o'clock. The singing was most beautiful. They all accompanied us down to where our boat was laying. We all shook hands and bid them goodnight and we went on board for the night.

The next day was Sunday and this day was entirely set aside for church. Everyone in the village went to church three times that day. I of course followed suite [*sic*]. The service was preached by a Native missionary who had much better control of his people than some white missionaries I have met. On other islands they are not there to protect but to get all the money they can get hold. Here they live in the same style as the people.

On Monday morning I awoke to very loud music right near the boat. When I got up I saw about a dozen Native musicians standing on the beach each one playing a home-made instrument made in different styles, some made out of tin cans and others out of a tree trunk. After a few minutes they marched through the village playing as hard as they could. I went ashore to ask Mr. Williams what they were up to—and he said that they wanted to give the crew another good day.[119]

On that day of departure, the entire village turned out to say goodbye. When Luxton was unable to get the anchor off the bottom—it had become fouled in the coral—one of the singers dived down and cleared it. This impressed Voss, who offered him a reward—which was refused by this helpful villager.

PUKAPUKA (DANGER ISLAND)

The trade winds carried the *Tilikum* over the horizon from Mani-hiki toward Pukapuka. Pukapuka is a small coral atoll in the northern group of the Cook Islands. The low coral islands are dry and sparsely populated. A developing gale with following seas forced them to heave to for thirty hours. Voss sailed close to the island but could not find a suitable anchorage.

A group of people on the beach shouted to them. One of them was a trader who could speak English. Voss put down an anchor and ran a line to the beach to keep the vessel in deep water while Luxton went ashore. However, the chief could not convince Voss to leave the *Tilikum*. Instead, he sent gifts of food, in particular four-dozen eggs and some pork. Since there was no suitable anchorage anywhere around the island, Luxton came back on board and they resumed their voyage to Samoa.

APIA, GERMAN SAMOA

It took three days to sail the four-hundred-mile distance to Apia, the major settlement in German Samoa. During this voyage, Luxton recounts a terrifying fight with Voss—threats supposedly made by both men to throw the other overboard and report it later as an accident—an epic struggle in which Luxton managed to get the "jump" on Voss after an altercation, lock him in the cabin and steer the *Tilikum* single-handedly to Samoa. In this unlikely retelling, Luxton purports to bend Voss to his will at the end of a loaded rifle, forcing him to cook while locked below. Curiously, this story surfaces again in 1956 in a note from a friend of Luxton's: "He [Luxton] spent the last week of the voyage with Captain Voss locked below decks and a gun across his knee ... but would not tell me why."[120] But perhaps just as interestingly, in Voss's account the same three days are reduced to a single sentence, glossed over, it seems, in haste to report their arrival in Apia. Whatever perils they faced on their transit, neither man made a claim against the other. When they finally reached harbour they observed flags flying at half-mast in answer to the news that us President McKinley had been assassinated the week prior.[121,122]

Sailing along the coastline of Upolu Island, they approached the entrance through the outer coral reef to Apia Harbour. The harbour was busy and no officials took notice of their arrival.

The *Tilikum* at anchor at Apia, German Samoa, 1901.
Voss can be seen in the cockpit.
Maritime Museum of British Columbia.

They dropped their anchor near the hulk of the German warship sms *Adler*, which was stranded high and dry on coral very close to the shore.[123]

SMS *Adler* had been a gunboat of the Imperial German Navy. She was launched November 3, 1883, in the Imperial shipyard in Kiel. She was wrecked together with other German and us vessels on March 16, 1889, in a hurricane at Apia, during the Samoan crisis. Twenty crew members lost their lives.

Voss and Luxton raised the British flag on the mizzen-mast. They hailed a woman in a nearby boat, asking her if she would report them to the customs. She asked them where they were from and Voss told her, "Victoria, bc." She expressed great skepticism but duly reported them to the port authorities. Samoa was then a Pacific possession of the German Empire, later lost after the First World War. A German customs officer, Mr. Burkheim, dressed in a starched, white uniform, hailed them in German. He also asked where they came from and demanded that Voss should tell him no lies. He stepped on deck to inspect the ship's papers and was surprised at how the *Tilikum* heeled over as he boarded. Once convinced of their bona fides, he took them ashore for refreshments and introduced them to Mr. Reinhardt, the collector of customs, and to the German governor. Voss's ability to speak German must have been a great asset in these transactions.

Voss stayed ashore in a hotel built partly over the water. The next morning, while he was in the sitting room reading an old edition of the *Daily Mail* and smoking a cigar, he was approached by a man who introduced himself as Mr. Harder. It turned out that Harder was a former schoolmate of Voss when they had been teenagers back in Germany, and he had subsequently settled on a farm in Samoa. He offered to host Voss while introducing him to his friends, later sending a buggy to pick up Voss at his hotel for a trip out to Harder's cocoa plantation. Voss enjoyed the scenery and birdlife from the buggy and was impressed by the house and its surrounding land.

Meanwhile Luxton was pursuing his own relaxation and tours, probably glad to be away from Voss's proximity. No doubt Voss was also enjoying a break from Luxton's company.

The following day Voss and Harder visited the tomb of *Treasure Island* author, Robert Louis Stevenson. Voss also paid respects at the graves of the fallen British, American and German soldiers who died during the war suppressing the Samoan uprising of 1888.

Voss was able to take advantage of opportunities in Samoa because he could converse in German. The German governor, impressed by Voss and Luxton's accomplishment, showed him a large Samoan war canoe. He described it as being almost 100 feet long and 7 feet in the beam. It was built of timber with a bridge across the middle and it carried just one large mast. This was, the governor claimed, the largest canoe in the world. The Samoans had no further use for it so they had given it to the German Empire. The governor wanted to send it back for display in a museum, but it was too large to put on board a freighter. Voss offered to sail it to Germany, but when he asked how much they were prepared to pay for the delivery he was told one thousand marks ($250). Voss told the governor that he'd better get another man.[124]

Voss attended a dance the evening before their departure, a European-style affair, and he enjoyed every dance. It went on until one o'clock when the floor suddenly collapsed. Voss was dancing with the landlady and the two of them fell through. He recalled, "It was a terrible disaster but as luck would have it the floor was only

A huge Samoan war canoe similar to the one offered to Voss.
Norman Luxton photograph in the collection of the Archives of the Canadian Rockies.

about four feet off the ground and not much damage was done either to my partner or myself. After this accident the dance broke up and we all shook hands and went home."[125]

Voss took on mail in Samoa for Fiji and Australia. The collector of customs sent his boat to tow the *Tilikum* out of the narrows. On October 17 the new friends of the *Tilikum* were lined up at the wharf, waving hands and handkerchiefs in farewell.

NUIAFO'OU, TONGA (THE FRIENDLY ISLANDS)
On the second night out of Apia, they sighted Nuiafo'ou, the most northerly island in the kingdom of Tonga, and they sailed around

the north end to the west side. In the morning they headed to a village and found a suitable anchorage in twelve fathoms of water about three hundred feet from shore. Soon a canoe with three Indigenous men on board approached and came alongside. The chief, sitting in the stern, spoke to them in English. He invited them to come ashore. It was blowing hard, so Voss remained on watch while Luxton went ashore. The chief owned the only canoe, meaning men and women interested in seeing the *Tilikum* had to swim out from the beach.

Voss found his visitors very good-looking and polite. When they asked him for tobacco, he felt he could not refuse them each a small piece. They were all very thankful. Returning to the shore, they made a second trip to the boat bearing fruit. Luxton remained on the island until dark. The crew then returned with the chief and Mr. Charles C. Flowers, a trader who lived in the island's interior and was worried about the presence of the *Tilikum*'s crew. Flowers told them that they had to have a government permit to land, even to anchor. Meanwhile, the chief related the

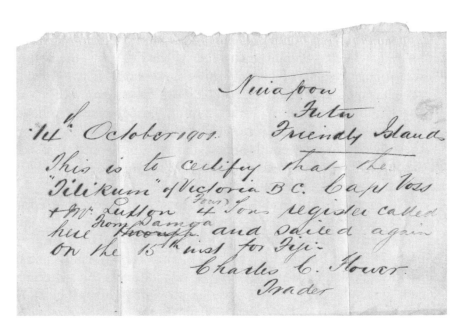

**The affidavit sworn by Mr. C.C. Flowers attesting to
the *Tilikum* having left the Friendly Islands.**

Archives of the Canadian Rockies.

story of how the volcanic island had experienced an earthquake
some years before that had killed many of his people.

Flowers signed an affidavit that read, "Nuiafoou [Futer?]
Friendly Islands, October 14, 1901. This is to certify that the Tilikum of Victoria BC. Captain Voss and Mr. Luxton 4 (four) tons,
register called here from Samoa and sailed again on the 15ᵗʰ inst.
for Fiji. Charles C. Flowers, Trader."¹²⁶

Luxton was taken to meet Folofile, the king of the island,
whom he found to be arrogant and unwelcoming. Flowers warned
that white visitors in the past had disappeared—and cannibalism
was suspected. Luxton didn't visit long, returning to the *Tilikum*
by late afternoon.

During their overnight stay at anchorage, Luxton related
a perilously close encounter with the inhabitants. Voss had
remained awake on guard in the cockpit observing several catamarans being lowered from a cliff. The night before, Luxton had
spread flat-headed tacks over the deck to discourage boarding.
He remembered this too late when he went back on deck, only to
have one embedded in his foot. Luxton recalled that Voss waited
for the islanders to board their boats before firing the brass
cannon. The loud boom had brought Luxton up from his sleep
below in time to watch the gun roll off the deck into the sea. It
was enough to discourage any further aggression and the *Tilikum*
sailed away unscathed. In his book, Voss makes no mention of
this thrilling event or of a brass cannon. Luxton claims to have
gathered all the paddles from the abandoned catamarans "selling
the collection for several hundred dollars later in Australia." He
accounts for Voss's silence as the captain's fear of going to jail for
shooting at the Indigenous people.

Voss indicated instead that he and Luxton shaped a course for
Fiji "at daybreak."¹²⁷,¹²⁸

After three days at sea they sighted a small island on the north
end of the Fiji Islands. This area has a number of small islands,
mainly uninhabited, among dangerous coral reefs. As a precau-
tion at night, whenever Voss was in proximity to land, he cau-
tiously heaved to and waited until daylight to approach. They saw
a long line of breakers on a coral reef that they followed to what
appeared to be an island. As they drew closer, they realized this
was still part of the reef but was dry enough to support coconut

trees. Running in the other direction, they reached smooth water and a soft coral bottom suitable for anchoring. While Voss ate dinner, Luxton, armed with a gun in one hand and a Kodak camera in the other, slipped over the side and started to wade to shore. Voss was concerned about the reputation of the Fijians as cannibals but Luxton, more adventurous, said that was exactly for what he was searching.

Voss knew that arguing the point with his mate was no good and dropped the matter. When he reached the shore, Luxton shouted to Voss that he'd be back in about one hour and then disappeared into the bush. Voss finished his lunch, cleaned up the boat and lit a pipe. He placed a loaded rifle at his side and waited for Luxton to return.

After two hours Voss fired a shot but received no answer. An hour later he fired three shots with no answer. His imagination ran wild. He imagined Luxton taken prisoner and roasting on a spit. Again he fired shots; still there was no answer. He then loaded the Winchester with cartridges. Carrying his clothes and rifle over his head, he waded to shore to search for his missing mate. When he was about twenty feet from the shore, he saw the dorsal fin of a shark heading straight for him. He rushed to shore, got dressed and walked toward the spot where Luxton had entered the bush.

He found the travel very hard going, but as he proceeded the bush got thinner. He had his rifle ready when he came across an Indigenous hut. It was made of small trees and covered with palm leaves and on inspection did not appear to have been recently used. He saw no signs of Luxton, so he continued up the beach past traces of old shipwrecks. Suddenly he came upon a spot he imagined as a cannibal feasting place. An underground oven was built nearby. He discovered an old shotgun and a human skeleton, which he assumed to be the remains of a victim of cannibalism. Without finding Luxton, he retraced his path back to the *Tilikum*.

Voss lit the stove and was about to start supper when he heard a voice—it was Luxton. Much relieved, Voss assisted his mate on board.

In an exceedingly different account with no mention of going ashore, Luxton shared a tale of shipwreck, referring to Voss's only deviation from good seamanship as he ordered his mate to steer toward the sound of breakers. This story involved the *Tilikum* slamming onto a reef and tossing Luxton from the cockpit. He struggled desperately in the shark-infested waters of a wave-tossed lagoon to reach shore but could only hang on to a jagged coral reef that left him "butchered." When he awoke hours later, face down on a sandy beach, he was able to observe Voss examining the canoe for damage, apparently convinced that his mate was dead. Luxton takes great pains to describe his condition: "What a mess my body was in … I had no toe-nails, no finger-nails … My knees were scraped to the bone and my shins also, such was the roughness of my treatment by the coral." He later discovered the name of the reef to be Duff Reef and remarked on the number of wrecks they passed on their voyage to Suva after spending several days repairing the *Tilikum*. Voss is credited with re-stepping each of the masts on his own and demonstrating "one of the few times that he [Voss] showed any fellow feelings, and in my weak state it helped me to come back."

Later, apparently neither man spoke of their adventures, and the next day they resumed their voyage to Suva.[129]

SUVA, FIJI

Back at sea, they soon fell in behind a trading schooner making for Suva, and as the water was smooth they sailed along with it. The captain warned Voss to be wary of Thacker Reef lying just ahead of them. As usual, in the darkness, Voss heaved to. In daylight they resumed their voyage, after passing a large ship up on the reef. The following day, October 20, they arrived off Suva and were met by Captain Clark (Luxton records this as a Captain Clark, the Harbour Master) in his launch, who reported their arrival in Suva to customs. A Captain Wooley returned to tow them into port, where they met the chief port medical officer, Dr. Carvey, along with a Mr. Thomas Horne.

With them was the Reverend Mr. Williams from New Zealand, a very large man, who was invited to have a look over the rail but not to come aboard. However he insisted on stepping aboard. When he did the deck almost went under the water. He stepped back as quickly as he had arrived, remarking that he was sure he could see all he needed from the launch. As the *Tilikum* passed other vessels in harbour, Voss and Luxton were given cheers from their crews.

Luxton and Voss were invited to dinner and in the afternoon toured the city with Captain Wooley. Voss received a request from Governor Sir William Lamond Allardyce, the acting governor of Fiji, requesting a trip on the *Tilikum* for himself, his wife and another woman. Voss offered to do so the next morning from the governor's private wharf. Accompanied by the harbour master's launch, they all had an enjoyable sail around the harbour.

LUXTON QUITS AND VOSS FINDS A REPLACEMENT MATE

Luxton had been considering quitting the voyage much of the way across the Pacific. It was not the fine adventure he had envisioned back in Victoria. In fact, it had turned out to be precisely the dangerous yet boring trip his family and friends had predicted when they initially tried to persuade him to abandon the idea. He had stubbornly persevered but now, months later, he found himself feeling let down and trapped by his circumstances.

The bad food, the cramped quarters of the *Tilikum*, the lack of sleep and privacy and the immediate proximity of the sea and his companion all combined to become negative forces, draining his desire to carry on to Australia. The problem on his mind then was finding a reason to quit that would not cast a shadow over his performance on the boat. "My newspaper man mate had by this time seen something of the world and also had quite a little sail in the *Tilikum*," Voss wrote. "We had sailed up to Fiji, a distance of 7,200 miles."[130]

At each island they visited Luxton grew more disenchanted with the voyage. Conditions were getting worse for him and the irritations born of close quarters were mounting. Although Luxton's actions at the time do not reveal any misgivings toward Voss, in his later writings he stressed that he began to feel Voss was becoming a threat to his safety—that every action or criticism of him was motivated by malevolence in Voss. However, it seems likely that Luxton was fed up and desired an excuse that would find him blameless and help him avoid the embarrassment posed by his failure to complete the voyage.

In Luxton's account of the voyage, he claims he made a

statutory declaration in Samoa: that if anything happened to him while they were at sea, the authorities in Samoa should inform law enforcement officials in the relevant jurisdiction. Presumably they would have investigated on suspicion of foul play. Despite having saved an impressive collection of ephemera related to the voyage—including tickets, receipts and correspondence—there is only an unfinished draft of this declaration in his personal papers but no copy of a notarized statement. He does not appear to have mentioned this declaration in his letters to his parents and friends at the time; nor does he make any suggestion to authorities that his life is in danger from Voss. It is more likely this story was developed well after the voyage to increase the high level of danger Luxton wanted to convey was ever-present while in Voss's company—no doubt a reflection of the newspaperman's penchant for suspense.

He may also have amplified the magnitude of an infection in his feet that he termed "coral poisoning" and used this as another reason for not continuing.

CORAL POISONING

Some types of coral produce toxins that can be hazardous to human health when in contact with skin. The symptoms can include fever, weakness, cough and muscle pain, and a reported bitter metallic taste in the mouth. Other symptoms can include chills, swollen glands and fatigue. This could have been a legitimate complaint for Luxton, having come into contact with coral on Penrhyn Island. If he was feeling ill, this would have amplified his physical and mental exhaustion.

In Suva, Luxton and Voss each relate conflicting accounts of how the replacement mate was secured. In Voss's retelling, Luxton arranged for a man to take his place as mate for the next long leg to Sydney, Australia, a distance of eighteen hundred miles. According to Luxton, however, Voss met the new mate in a bar, then introduced him to Luxton after declaring that the doctor had advised Voss that Luxton *could not* continue the voyage. Regardless of how it came about, Walter Louis Begent, just twenty-five years old, had arrived in Suva on a sailing vessel from New Zealand and left his ship to join Voss on the *Tilikum*. Begent, who went by the name of Louis, was born in Georgetown, Tasmania. He was the son of Captain Clarence Begent, pilot and master of ships on the Tamar River in Tasmania.[131,132]

Luxton promised Voss that he would take passage on the Australasian Steam Navigation Company steamer *Birksgate*[133] to Sydney. He assured Voss that on his arrival it was his intention to rejoin the *Tilikum* and complete the voyage to Europe. Instead, he had already firmly decided to quit the voyage, sell his share in the *Tilikum* and return to Canada. From Sydney, Luxton wrote to his parents, "In Fiji I was none too well, the trip had been harder on me than I supposed. So I worked a deal with the Suva newspaper and he got me a pass to Sydney. I got some coral poisoning at Penrhyn Island in my feet which gave me a good deal of bother, and the doctor said nothing but rest would cure them."[134]

On arrival in Australia, Luxton took lodgings at Manly in a private hotel to recuperate and await Voss's arrival. Years later, in writing his account of this time period, Luxton states that "I regret very much that I lost, later in my travels, my diary on Suva ..."[135] It is, perhaps, no wonder that the two accounts by Luxton and Voss of the first fifty-eight days together are so remarkably dissimilar.

8

THE MATE WALTER LOUIS BEGENT

DEPARTURE FROM FIJI FOR AUSTRALIA

On October 22 at 1600, Voss said goodbye to his new friends in Suva. He shook hands with Luxton, who asked him how long it would take him to make Sydney, Australia. Voss estimated that the journey would take eighteen to twenty days, and Luxton promised to be in Sydney to meet him.

When Voss arrived back at the *Tilikum* ready to resume the voyage, Louis Begent was already setting the boat's sails. People on the waterfront gave three cheers on departure and Captain Wooley accompanied them in his launch to the harbour entrance. Before the water got rough, Wooley drew alongside and shook hands with them. Wooley then turned back to Suva and the *Tilikum* continued sailing for the Pacific Ocean.

By evening, still in Fiji, they anchored a little southwest of Suva Harbour under the lee of Beqa Island (also known by other names such as Mbenga Island) in three fathoms of smooth water. They put a riding light on deck and had a little tea. After a few hours of conversation they turned in for the night. The next morning, they tried to raise the anchor but it was fouled in the coral. Voss told Begent how the same anchor had become fouled on a reef at Manihiki Island and how a local islander had brought it up out of four fathoms of water. Neither Begent nor Voss could swim so an underwater recovery was out of the question. Voss was forced to cut the anchor rope and head to sea without one.

The *Tilikum*'s new mate, Walter Louis Begent.
Courtesy of Meg Daly (née Begent, Walter's great-grandniece) in Australia and Nancy Salter via Simon Begent.

Voss found his new mate, Begent, to be good-natured and sociable; further, he proved to be a first-class seaman and always on hand and ready when he was wanted on deck. They spoke of past voyages and ships. Begent asked if Voss knew of a Captain Cotswald and the American ship *Hawaiian Isle* (a four-masted steel barque built in 1892 by C. Connell and Company, Glasgow).[136] Voss replied that he did know this vessel, and that the captain and his wife were his friends. Begent remarked on the coincidence as the captain was, in fact, his brother-in-law, whose wife was his sister. The couple had travelled together at sea and Voss had met them in Victoria, BC, when they stayed at the Hotel Victoria while Voss was its proprietor. Voss recalled that after this he naturally became much interested in his new mate and lost his afternoon nap while chatting to him.

On October 29 at 1800 they had dinner, and afterward Voss relieved him from the helm. They each had one of the four hundred cigars given to them by Captain Wooley and a Mr. Cox in Suva. They continued chatting until 2000, after which Begent retired as he was scheduled to go on watch at midnight.[137]

A HARSH LESSON LEARNED

The *Tilikum* kept sailing before a fresh easterly breeze and Voss kept her at or near her course. He wrote:

> The sea was running high and once in a while a breaking sea struck her under her weather quarter and she would give a heavy roll and run 2 points up on her course. It was the kind of wind that allowed *Tilikum* to make her best passages. While I was sitting watching the compass I noticed the compass light got very low and soon went out altogether. I struck a match and looked at my watch which showed 2330. A bright star about 25 degrees above the horizon was a little to my weather bow. As I did not care about calling my mate until his time was due I steered the boat by the bright star and got along very nicely until midnight.[138]

Begent was a sound sleeper and as a rule Voss was obliged to call him two or three times before he could manage to rouse him out of the confined if not comfortable bunk. Voss shouted out, "Louis, its twelve o'clock. The compass light is out and I wish you to come on deck to take the helm so I can light up again."[139] This time, his call brought Begent immediately up on deck. The seas were running high, breaking close to the boat and throwing a lot of heavy spray on board.

Voss told his mate to put on his oilskin, take the helm and steer a course aligned with the star on his weather bow. Voss took the lamp into the cabin to fix it, but as there was no particular hurry he lit two cigars, passing one to Begent and smoking the other. Begent took the cigar and thanked Voss, saying that his treatment on board was the best of any vessel he'd been in. He also indicated he would gladly make the rest of the voyage in the event that Luxton did not carry on. Satisfied with the

" REGENT LOST HIS BALANCE AND WENT OVER THE SIDE WITH THE COMPASS IN HIS HAND,"

**Louis Begent is shown being swept over the side in the
dark with the compass firmly in his hands.**
World Wide Magazine, 1904.

easy air between them, Voss was more than happy to secure
Begent's interest.

By this time Voss had the lamp ready. He passed it out of the
cabin, and Begent placed the compass box (or binnacle) in front
of where he was sitting so he could steer. Suddenly, just as he
stood with the compass in both hands, a wave struck the canoe
under the weather quarter, which caused her to lurch to leeward.
Begent was unprepared for this and lost his balance. He went
headfirst over the lee rail.

Voss had been looking at Begent as he rose and was about

to tell him to keep his seat when, with shocking suddenness, Begent disappeared over the side. In a second Voss was on deck, throwing out the lifebuoy as far as he could. He then lunged for the helm and swung it hard over to bring the *Tilikum* around in very few minutes. He hauled in the sheets as she came around with the intention of putting her on the other tack and sailing back to his mate.

As the *Tilikum* came up into the wind, Voss shortened sail to keep the boat from turning over, but she refused to come about. At this point he took in all the sails and put out the sea anchor to keep the boat from drifting. Throughout this manoeuvring he was calling out to Begent. In agony, he shouted and shouted, but all in vain. He recalled, "My poor mate was done for and the moon was full and overhead light clouds were drifting from the east to the west, now and then shutting off the light."[140]

Tony Gooch and Jeanne Socrates, two modern-day Canadian solo circumnavigators who have each embarked on numerous voyages, believe that once Begent went overboard he was doomed. They both note that his heavy clothes would have become water-logged and weighed him down. In the dark it would have been impossible to see him even if he was nearby. The time passing while the vessel was brought around and the sail shortened would preclude a rescue unless the vessel returned to precisely the spot where Begent went into the water.[141]

Voss recalled in his original manuscript:

… it was the longest night that I ever experienced. In the morning at daybreak I got on top of the little cabin and swept the horizon with my eyes for hours but could see nothing but the blue waves with their little snow white caps passing me one after another. I kept on watching the waves all the forenoon until 1130 when I was certain that my mate was dead. The only thing left for me was to do the best I could. I made up mind to go under sail and steer for Sydney, but all by myself. I was then just going to take a look at the compass when it struck me for the first time that it had gone overboard with the unfortunate mate. I remembered that when I left Victoria my mate had a small pocket compass in one of his valises which I was unable to find—[as] all his luggage was ashore with him in Fiji … I had a Master's Certificate but I never read in detail about making a course at sea without a compass to find a destination."[142]

Voss considered letting the vessel drift with the sea anchor until he encountered a ship from which he could get a map and compass to sail to Sydney. But chances were remote that he would encounter another vessel.

At 1200 I took my quadrant [*sic*: sextant] up on top of the cabin with one arm around the mast and the quadrant and watch in the other. It struck me that I could get the direction of the wind and calculate the compass bearing at noon. I found my course to Sydney to be southwest and immediately set a course.[143]

The *Tilikum* soon left the watery grave of Voss's unfortunate mate behind.

Circumnavigators Gooch and Socrates both agree that navigating without a compass is not a significant technical difficulty given that Voss had his latitude; by heading west he would have eventually hit Australia. It may have been the shock of the loss of his mate that caused doubt in Voss's mind.

The trauma of the accident upset Voss tremendously, preventing sleep, and his hunger was forgotten. He kept on sailing until the following noon when, by his observation, he found he had made 125 miles and was off course by only about ten miles. He was satisfied then that he could sail the remaining twelve hundred miles to Sydney without a compass.

After taking his position, he had a little bread and tinned meat. He had two uneventful days of sailing with a fresh breeze and light variable weather. He tried to cook a little to eat but when he got into the cabin he became discouraged and went back out on deck again. He took in sails, put the boat under a sea anchor and went to his bunk to sleep. As soon as he closed his eyes, the horrible night returned to his mind, disrupting his rest.

Reflecting in his original manuscript, Voss wrote:

My readers may think that I was a little bit of a coward but I assure you that nobody knows what it feels like when you are way out in the Ocean in a small vessel and you lose your only companion. On one occasion in my life I saw 57 people (men women and children) drowned like rats in a trap. I helped to fish them out of the water and many other accidents but I have never even had a tear come to my eyes. But on this accident where I was left alone on a small boat 1,000 miles from land, nobody to speak to, nobody to express my feelings—nothing to do but think over my misery. The more I thought the worse I felt. For five days and five nights I could not sleep and hardly had I got an idea that I would never see land again and that I would die of exposure on board my little boat and provide food for a hungry shark.

On the fifth day after the accident I was sitting at the helm when I fell asleep as the weather was warm. It was the first time on the whole voyage and it nearly cost me my life. Southerly Boosters are winds with a tremendous force which blow off the Australian coast. One of these hit the *Tilikum* under full sail when I was sitting on the Port side. As the wind struck her fair it threw the *Tilikum* over on her side and I fell and struck my head [with] a sharp crack after which the *Tilikum* righted herself. Having a look around I found the foremast had broken and it was that which had saved the boat and my life.

But after all I found the old saying [that] where there is life there is hope and where there is a will there is a way.

This last accident, or more correctly speaking, carelessness, brought me to my senses. The spars and sails hanging over the bow of the boat kept her nearly head on to the sea. It gave me two hours and I sat in the cockpit never moving a hand during the time I made up my mind that I would do all what was in my power to bring my boat safely through the gale which was blowing and sail her to Sydney Harbour. I then put on a lifeline around my waist with one end fastened to the main mast [and] left slack enough to allow me to go right to the forward end of the boat. I went forward and secured the broken spars and sails. I then made myself a nice cup of tea, and with some biscuits and butter and some canned meat, I enjoyed the first warm meal in five days. At dark I put a riding light on deck and laid down in my bunk for the night. I woke up again after midnight from a bad dream. I got up in the morning and had breakfast at 0630.[144]

For three days Voss was becalmed and used the time to fish. He was annoyed when sharks would attack any fish that went onto his hook, shooting at sharks that came close to the surface near his vessel. He never managed to land a fish that he caught on a hook—all were lost to sharks.

Voss reflected, while writing his original notes for publication many years later, that when the sky turned dark and threatening, he and Begent should have turned around and gone back to Suva. Instead, he made the fateful decision to press onward. He wrote "… we poor human creatures never know what may happen to us the next second. I put to sea and went through an experience which I presume no man in this world should go through. I hope and trust that I shall never meet with such an experience again."

WAS LOUIS BEGENT MURDERED BY VOSS?

Over the years the story of Begent going overboard has become exaggerated leading some writers to suggest that Begent and Voss had a violent argument resulting in Begent's death by Voss's hand. At the time, when the accident was reported to port officials in Sydney, there was no indication from anyone that Voss was suspected of murder.

When Luxton's daughter edited his manuscript, she included an explosive footnote containing an unsubstantiated accusation Luxton had not included in his original account. This literary time bomb holds a shocking revelation. It powerfully states:

> I feel sure [Voss] killed Begent. It was a drunken fight without doubt that finished Begent. In fact [Voss] refused to say he did not when I accused him of it. Begent was not his first according to his own stories. I might have been one as well, but knowing him as I did, I was always ready for him. Voss landed in Australia days overdue, and was in hospital for weeks from exposure and sickness he contracted through the women on the islands.[145]

This accusation has subsequently been repeated many times in articles and discussions and is often accepted as fact by some writers and bloggers. Many writers have taken Luxton at his word, making a villain of Voss and branding him a murderer. Luxton made other careless and inflammatory observations elsewhere in his draft text.[146]

It is true that Voss's description of the incident is the only first-hand account we have. But it is a compelling account that rings true in its specific sincerity. Voss would repeat this story freely when asked, and the details he recounted remained consistent.

It's worth taking the footnote quoted above line by line to examine Luxton's claim as well as exploring the possible motives behind it. It cannot be overstated, however, that Luxton never intended for his manuscript to be made public. His sole purpose in writing it was to give his daughter an account of his time at sea and perhaps to satisfy his own need to get his experiences—however he chose to remember them—onto paper.

LUXTON'S ACCUSATIONS REFUTED

Luxton never publicly accused Voss of murder during the latter's lifetime—when Voss could have defended himself. As well, in his original manuscript, Luxton never alluded to harbouring any suspicion toward Voss that he murdered Begent—or anyone else. In fact in the subtitle of Luxton's eleventh chapter, the Begent incident is referred to simply as "Voss's terrible experience."[147]

The unsubstantiated footnote's claim that "it was a drunken fight without doubt that finished Begent" seems an unlikely explanation as no alcohol was known to have been carried aboard the *Tilikum*.[148] Both Luxton and Voss liked to imbibe ashore —and both men tell stories on themselves in this regard. Many sailors liked to drink when ashore but, for Voss, there is no hint of a problem at sea except this accusation from Luxton.

In Eleanor Luxton's published version, Luxton wrote, "In fact [Voss] refused to say he did not [kill Begent] when I accused him of it." But since we do not have any corroboration of this discussion and since it was recounted decades after the fact, it must be considered hearsay. Voss no doubt had a highly developed sense of responsibility to his vessel and his crew. As master of the vessel, he would have felt personally responsible for his mate—and probably wished he had done more to prevent the fall and to rescue him afterward.

"Begent was not his first according to his own stories," Luxton went on. There is little doubt that Voss was referring to Begent as not his first *mate to go overboard* rather than not his first *victim of murder*. Voss's tales of events when he served as mate and master in ships under sail likely included stories where crewmen fell from the rigging or were swept overboard.

"I might have been [a victim] as well, but knowing him as I did, I was always ready for him." Luxton was vulnerable, inexperienced and aboard a small boat at the mercy of a man he knew little about, and at times was fearful of Voss. But is this evidence enough to accuse Voss of murder, or is it instead an understandable paranoia developing from the stresses of the voyage?

"Voss landed in Australia days overdue and was in hospital for weeks from exposure and sickness he contracted through the women on the islands,"[149] claimed Luxton. The Australian papers make no mention of a hospital stay and there wouldn't have been enough time between Voss's public appearances to permit a long recuperation. Regarding the accusations of STDs and dalliances with island women, there is no evidence at all to support these allegations.

The unsubstantiated information contained in the footnote of *Luxton's Pacific Crossing* has worked to unfairly discredit both men: an intentional character assassination of Captain Voss and an unfortunate inclusion in a manuscript never intended to make publication, with Luxton reaching out from the grave to accuse his long-dead shipmate of murdering Louis Begent.

IS THERE AN EXPLANATION FOR LUXTON'S BEHAVIOUR?
The impact on the psyche of single-handed long voyages is now well known and has been studied extensively. For the *Tilikum* voyage, there were no precedents that could prepare the crew for the conditions they would face. Although there were two persons aboard, alone on alternating watches they may have experienced stressful conditions similar to those of a solo circumnavigator.

As a deep-sea master mariner, Voss would have assumed that he had absolute command of the vessel. He would likely have behaved as if he were on the quarterdeck of a full-rigged ship, using rough, salty language to communicate his instructions, perhaps even peppering them with threats—traits commonplace among captains and senior crew. Moreover, Voss was a "water-front character"—colourful and charming but capable of decisive and ruthless action. He was an authoritarian—the masters of sailing vessels had to be ultimate forces on board who brooked no questions, particularly in moments of danger.

Luxton, on the other hand, was a "green hand" with little practical experience at sea and no experience in a small yacht on the ocean. He was learning on the job—unprepared for most of the conditions he experienced. Despite Luxton's inexperience, Voss had readily aligned himself with the green hand, assuming he would learn—on the job. Voss does make mildly deprecating observations about Luxton's lack of experience and knowledge of seamanship.

Travelling in a tiny boat with no private space and barely room to get more than a few feet away from each other must have been an ordeal for both of them. The stresses of loneliness, constant danger, coping with the unknown, continual thirst and hunger as well as fear would have been powerful influences on their mental health. They both likely would have suffered from chronic cabin fever, causing irritability and restlessness. It is not surprising, then, that Luxton developed a strong distrust and fear of Voss. In a letter written to his future wife, Georgia Elizabeth McDougall, Luxton revealed a very strong sentiment toward his sailing companion. "Dangerous as were the storms and calms of the Pacific, they were as nothing compared to the clash of our personalities. Before we ever reached Apia, Samoa, we hated each other, and I was certain Voss intended to do me harm."[150]

Luxton describes Voss as "not what any person would term a daredevil or even a fearless man. At his best he was quite methodical and sure of himself, always, before he acted. When roused and in his black moods it took a lot to stop him. Neither could he handle liquor, so that outside of a few ounces that I carried in the medicine chest, no spirits of any kind went into the stores of the *Tilikum*."[151] He further states that Voss was a violent binge drinker, but there are no indications of this later in the voyage when Voss is repeatedly entertained in the ports he visited. If he were an ugly drunk, wouldn't word have spread quickly to potential hosts at yacht clubs and other venues? His social hosts have left no record of such behaviour.

Luxton, like Voss, was prepared on several occasions to use firearms against the inhabitants of the islands they visited. Luxton wrote that at the outset of the voyage he had installed a small brass cannon on the bow of the *Tilikum*—able to dispense awful damage against foes. He was clearly able and willing to wound or kill.

If Luxton had accused him of murder directly, Voss makes no mention of it in his own account of the voyage. If we analyze the available evidence, what is known for sure?

- Voss made statements to the port authorities in Sydney immediately upon his arrival, explaining the circumstances of Begent's demise.
- The port officials exonerated Voss of blame. There is no record of a formal inquiry.
- Neither Voss nor Begent could swim. Any "man overboard" situation was likely to end in tragedy.
- The cockpit of the *Tilikum* was tiny and shallow, without handholds or railings for protection. It would have been easy for an occupant to go overboard in a storm with breaking seas.
- The crew did not routinely use a lifeline to secure crew on deck, nor did they wear flotation devices.
- The Begent family accepted Captain Voss's account of the loss after speaking directly with him about the incident. Begent's father was a master mariner who would have been quite capable of evaluating the story and its teller's credibility.
- Voss described the loss in detail to the Australian newspapers, and the story was widely reported around the world. The reporters did not detect any hint of foul play in the telling.
- None of the later mates reported the behaviours in Voss that Luxton found abhorrent—drunkenness and violence. In fact, unsolicited testimonials to Voss's gentle demeanour were published in some newspapers. He was regularly feted by community and business leaders in every place that he visited and was never suggested to be anything other than a gentleman.
- In his newspaper interviews in Australia, Luxton gave no indication of his suspicion of trouble or foul play. He made no public accusations of negligence or wrongdoing. His letters home make no mention of this suspicion or accusation. The

murder theory seems to have developed in later years through
the telling and retelling of his story.

- Luxton and Voss continued to communicate after they met
in Manly, near Sydney, worked briefly together and then separated again. Luxton claimed he never communicated with
Voss after they parted in Australia, but in fact he received a
letter from Voss in late 1904 when Voss announced his intention to write a book about the experiences and asked Luxton
if he would send him a portrait to include in the book.[152]

VOSS'S REACTION TO THE EVENT

Voss's statements from his manuscript tell a compelling story of
how he agonized over the loss of his mate.

> I could not understand that my mate went overboard. I was
> looking at him at the time that he fell and I put the boat around in
> a very few seconds. When she stopped headway the boat should
> have been close to the place where he fell and gave no answer
> to my calling.[153]

> After getting a full headway on the boat all sails nicely draw-
> ing the wind two points abaft the beam I went through the
> same performance again as I did at night during the accident.
> I dropped a stick of wood over board in the spot where the man
> fell out of the cockpit. I then put the helm over and swung round
> and as she came head to wind I was about 100 feet off that piece
> of wood. By that I know the boat was not any further off the man
> at night when she stopped headway. If the man had been able to
> swim he should have been able to swim up to see me.[154]

> I made this statement before the authorities in Sydney and
> was told then that I had done as good as any man could have
> under the circumstances. No blame was put on my shoulders
> and I myself was quite satisfied that I had done the right thing.[155]

> I want to state here that later on by experimenting I have
> found that I acted wrong but as this is not known to many in fact

that I have never met a man yet that did not say that I acted correctly in manoeuvering [*sic*] the boat. However through experimenting I found if a man falls overboard from a large or small sailing vessel regardless of the direction of the wind bring the vessel around before the wind keep the sails in trim as she comes around then the vessel will most likely run right on top of the man or the boat will be very close so that a rope can be thrown on top of him.[156]

THE UNANSWERED QUESTIONS

There are too many unanswered questions in this case to believe that Begent's untimely death was anything but an accident.

- Why would Voss murder his mate—what was to be gained by doing so?
- Why did Luxton claim to have reported Begent's loss to the port authorities? And why *after* the Manly exhibition rather than upon Voss's arrival in Sydney? In fact, Voss had reported Begent's accident to the port authorities immediately upon his arrival. The story was reported in the newspapers that very day.
- Why did Luxton assert that Voss had been dropped by the Australian press at the news of Begent's death? A long, detailed press report in March 1902 addresses the tragedy head on, in detail and in a positive light.[157]
- Why would Luxton claim to still be acting as mate in the *Tilikum* throughout the travels in Australia—when he had obviously parted ways with Voss in Sydney—and risk being associated with such a scoundrel and murderer?
- If Voss had truly murdered Begent, why did he continue to relate the story of his mate's accident to audiences on his post-voyage tours? It does not seem likely that Voss would continually raise the subject had he been involved in foul play.
- Why would Luxton state categorically that Voss was a "superior mariner and that he would not hesitate to go to sea with him in a larger vessel" if in fact he feared for his life and was sure Voss had murdered his successor?

The simplest explanation is the most likely: Louis Begent,

unsecured to the boat, fell overboard by accident. He was either unable to swim and quickly drowned or was swept away in the rough seas and wind into the darkness and drowned. Voss's sad account of the event reads true. Luxton, writing his memoirs of the trip in response to Voss's book and harbouring resentment over his former shipmate "stealing" his story, rewrote events to support his own version of the voyage.

It is our assertion that had Luxton intended for his account to be published he would have done so in his lifetime. His daughter Eleanor, with pride for her father her only motive, published a manuscript that could no longer be corroborated by the original author.

Interestingly, despite all the grief and tension of those first fifty-eight days at sea, in both Voss's and Luxton's versions of the voyage, each man paid compliments to the other.

Luxton parted with Voss in Sydney on good terms: "When Jack and I separated in Australia it was the last we saw of each other, though through the press and mutual acquaintances I often heard of him for years. After a wonderful and eventful voyage with the *Tilikum* across the Indian Ocean and the South Atlantic twice, he finally landed in London England, and as mentioned in this script, I can recommend his book to all who love adventures."[158]

As for Voss, he wrote of Luxton in parting with him and the *Tilikum*: "Mr. Luxton was a good shipmate in every way, and also a very careful man on board the boat and I am quite certain that if he had remained on the vessel in Suva and made the trip with me to Sydney the accident would not have happened."[159]

The men—and their stories—contrary to their last words.

9

AUSTRALIA

As he drew near to the Australian coast, the worry of being run down by a larger vessel grew in Voss's mind. The courses of ships sailing to Sydney tended to increase in density the closer they came to the port's entrance.

Even more worrisome for him was the risk of running ashore. He was unsure of his exact position and felt it necessary to keep watch all night in case he was too close to the coast. This growing fear confirmed his aversion to single-handing in a small boat.

After weeks of very little sleep, Voss was exhausted. Every possible threat to the *Tilikum* was magnified, and new threats seemed to be constantly appearing. On one occasion, to avoid an impending collision at night with a large vessel, he soaked one of his socks in kerosene and lit it on fire as a warning signal. This was spotted by the other ship, which passed within five hundred feet of the *Tilikum*.[160]

On November 17 he encountered a waterspout that appeared within three hundred feet of the boat. A waterspout is a small tornado occurring on water. It does not suck up water; rather, it is a rotating column of air over the water. Direct contact with a vessel could be disastrous, but such incidents are actually quite rare. Voss perceived the spout as a threat and was frightened by its proximity. He invoked a folk remedy to counteract it and fired a rifle shot at the middle of the water at its base, feeling vindicated when the waterspout apparently began to dissipate. He fired shots at others but decided that they were too far away because the shots had no effect.

On November 20 he sighted the Sydney Harbour Light—visible twenty-five miles distant. He had been sailing for twenty-two days without a compass and with only a watch for a chronometer and a sextant that had cost him fifty cents in Victoria.

The port of Sydney took note of the arrival of an unusual craft in the harbour approaches:

> The lookout at Sydney Heads has been called upon to report the arrival of all kinds and conditions of craft, from the stately 13,000-ton palatial liner down to the diminutive coaster of barely a score in tonnage measurement. Yesterday (says the Sydney "Daily Telegraph" of Wednesday), however, for the first time in the history of the port, "colours" were hoisted indicating a 4-ton craft. "A schooner from Canada" was the signal run up at the Fort Phillip station, and speculation was rife as to the name and nationality of the vessel. She was such a small craft that the signal-master at South Head had to place the glasses to his eyes a second time to make sure that she was not one of the pleasure craft from one of the resorts on the coast. Her name, in bold lettering on the bow, however, soon showed that she was the Canadian yacht 'Tilikum', which had made Sydney as a part of the programme of her voyage round the world. So fragile, so diminutive did she seem as she sailed in with the Canadian flag flying at the mizzen, that one wondered and admired the pluck, perseverance, and skill displayed in bringing her across the 9,200 miles of trackless ocean.[161]

Voss was hailed by a tug whose master had read about his expected arrival—which was now overdue. Although he was offered a tow, Voss chose to wait for the wind to change so he could sail into the harbour unassisted. Opposite the signal station at Fort Phillip he hoisted his little Canadian flag at half-mast, and on November 20, 1901, he sailed into the harbour.

He was hailed by the quarantine vessel and was boarded by a port medical officer to clear the pratique, a licence giving permission to use a port after quarantine or on presenting a clean bill of health. After Voss presented the ship's papers, he had his first opportunity to report the details of Begent's death, making an official statement about the accident. In the boat alongside him was Mr. Walsh, the customs officer, who asked Voss to declare any contraband goods. He offered Voss a tow up into the harbour to an anchorage, which Voss readily accepted.[162,163]

It must have been a great relief for Voss to be safely in port. Having previously lost his second anchor, he now had to make use of a thirty-pound piece of lead on a line. This temporary measure was ineffective, and the *Tilikum* began to drag in the wind, drifting near another anchored yacht with the danger of drifting farther. Voss received a proper anchor from shore and anchored again. Finally, he arranged for a boatman to take him ashore. He went directly to the Sydney general post office. A large number of letters were waiting; some of them had followed him across the Pacific. One letter contained an invitation from Luxton to come to Manly, where he was staying.

While Voss was struggling alone across the Pacific in the *Tilikum*, Luxton had travelled from Fiji to Sydney by passenger vessel. On arrival in Sydney, Luxton had taken lodgings in nearby Manly in a small private hotel. Voss was anxious to see his old mate. He arrived in Sydney harbour about 1400—his passage the night before had been a combination of sailing and sleeping, covering the last fifteen miles in four hours. Securing the *Tilikum*, he picked up the mail and sought out Luxton. He took a streetcar to Circular Quay, where he caught the ferry to Manly and walked to Luxton's hotel.

In his book, Voss wrote: " 'Well John,' Luxton said, 'I thought sure that you and your mate and the *Tilikum* was [sic] on the bottom of the ocean! How did you get through the last heavy gale sea that

LETTERS FROM HOME

Receiving mail from home was a challenge for Voss and Luxton. They did not follow their original sailing plan to go to French Polynesia so their early mail was misdirected. Each envelope told a story.

An example of an envelope addressed to Norman Luxton from his brother George. It is addressed to Tahiti but the sender asks the postmaster to forward it to Sydney, Australia, if not received there. Helpful postal workers who knew of the exhibition site of the *Tilikum* at Manly redirected it again, where it finally reached its intended recipient.

Archives of the Canadian Rockies.

frightened people around here? You actually weathered the heavy gale in that little dugout. Well, well, you are a brick!' "[164]

After they got through the handshaking, they both sat down and Luxton asked about Begent and the *Tilikum*. Voss recounted the story of Begent's death. In Voss's original manuscript, he wrote that Luxton was so overcome with emotion that he nearly fainted. The erstwhile mate told Voss that, having sailed the boat, he knew only too well what an ordeal the captain had been through over the last twenty-three days on the boat alone.

Voss recalled, "My mate said that owing to the accident he would never put a foot on board the *Tilikum*. He asked me to abandon the trip and go back to Canada. No doubt his advice would have been suitable for a good many but my belief is, and always has been, that when I start a thing I put it through. The accident was a bad one but accidents will happen on board any vessel."[165]

A couple of days later Voss spoke to the newspapers. They reported that "the schooner yacht *Tilikum* arrived at Sydney on Tuesday last, when the commander reported the loss of his mate and only companion Mr. Walter L. Begent, a Tasmanian. 'We had an awful time of it' was the first remark made by Captain Voss to a representative of *The Age*. 'The weather was simply awful off the coast, and I am sorry to say that I lost my companion. He fell overboard and was drowned and I have been entirely on my own ever since. Such an experience I have never had during my long term at sea.' "[166]

Years later, Luxton repeatedly wrote that once the Australian newspapers learned of Begent's death, "every paper dropped us as if the *Tilikum* had never existed."[167] But the favourable local press coverage continued almost daily—with no hint of a suspicion of trouble. Clearly, reporters, who undoubtedly would have been right onto a story with suspicion of murder, were silent on the subject. Instead, Voss became a media sensation and reporters interviewed him almost daily, reporting every new development in the story of the *Tilikum* being followed by their readers.

Also, if the port authorities had suspected foul play, they would have arrested the vessel, ordered a formal enquiry and turned Voss over to the police. None of this occurred. Instead, the authorities accepted Voss's version of the story. The shipping master of the port of Sydney sent a formal letter to Voss requesting Begent's wages (which were still owing) to be transmitted to his parents: "Dear Sir: Would you kindly pay into this office the Balance of Wages due L. Begent late of the Tilikum."[168] He would not have been so matter-of-fact given any hint of foul play on Voss's part. Voss recalled:

My mate [Luxton], who had a half interest in the Tilikum came
to a conclusion with me that we should bring the boat over to
Manly for exhibition. Luxton reported to The Victoria Daily Colonist November 30, 1901 that he had not abandoned the voyage
as was previously reported, but that he was arranging to exhibit
the boat and his collection of curios. He made no mention of
his private decision never to go to sea in the Tilikum again. The
Mayor of Manly offered us a nice position free of charge for
showing the boat. The steamboat company running between
Sydney and Manly offered to advertise the exhibition.[169]

Voss returned to Sydney and sailed out of Rushcutters Bay but
ran onto a sandbar on a falling tide. He drifted around Sydney
Harbour all day, finally reaching Manly Bay late in the afternoon.

To get the *Tilikum* ashore they had to pull the boat over a
six-foot stone wall with blocks and tackles to get her out of the
water. She was shown under a tent in a little park among the
trees. At that time Voss was inexperienced in showmanship and
simply stood in the crowd, watching. Some visitors said the boat
represented a really skillful accomplishment; others remarked
that it was a fraud executed by some Yankee who had carried it
across the Pacific on a freighter. It would not be the last time that
people would doubt the veracity of the Lloyd's certified claim
that the *Tilikum* had been sailed there from Victoria, BC.

Initially shy of publicity, Voss had much to learn as a showman. Presenting himself to strangers in large numbers was something with which he was quite unfamiliar. Manly represented the
first attempt at displaying the *Tilikum*. Using a large tent draped
with flags, Voss hung numerous photographs of the South Sea
Islands to make the exhibit "look attractive." Here he admits his
reluctance to speak publicly. "The next thing I had to do was to
act the part of a showman, and this I soon found was the hardest
proposition that I had tackled so far on this cruise, and I very
nearly gave it up at the beginning."[170]

He was tested with his very first customer, an elderly visitor
who paid her sixpence entry fee, came on board and sat down in
the cockpit. She sat for some time without saying anything.

"Well, madam. How do you like my little boat?" Voss asked.

"Like what?" she said. "I don't see anything to like about your little boat. But when is she going to start?"

"Start for where?" Voss asked.

"I don't know," she retorted. "You ought to know; I paid a six-pence for a boat ride, and I'm going to have it."

"Madam," he explained, "you are mistaken; this boat is not here to ride about on, but on exhibition as a novelty." To his great surprise, the old woman went off like a stick of dynamite.

"Boat on exhibition as a novelty! You must think I'm crazy. I can see hundreds of boats every day in Sydney Harbour for nothing, and you are very mistaken if you think I have come here to pay you sixpence to see your old boat!"

Voss returned her entry fee and she departed.[171]

One day a wildlife showman erected a tent next to the *Tilikum*'s venue. He introduced himself as Louis de Rougemont (his real name was Henri Louis Grin, born in Switzerland), a colourful character and a relentless self-promoter. His invented exploits were published internationally in issues of *World Wide Magazine*. In his articles, de Rougemont claimed, among other things, that no one could effectively ride a turtle. He made this statement to create interest in his sideshow adjacent to the *Tilikum* exhibit.

Luxton was fascinated by the operation. To generate some income for himself, he helped out de Rougemont as a casual show worker. He listened to the yarns spun by the showman and learned the art of generating publicity and attracting visitors.

A complimentary ticket distributed to a member of the press at Manly, New South Wales, to attend the exhibition of the *Tilikum*.

Archives of the Canadian Rockies.

INDIAN WAR CANOE — TILIKUM

No. 1. "TILIKUM" is now on exhibition at the Corner of George and Gipp Sts., Sydney. This little craft was made by the Indians of Puget Sound over **40 Years** ago for the purpose of carrying war parties between the different Islands. The wonderful feature of the Canoe is that she is a DUG-OUT FROM ONE TREE, having a length of 32 ft. keel, 6 ft. beam, 3 ft. deep, and 4 ton measurement. From the port of starting, Victoria, B.C., Canada, to Sydney, viz., Penrhyn, Humphrey, Danger, Samoa, and Fiji Islands, she has covered a distance of 9,400 miles.

Some of the Things you see .. when you call on the "Tilikum"

No. 2. The DEEP SEA ANCHOR which took the "Tilikum" safely through many gales.

No. 3. CHART of NORTH and SOUTH PACIFIC OCEAN, with the track of the "Tilikum," showing the Islands stoped at; the gales encountered is all cheerfully explained by Captain J. C. Voss.

No. 4. INDIAN FLAT HEADS.--Skulls and bones of the Indians of Puget Sound.

No. 5. WHALING HARPOON of the Indians.

No. 6. TOOLS the Indians use in making their canoes.

No. 7. MODELS of Indian canoes.

No. 8. INDIAN PADDLES.

No. 9. INDIAN BASKET WORK.

No. 10. INDIAN WATER BOTTLES.

No. 11. INDIAN ANKLETS used when dancing.

No. 12. IMPLEMENTS used in basket work.

No. 13. PAPOOSE CARRIER.

No. 14. INDIAN FISHING BASKET.

No. 15. PEARL SHELLS from Penrhyn showing the growth of the pearl stone.

No. 16. NATIVE HATS of Humphrey Island, made from sugar cane, cocoanut, sweet grasses and pandanus.

No. 17. FANS from Penrhyn, Humphrey, Danger and Samoa Islands.

No. 18. BIBLE BASKETS used by the South Sea Islanders to carry their bibles.

No. 19. SOUTH SEA ISLAND MATS

No. 20. PANDANUS Strips used in making hats, mats, baskets, etc.

No. 21. MODEL of South Sea Island Canoe known as the Catamaran

No. 22. TAPPA CLOTH, made by the natives out of bark known as "Masi"

No. 23. SAMOAN MAT, made out of the bark of trees.

No. 24. NATIVE ROPE, made from cocoanut fibre.

No. 25. TOBACCO grown by the South Sea Islanders.

No. 26. PEARL FISH HOOK

Numerous other Curios are on view, and remember it will in all likelihood be the last time a vessel made from one tree—a North American Indian DUG-OUT—will ever visit the Australian Colonies. Now is your chance. Leading Newspapers will chronicle future movements of the "Tilikum" for the next four or five years.

On EXHIBITION at
Cor. GEORGE & GIPP STS.
Opposite ANTHONY HORDEN'S
ADMISSION: Adults, 6d; Children, 3d.

The advertising poster that was distributed for the exhibition of the *Tilikum* at Sydney.

Archives of the Canadian Rockies.

De Rougemont also taught Luxton to ride a large turtle in the show whose head was reined to keep it from retracting. This was billed as a "world's first" attraction. Luxton thoroughly enjoyed being the centre of attention in the turtle show.

After Voss left Sydney, Luxton was hired to manage de Rougemont's show. At the next engagement on their tour an angry audience ran them out of town, and a disappointed Luxton never saw de Rougemont again.

Luxton had made up his mind that he would not continue the voyage. "I am offering up daily prayers for a buyer for my share of the canoe," he wrote to a friend. "I have tried for days."[172] Luxton never did find a buyer. In the summary of his account, Luxton claimed that "… to this day I own two-thirds of one half of the *Tilikum*, one-sixth of it being used to pay the wages of the sailor at any time I was away from the boat."[173]

Meanwhile Voss would have to find yet another new mate.[174] (Regarding the mate, the Charters Towers *Evening Telegraph* of Friday, December 6, 1901, stated that although "only one of the two referred to is a sailor, there are nevertheless two pairs of hands in an emergency.") He received several applications, including one from a woman. Intrigued, Voss interviewed her and found her "a fine looking strong able woman who had been yachting in Sydney since she was eight years old. She stated that she could sail any kind of vessel, could steer, set sail, reef and take in sails and come to an anchor. She could also cut and sew sails, splice." She insisted strongly on being taken on for the voyage, but Voss felt it would be improper for a married man to take along a female mate. Finally, she admitted to Voss that she could not navigate and he was able to turn her down.[175]

He then received an application from Peter Drummond, the secretary of the Sydney Canoe Club, who was well known on the Sydney waterfront as "Peter the Sailor." Drummond reported that he was determined to travel in search of "novelty and adventure." Thirty-two years of age, he was a native of Sydney and an enthusiastic sailor who owned and sailed a range of craft including a boat he had built himself—the 22-foot *Shannon*. Drummond said he "looked forward to a unique experience and had no misgivings in respect to the cruise but rather embraced it as an admirable opportunity of experiencing life at sea." Voss hired him.

At this point Voss's next preferred route was reported by Drummond to be "Hobart [Tasmania], Melbourne, Geelong, Sydney [again] and Brisbane." Drummond looked forward to visiting "the Torres Strait, Singapore, the Malay Archipelago to Ceylon [Sri Lanka] and on to Aden, the Red Sea, and the Suez Canal to England." The final port would either be Halifax, Nova Scotia or New York. Drummond said, "The only possible danger was that of collision, or the remote chance of being run down. On the score of weather [Voss] had no misgivings."[176]

Voss and Drummond sailed the *Tilikum* across Sydney Harbour unballasted from one display site to another so that she sailed very tenderly. Any gust of wind was able to put her over on her beam-ends. In spite of these gusts of wind, they got across the harbour successfully. But the impression on the new mate was

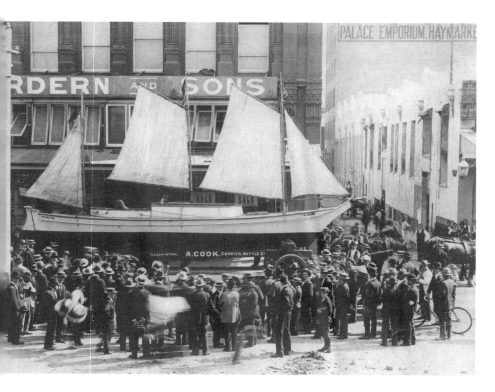

A large crowd gathers to view the *Tilikum* on exhibition at the corner of George and Gipp streets, opposite Hordern and Sons store, in Sydney. Admission was sixpence for adults, threepence for children.
Archives of the Canadian Rockies item lux_i_b1_13_17

traumatic. Once the boat was secured, Drummond apparently went ashore and was not seen again. The "tender" behaviour of the *Tilikum* was too much for "Peter the Sailor," who quit the voyage before actually going to sea.[177]

To further complicate his life, Voss was summoned to the Sydney Harbour Board office, where he was advised that he owed them pilotage dues for his entry to the harbour. Because he had never had a pilot on board, Voss objected to paying these fees. But the harbour master declared the dues must be paid before Voss could sail back out of the harbour. A long discussion with the port officials ensued. Determined to avoid payment of the pilotage fees, Voss called at the railway office to arrange to ship the *Tilikum* by rail to Newcastle. He was later told that the *Tilikum* was the first deep-water vessel to ever enter Sydney Harbour and not depart by sailing out the same way.

NEWCASTLE, AUSTRALIA

At Newcastle, Voss was still evading the bill for harbour dues at Sydney. Since Luxton was still in Sydney and Voss was anxious to settle up with him, divide the gear and deal with the debt, he prevailed upon his erstwhile mate to intervene.[178] Government officials denied Luxton's request for them to waive the pilotage fees, and it is presumed that Luxton later settled them.

While in Newcastle, Voss overhauled the *Tilikum* and painted her inside and outside. A Mr. A. Hamilton was engaged as the new mate to sail the leg between Newcastle and Melbourne.[179] On the day before their departure, Voss received a letter from Luxton in Sydney, saying that he had consulted a clairvoyant who predicted disaster if Voss carried on to Melbourne. Luxton urged him not to go.

On February 10, 1902, ignoring Luxton's warning, Voss had several Newcastle yachtsmen tow the *Tilikum* out with a steam launch, and in a few minutes they were outside Nobbys Head Light. The launch blew three whistles to indicate Voss should hoist his sails and let go of the tow line. The ocean swell was tumbling, and up came the mate's breakfast. Voss was obliged to hoist the sails and let go of the tow line himself. The wind laid the *Tilikum* over on her beam and occasionally heavy spray covered her. It was very uncomfortable for Hamilton. He was a poor helmsman, and when questioned further he revealed that his only experience was on a coasting steamer from Sydney to Newcastle.

However, Hamilton proved to be a quick learner and he soon gained skill and confidence in boat steering. Unfortunately for him, he could not get used to the motion of the *Tilikum* at sea and was constantly seasick. For five days they continued on one course and then rounded Cape Howe. On the eighth day they entered the Bass Strait, where they had to shorten sail. Finally they had to heave to on the sea anchor with the weather increasing to a gale.

Hamilton had not eaten a meal since their departure from Newcastle. He had managed to eat only a dry biscuit from time to time (which apparently came up as soon as it went down). The mate complained that he felt so ill that he thought he would never see land again. In agony, he lay on the bunk in the cabin. Voss saw a sail to the southwest of their position, and observed that the vessel was approaching them. When he asked Hamilton if he would agree to go aboard the approaching vessel, his mate asserted that he would make the trip on the *Tilikum* or die on board.

The sailing ship continued to approach the *Tilikum*. Voss wondered if the master had mistaken them for a lifeboat from a ship sunk in the blowing gale. Voss recalled:

> It was a wonderful sight—one that people would give a lot to see such a wonderful living picture. It was a full-rigged ship running under her fore and main lower topsails before a heavy westerly gale. In the large sea she was rolling from one side to the other such that her yards were almost touching the water every now and then. The vessel's tall mast was out of sight at times, hidden behind the seas. One minute she was entirely out of sight and the next second her bottom was almost in sight. As she came closer we could see plainly that the large seas were breaking over her stern and kept the deck awash.
>
> She was coming straight towards us and when she got within about 300 feet it looked like she was going to run the *Tilikum* down, but she changed course in time. Within a minute she was alongside of us. The Master was standing on the quarterdeck with marine glasses to his eyes watching the *Tilikum*. His crew

were arranged along the deck hanging on to the rail and rigging. Two men were at the wheel twisting it from one side to the other and it was all they could do to keep the vessel on her course. They were all busy watching us when the vessel shipped a sea over her forcing some of them to leap into the rigging while others were covered by the water. The unfortunate Captain, a rather short and stout built man and therefore slow in movement was slow to react. As he was caught by the breaking sea he got hold of the mizzen mast and hung on until the water ran off.

The *Tilikum* was laying quite comfortably with her mizzen storm sail and sea anchor over the head rising as the large waves came along. My mate had just crawled out on deck to have a look at the passing ship. I was sitting in the cockpit smoking a pipe. The Captain of the passing vessel was standing on his quarterdeck shaking off the water [and] at the same time looking at us. I was waiting for him to say something as he had the largest vessel and therefore his place to speak first. But he only looked at us not saying a word and I allowed a little for him not speaking on account of getting a soaking. When the vessel was right alongside of us I asked the Captain if he required any assistance. I got no answer to my question as he kept on going. I put it down for granted that he could get along without our assistance. In another half hour the ship was out of sight.[180]

The next morning, the wind subsided, and they made for Wilsons Promontory, which they rounded after being at sea twelve days. Late in the day, close to Cape Liptrap, the wind freshened across the westerly swell. Hamilton once again fell seriously ill. On the chart, Voss saw a place where he could run for shelter—a little inlet at the head of Waratah Bay called Shallow Inlet. The name worried him but he felt compelled to get his mate to shore.[181]

WARATAH BAY
At horseshoe-shaped Waratah Bay, the wind was blowing straight into the beach with a heavy sea running. The bay, located in south Gippsland, Victoria, is an arc of twelve miles of flat, sandy beach framed by Cape Liptrap to the west and Wilsons Promontory in

the east. The wind pushed the *Tilikum* closer to the shore despite the many tacks Voss made to try to run toward the open sea. Voss warned Hamilton to prepare for the worst, certain they were going to wreck. As they entered the breakers, Voss dropped the sea anchor over the stern. He tripped the sea anchor bag when breakers ran up, and the anchor alternately filled and emptied when it was necessary to stop headway. The *Tilikum* responded, her stern lifting to the tempestuous breaking sea without taking any water.

They crossed another half mile of breaking seas, but at the end, the water was not deep enough for the *Tilikum* to get safely through to shore. At the end of the inlet they became stuck on the sand, with an ebbing tide leaving them high and dry. But the end of sea motion was just what Hamilton needed, and he was soon well again. By the time lunch was ready, he was able to eat his share.

As they finished their lunch, they expressed satisfaction with their good luck in getting through the breakers without a scratch. But the tide now began to rise quickly and the breakers encroached upon the *Tilikum* until it was lying broadside to the waves. When the vessel began to roll and tumble, they had to abandon their meal to try to get out of this new difficulty. The waves caused her to bump up and down on the sandy bottom, piling sand on the lee side of the boat until the sand almost hit its surface. On the weather side, a deep groove in the sand was being eroded.

They hoisted the sails, but this made little difference as the breakers smashed over her top and the bumping grew worse. Finally, a big breaker lifted the *Tilikum* and pushed her over the sandbar, dropping her into deep smooth water behind it. Voss and Hamilton, much relieved, were determined to remain with the *Tilikum* as long as they could.

"BOYS, I BELIEVE I READ ABOUT HER IN THE PAPER"
This episode was duly reported in the newspapers from an eyewitness account from local fishermen, the Winchester brothers. They surmised that the *Tilikum* had entered over the sandbanks at high tide but would have trouble getting out again at lower water when the danger of touching bottom became greater.[182]

Once free, Voss and Hamilton sailed half a mile up the inlet where they sighted four men fishing. Voss learned that they were farmers who lived about five miles away and were fishing on their Sunday day of rest. Two of the onlookers, the Pilkington brothers, who owned a large farm and raised cattle in Gippsland, invited Voss and Hamilton to their house (in Voss's account they are incorrectly named as Pinkerton). They would ride there on their horses. Hamilton eagerly jumped on one, but Voss explained that he was not a farmer and would prefer to walk. The brothers assured Voss they would ride slowly and that after what he had just come through in the boat, he need fear nothing. All went well until he had to cross a stream. The horse cleared easily but Voss fell into the water.

The Pilkingtons offered the men some refreshments and Voss a change of clothes. But both of the Pilkingtons stood six feet and Voss only five foot four, so the clothes did not fit well. They were invited to stay overnight but Voss was reluctant to leave the boat unattended, so late at night they decided to walk back. They found the *Tilikum* high and dry on a sandbank, and in the morning they once again rode back with the Pilkingtons to their farmhouse. Decades later, one of the Pilkington brothers (he is unnamed in the narrative) wrote of his experiences while living at Sandy Point, including his recollection of meeting Voss and Hamilton:

> We shouted and waved to them, and they waved an answer in return, and were presently along side the Channel's bank where we stood, joining us without further mishap. We gave our visitors a hearty welcome and warm congratulations on escaping from what was undoubtedly a perilous experience. We quickly intro-duced ourselves to one another, while Capt. Voss explained that, having had his rudder damaged, to make a landing for repairs at the first opportunity, was necessary. By the chart of our coast-line, he saw that an entrance to Shallow Inlet, "available for small craft only" would answer his purpose, so he took the risk, entering the "New Channel" that, at all tides was both difficult and dangerous to approach. Our visitors were of very different types. The skipper was the typical Scandinavian, squarely and strongly built, fair haired and blue eyed, with the firm strong

mouth and chin that clearly showed the stuff he was built of. I
should judge he would have been in or about 40; his mate, Hamilton, was an Australian born and bred, having joined "The Tilikum" at Sydney, following the loss of the skipper's previous
mate, a young Tasmanian, Louie Begent, who, with the binnacle
box and compass went overboard when about twelve hundred
miles from the Sydney Heads. Young Hamilton, we later learned,
had had but little experience of the sea, that much being gathered from a few trips on Australian costal steamers, but, though
a martyr to the worst form of sea sickness, Capt. Voss valued
him as a good mate, and an active and willing seaman.[183]

The hospitality carried on for ten days. Both hosts and visitors enjoyed themselves immensely, if only for the break in the
monotony of their routines. One further anecdote concerning
the mate Hamilton: "At one point of his varied career, Hamilton
practised as a distortionist [sic], and he gave us quite an exhibition of his prowess as such this evening on the floor of the living
room, that was truly the highlight of our entertainment."[184]

Voss announced that they must depart. Sailing back out
through the breakers, the *Tilikum* shipped seas and the motion
made Hamilton sick again. They entered Port Phillip Bay on a
slack tide, and in light air they dropped anchor in Williamstown
Harbour at Melbourne.

HOBSONS BAY

After rounding Gellibrand Point, the *Tilikum*'s arrival at Hobsons
Bay aroused considerable interest. The boat was unexpected; she
was presumed to have been still stranded in Shallow Inlet and
in distress. Voss had passed Cape Schanck and had entered the
bay without any telegraph notification from the signal station of
her arrival.

The port doctor and customs officers came on board the *Tilikum* to inspect the certificates. Voss then went ashore to search
out a venue for displaying the canoe. He had his own collection
of artifacts and curios to display, including photographs taken
while voyaging down the islands, the head of a rare species of
sawfish and "endless Native implements and manufactures."

They were very popular with visitors and created almost as much interest as the canoe itself.[185]

In St. Kilda, Voss arranged with Captain Canny (sometimes spelled *Kenny*) to exhibit the *Tilikum*. He sailed the vessel from Williamstown to St. Kilda. The boat was dry-berthed and put on display for a week. She was then moved to a shore venue for display for a few days before moving on to the Melbourne exhibition grounds.

MELBOURNE

Voss arranged with a large carrier firm to haul the *Tilikum* out to the exhibition building and afterward to take her back to salt water. After the exhibition was over she was taken outside the hall, and using shear legs and tackle, she was prepared to be hoisted and placed on a horse-drawn wagon. Voss directed the work but used block and tackle supplied by the carrier.

A heavy strap was placed around the middle of the boat and hooked onto a block. Voss gave orders to heave up and four men got hold of the winch handles, lifting her until the *Tilikum* was high enough to place on the wagon. Then Voss gave the order to stop heaving. Just as two men began to remove the cradle from the ground, the *Tilikum* dropped with a crash. Fortunately the men escaped without injury.[186]

However, the canoe was seriously damaged. Voss was appalled as he surveyed his broken vessel. Disaster was now staring him in the face as he saw his dreams of future achievement suddenly evaporate.

A HOOK, A CROOK AND A VICTORY

Voss recalled:

> It almost broke my heart when I saw her dropped like that. However I took courage enough to have a close look at her and found that she had been split in five different places. The splits ran from the stern to forward from 15 to 20 feet long. They were large enough for a man to put his hand through. I thought that this was the end of the *Tilikum* and that the fortune teller in Manly that told Luxton not to go to Melbourne was right. I then

looked around to find the cause of the accident—it was the top
hook from the tackle that had broken in the neck of the hook.

I took one piece and put it in my pocket after which I tele-
phoned for the Manager of the carrier company. He came as
soon as possible. When he arrived and saw my little boat laying
there all in pieces he seemed to feel as sad as I did about it. In
fact he said that he'd rather lose one of his relations as to see
that little boat which then held the world's record for crossing
the Pacific laying there in pieces.

"What caused the fall Captain," he asked? I said that the
hook tip broke and it was too bad. He said he was sorry, so
sorry. After a few more words of consolation he gathered up
the pieces and transported them into town and put them in Mr.
Carlson's back yard.[187]

In a subsequent letter to the carrier company, Voss asked
whether they would be willing to repair the *Tilikum* under his
instructions. If they would, Voss said he would make no further
claims. The offer was refused. But a few days later the owner came
down with a young boat builder, who offered to make repairs for
C$22.10. The owner stated that he was willing to pay half the
cost. Voss refused, stating that the carpenter was not competent to undertake the work. The owner produced an older, more
experienced carpenter, James Cowan, who offered to do the work
under his direction for C$37.00. Voss was prepared to accept
this offer, but the carrier company owner stated firmly that the
damage was the result of an accident and therefore it was not his
responsibility to cover repair costs.

Voss had received an outpouring of public sympathy after the
accident. He was advised to put in a claim for damage, and after
consulting a lawyer, learned that he was entitled to compensation.
Mr. W.J. Woolcott, a Melbourne lawyer, was engaged as his solici-
tor, who instructed his barristers, Mr. McArthur and Mr. Cusson.
Voss put in a claim against the company for five hundred Australian pounds. For the defendants, Mr. Kilpatrick was retained.

Voss had to wait three months before the case came to trial.
County Court Judge Chomley heard the case. The suit was against
Messrs. Warr and Company, the carriers.[188,189] During this time

Voss was living with Mr. W.E. Smith, a new acquaintance who had offered hospitality to an interesting stranger. Smith was a building surveyor in Melbourne who was also a carpenter by trade with a shop well equipped with tools. Smith was also a Canadian by birth.

Voss's barrister, Mr. McArthur, had the task of representing him in court. Voss was able to produce only one witness—a labourer. The others who were present at the accident scene had accepted inducements to testify for the defendant. In Smith's workshop, Voss built a scale model of the *Tilikum* including the shear legs, block and tackle.

When the case was called, Voss was the first to testify and answer the questions, which were principally about the breakage. After describing the incident, the defending lawyer asked whether the iron in the hook was good. Voss thought the iron was not good, and he was asked what he would say after the court heard from an expert, Professor Kernot (a professor of engineering at Melbourne University), who would testify that the hook was made of the best Swedish iron ever produced. Pressed, Voss suggested the iron might have been good but the hook had been spoiled in workmanship.

Voss claimed that the hook had been fabricated out of two pieces of iron, the eye part and hook. The two pieces were welded together, a process that had created a flaw on the inside of the hook about one-sixteenth of an inch deep and nearly the circumference of the hook outside where the weld came together. It appeared the hook had been hammered too long after the iron had cooled. This caused the metal to crystalize, making it susceptible to breaking like glass. Black paint then covered the iron-smith's defective work.

The professor testified that he had tested the other hook. He acknowledged there was a small flaw in the hook and it broke only after a strain of almost four tons. When asked whether he would use such a hook to lift the *Tilikum*, his answer was negative. This made the professor's earlier testimony look contradictory in the eyes of the jury.

The old carpenter who had offered to repair the *Tilikum* was also called as a witness. He tried to put the blame on Voss, stating that shear legs should not have been used but rather a lifting derrick. He stated that the derrick would lift twice as much weight but that he didn't have enough men to winch the boat up slowly. The jerking motion, he said, was what caused the hook to break, and it was Voss's fault for not directing the work properly.

In rebuttal, Voss brought out his model. Using a spring scale, he showed that two legs caused a breaking strain (the weight needed to make the gear snap) of six pounds. Then he attached a third leg, taking the strain to the breaking point with the scale showing fourteen pounds.

Voss then asked the witness how much weight there had been on the winch handles for each man to heave. The old carpenter answered that he did not know. At this, the judge became angry, asking how the witness could state that there was too much weight for each man when he didn't even know how much weight there was in total.

Voss, however, was able to show that each man had only fifty pounds to heave, according to the tackle, the great wheels on the winch and the size of the winch handles. Satisfied with Voss's technical explanation and ability to demonstrate true competence, the judge did not need to hear any further testimony. The jury quickly returned a judgement in favour of Voss of two hundred Australian pounds, which was paid to his lawyer.[190]

Smith and Voss decided to repair the *Tilikum* themselves. They put a chain around the boat and twisted it so that the splits slowly closed until they were hardly visible. Voss put in steel straps fastened with bolts driven from the outside. He set up a screw on the inside after having the straps well fastened. He caulked the cracks and covered them with pitch, and the *Tilikum* became as tight as ever.[191]

BALLARAT

While in Melbourne, Voss received an invitation from a man from the city of Ballarat to sail the *Tilikum* on Lake Vendoree, a small inland lake fourteen hundred feet above sea level. Voss put the *Tilikum* on a horse-drawn wagon and took her to Geelong, and from there to Ballarat. Lake Vendoree is about a mile square and shallow, with an average depth of about six feet. The name is also spelled as *Wendouree* in contemporary literature.

In Ballarat, Voss placed the *Tilikum* on exhibition for a short time on improvised stocks constructed near the boat shed. Later, she was displayed in Camp Street where an admission of three-pence was charged. Several local celebrities attended including Mr. F.J. Martell, the director of the School of Mines.

Voss gave a public lecture about his voyage on October 20, 1902, and kept the *Tilikum* on display for several weeks. He also gave it some time at anchor in Lake Vendoree.[192] He used this opportunity to bend on a new suit of sails that he received from some Ballarat yachtsmen. The old suit was tacked up in their boat shed by the members of the yacht club to keep as souvenirs. The *Tilikum* had the unique distinction of being the very first deep-water vessel ever to sail on the shallow lake.

Hamilton seems to have either quit as mate, or was dismissed. In any case, Voss needed another new mate so he put a small advertisement in the Ballarat paper and the next morning he had six applicants. He picked the one thought to be most suitable, Mr. W. Davis, and together they brought the *Tilikum* back to Geelong by rail, where she was re-ballasted and put back in the water.

GEELONG

With the *Tilikum* back in the water, Voss and Davis went for a trial sail to vigorously test the boat. She pitched heavily in the choppy waters of the bay, which made Davis seasick. Voss reflected that the *Tilikum* could make any man sick in a rough sea whether he was experienced or not. He felt that if a man could sail the *Tilikum* without sickness then that man could sail in any vessel anywhere.

Voss announced to Davis his intention to sail to Adelaide. Before they departed, his mate advised Voss that he needed to return to Geelong to fetch his clothes and gear. But Davis did not come back and Voss was once again without a mate.

Voss wired the Melbourne Sailors' Home, requesting that they send him a new mate. (The Melbourne Sailors' Home was built in 1864 to house visiting seamen until they received notice of their next voyage.) While waiting for his mate to arrive, Voss spent time with some Geelong yachtsmen. Late in the evening, Voss was approached by a man carrying a kit bag and rolling from one side of the wharf to the other, occasionally dropping the bag and cursing. Voss observed, "I could see from his appearance that he was a proper old shellback." (A shellback was someone who had crossed the equator—and could also refer to an old, experienced sailor.) Voss later recalled:

> I stood there pretending not to take any notice of him when he got close up to the end of the wharf where I was standing. He dropped his bag and sat down on top of it. He pulled out a bottle from his pocket and had a good drink, after which he looked at me and passed the bottle over and said, "That is damned good stove governor, have a drink old man." I thanked him and said that I did not care about [alcohol] and don't like to drink with an old sailor. He replied that this was alright—he would have another. He said to me, "I say governor I want to go out to board that there ship (pointing to a large vessel laying [sic] out in the harbour at anchor). Would you mind to put me off in this boat (pointing to the *Tilikum*)." I told him that the boat did not belong to me. "Don't she?" He asked, "Well I will take a chance at her myself" and was in the act of putting his bag on board.
>
> It was then time to act, to stop him. I said, "Hold on young man this boat does not belong to you." He protested that he had to get there somehow—explaining that he had been sent from the Melbourne Sailor's Home to go on that windjammer to London. He had been told that she was all ready for sea and just waiting for his arrival.[193]

Voss asked him whether he had a letter to the captain. The sailor pulled out the letter and handed it over. On the envelope it read, "To Captain J.C. Voss of the *Tilikum*." He was shocked to realize this was his proposed mate for the next leg of the voyage. He needed to get to sea, but taking a man in such a condition was unthinkable. In his experience, Voss had often seen men coming on board crazy with drink, but there was always a large crew and the loss of one man for a few days mattered little.

In British vessels, officers told such men to go to their bunk until they sobered up. The other crew members had to pick up their share of the work. In American and Nova Scotian vessels, the officers used a different method to treat men in that condition. They fed them on "belaying pin soup" (beating the men with clubs), which made them come around very quickly. It happened very often that when these men sobered up, they turned out to be very good seamen. Voss made up his mind to take the man and give him the "British treatment," since he was quite able to handle the boat alone.

Voss informed the man that the letter was addressed to him. The sailor asked if he was the captain of the *Tilikum* and bound for London. "He looked at me as much as to say 'you are a damned liar.' " Voss eventually convinced him to get on board, and in the afternoon they let go the lines, set the sails and left the wharf. A crowd on the wharf gave three cheers and the *Tilikum* left Geelong Harbour astern.

The new mate, Mr. McConnell, lay down and had a good sleep. Voss sailed the boat alone and at dawn dropped anchor, put a riding light on deck and had a small meal. Afterward, he too lay down and slept for a long time. When he arose the wind was blowing freshly. He called for his mate to come on deck.

McConnell, now sober, raised the anchor and set the sails and they sailed toward Queenscliff near the entrance to Phillip Bay. Much to Voss's relief, McConnell proved himself to be a first-class seaman. After a brief stay there, they were towed back to sea.

GLENELG

They sighted the east end of Kangaroo Island and passed through the Backstairs Passage, arriving at Glenelg, a seaside village that sits in Holdfast Bay near Adelaide, South Australia, where they moved on to the Semaphore Anchorage to await the customs service boat. The master of the customs boat declared the *Tilikum* to be "the queerest looking craft that he had ever seen." "Do you mean to say that you have come all the way from British Columbia in that little boat?" he asked.[194]

At the end of their stay a farewell social for the *Tilikum*'s crew was held at the Jetty Hotel in Glenelg by members of the Glenelg Dinghy Sailing and Aquatic Club, whose vice-captain W.H. Varley presided.[195] It was here that Voss first mentioned a Mr. McDonald, who was by this time apparently acting as Voss's manager and advance man. McDonald was also present.[196]

The *Tilikum* causes a minor sensation as a crowd
gathers to watch at the Glenelg waterfront.
John MacFarlane collection.

ADELAIDE

They sailed up the Adelaide River to Port Adelaide the following day, where Voss arranged to exhibit the boat in the Eagle Tavern (five doors down from the Theatre Royal)[197] at Hindley Street. The doors were not wide enough to move the vessel inside so a picture window was to be removed to facilitate her entry. McConnell was instructed to prepare the site while Voss returned with the *Tilikum*. With the ballast removed and assistance from some volunteers, Voss put a strap around the boat and lifted her out of the water with a hand crane onto the bed of a truck. But when they arrived the mate had not undertaken any of the work and was fast asleep on a pile of lumber, passed out from drink. Voss left him asleep. Before they could get organized, hundreds of people had gathered to see the *Tilikum*.

Voss blended into the crowd to hear their reactions to the little vessel. The comments were a mix of wonder and scorn. Voss was just about to introduce himself when he overheard a woman

**The dry-berthed *Tilikum* on display at Glenelg with Captain Voss in the cockpit.
Voss found it easier to pull the vessel ashore for exhibiting than to leave her
in the water. He could also paint and undertake repairs at the same time.**
John MacFarlane collection.

state that the owner should be tried for murder and that if she
was on the jury she would certainly vote for conviction in the
first degree (for so recklessly endangering himself and his mate
in such an unlikely looking craft). This argument was taken up by
another woman, Mrs. J. Jewel, who had apparently survived the
sinking of the ship *General Grant*. (The ship-rigged *General Grant*
was wrecked on May 13, 1866, at the Auckland Islands. Sixty-
eight people drowned and only fifteen people survived. After a
year on Auckland Island, four of their number sailed the ship's
boat to Australia to report the incident.)

Eventually the *Tilikum* was placed inside the store for exhibition. Voss hired a man to greet people at the door, much like a
carnival barker. This man was a "theatrical manager" who anticipated the questions that would be asked and then "hooked" pass-
ersby into buying a ticket to enter the exhibition. His spiel went
something like this: "Ladies and Gentlemen! Allow me to tell you
that I've got the greatest novelty in the whole world. Captain Voss

is the most wonderful and most intrepid mariner that the world has ever known. You have heard about Captain Cook, who is considered to have been the greatest navigator in the world. This intrepid mariner has simply put Captain Cook in the shade."[198]

Voss was standing behind the door listening and became embarrassed by this bold stretch of the truth. He told the barker to "hold on out there, do not stretch the truth any more than you have to!" Just at that moment the barker declared that "this intrepid mariner sailed ten million miles." "Hold on, hold on!" Voss shouted. "I sailed ten thousand miles up until now."[199] The barker ignored the advice and went on to declare that it was ten *million* miles in a boat only thirty-eight *inches* long. Voss figured that if people swallowed that tale they would believe anything.

The barker would not allow anyone to enter until he got through telling them about the large whales and sharks and other things Voss had seen on his travels. When he got through with his "fish tales," people simply rushed to the door. He could hardly take the entry money fast enough. Voss went out through the back door, afraid to face the people who had been listening to this hyperbolic banter. Once the place filled up the barker went inside and, failing to find Voss, delivered an even taller tale to the crowd.

GLENELG AGAIN

Afterward, Voss took the *Tilikum* back to Glenelg where they stayed until January 8, 1903. While he was there he was made an honorary member of the Holdfast Yacht Club, which honoured him at a farewell banquet. The club had been established at Adelaide in 1883. In 1998 it amalgamated with the Glenelg Sailing Club to form Adelaide Sailing Club. In addition, there is the Port Adelaide Sailing Club, which was established in 1897.

The response from the public to this visit was overwhelmingly enthusiastic. A letter to the editor of the *Adelaide Register* stated:

To the editor: The Canoe *Tilikum*

Sir—Two things break the monotony of a deep sea trip—sometimes, alas! We ship a sea and sometimes we see a ship.

In passing through Hindley sum a day or two ago I saw the

word "Tilikum" on the wall near the Eagle Tavern and by making enquiries I was informed that a ship of the above name was on exhibition inside. The word "Tilikum" awakened pleasant memories of the past, at it means friend. Just then the star navigator, Capt. Voss, appeared on the scene, and when the compliments of the day was passed in the Chinook language he gave me a hearty welcome to inspect his canoe. ... The sea anchors are made of canvas, and are a wonderful invention, and should be examined by every person who goes aboard of a boat or a ship. The canoe is trim and shipshape, and has acted nobly in all weathers up date, and her captain, on his great feat deserves unbounded praise, for there is not one sane man in 10 million would risk such a voyage. Just fancy being on the wide, wide ocean in a raging storm, your mate and only companion washed overboard, never to be seen again? The next wave carrying away all the nautical instruments, and Capt. Voss has to navigate his frail 4-ton canoe by observation a distance of 1,700 miles. When worn out with fatigue for the want of sleep he quietly camps on the crest of the wave, like the noble albatross. He lays her to, round comes her head, out with her sea anchors, bells go, and the Captain "douses the gilm." and turns in for the night. Next morning hot coffee, reefs shaken out, the tiller unlashed, and the captain is steering by observations to the sunny shores of Australia. I have been a bit of a cuckoo sailor myself and I sailed and paddled all varieties of canoes, viz. dugout, bark, canvas, green hide, and wattle and daub. Capt. Voss has for sale a very instructive pamphlet containing many useful hints to persons traveling by water. Capt. Voss, who will shortly start for homeward bound, is a naturalized British Columbian, and started from Victoria, Vancouver Island to make a trip around the world for a wager, and I hope he arrives safely at his destination in good cowl at Victoria, where I spent a few pleasant years of my life in the fifties.

I am, Sir, Etc. R.T. CLARK.

Adelaide, December 27.[200]

10

NEW ZEALAND

It does not seem to have occurred to Voss to be concerned about the time it was taking to complete his voyage. He appears to have been more interested in visiting intriguing new places. After Australia he headed for New Zealand, which gave the appearance of backtracking. The winds were favourable for the voyage and he knew the coastal cruising there would be enjoyable. Until he had visited all the larger ports he was not anxious to head north on his route across the top of Australia.

A NEW MATE FOR THE VOYAGE TO NEW ZEALAND
The conditions on the *Tilikum* caused many of the mates who engaged for the voyage to have second thoughts. Many of them only lasted a short time, particularly if they completed a voyage leg at sea. Once again Voss was obliged to engage a new mate for the voyage to Dunedin, New Zealand. He was Edward O. Donner,

Voss (standing) with his mate Edward Donner, "the Tattooed Man of Australia," probably taken at Glenelg, Australia.
John MacFarlane collection.

more famously known as "the Tattooed Man of Australia." Voss particularly enjoyed his company and his storytelling.

ON TO HOBART, TASMANIA AND A NEAR DISASTER

At short notice Voss announced that the wind had become favourable and they must depart.[201] The *Tilikum*'s departure again attracted a huge crowd at the Glenelg harbour, and they were given a rousing send-off. They were towed out of the harbour by some small boats in the company of several yachts. After dropping their tow line, the crew set the sails. They sailed past Cape Willoughby, a headland located on the east end of the Dudley Peninsula on Kangaroo Island in South Australia, in company with a barque bound for Hobart, Tasmania.

When poor weather threatened, Voss went forward and took in the sails as Donner was not yet used to the motion of the boat. With the storm sails set, the new mate hauled the lines taut to keep them from swinging about. When Voss got back into the cockpit, much to his satisfaction, he saw that the ropes were in their proper places. As a principle, when on board a boat it is essential that there is "place for everything and everything must be in its place."[202]

But as he surveyed the scene, Voss noticed that the throat halyard had unbuckled, and the taut ropes had caused the clip hooks to go up to the block on the masthead. He spoke to Donner about it and told him to be more careful the next time. Donner volunteered to climb the mast and get the line down. The *Tilikum* was tossing about in a heavy sea and could not set sail while it was blowing so hard, so Voss told him to wait until the weather got better. After this Voss went below and lay down to have a nap. When the *Tilikum* was under storm sails or sea anchor, the helm was lashed and there was nothing to do but look for other vessels.

Voss had been down in the cabin about ten minutes when he heard a noise from the bow of the boat. It sounded like something falling from the mast, and he jumped out of the bunk and onto the deck. Donner was not to be seen. He shouted, "Where are you?" but there was no answer. He looked over the weather side and there he was—in the water, apparently helpless. Voss called his name without answer and watched as his mate went down for a second time. The *Tilikum*, under storm sails with sheets hauled well in to amidships, crawled along very slowly. Voss must surely have been recalling with dread the gruesome fate his former mate Louis Begent had met.

Voss recalled later that many things passed quickly through his mind.

> How well I remembered that I promised the good woman to take care of her husband and my mind was made up in a second that I would stick to my promise either to save him or die with him in the ocean. By the time my mate had come up the second time and was then about six feet to windward of the cockpit I took hold of the lifeline which was always ready for such occasions and jumped overboard. In a second I was up to him and shouted at the top of my voice "You are safe!" but I got no answer. I took hold of his hair and by giving a quick pull I turned him on his back and then put the lifeline around his body just below his arms. As I got back on board I pulled the mate on board—and never felt better.[203]

In those days, the lifeline was used to save people already in danger. In modern use, blue-water yachtsmen attach themselves with a line to the boat at all times. But the situation was still grave. Voss looked into Donner's bloodshot eyes and realized he was not breathing. He rolled him over but could not bring him back to life. (This was before modern techniques of artificial resuscitation had been popularized.)

Suddenly an idea occurred to Voss, as he recalled an incident he had witnessed years before when he saw a drunk lying unconscious in the street. A policeman had grabbed the drunk by the back of the neck and given him a good shaking to no avail. He then took off his boot and struck him with a few heavy blows. Incredibly, the drunk recovered his senses as if nothing had happened. Voss tried this remedy on his mate. When he struck him the first blow, a shiver passed through Donner's body. With such a response, Voss immediately struck him again with a few more blows until Donner began to move.

Voss removed the man's wet clothes, gave him a good rubdown and took him below to the cabin, where he laid him in his bunk and covered him up. Voss repeatedly poured some Worcestershire sauce on Donner's lips, and soon his mate was breathing freely. Once the danger had passed, Voss asked for an explanation.

Donner described how he had climbed up the foremast to get the hook of the throat halyard down to make it ready to set the sail. Just as he was high enough to reach the hook, the boat gave a quick lurch, his legs slipped away from the mast and he was left hanging by his hands. As the boat swung back, he struck his head against the mast and recalled nothing else until he awoke in the bunk.

It was his fall from the mast and striking the deck that drew Voss's attention. If Donner had fallen directly into the water, Voss would not have heard a thing and would never have known about the tragedy until some time later. It was a "lucky" accident for both men and a dramatic start to their voyage.

On January 21, 1903, they entered Hobart Harbour, where they stayed for three weeks. During this visit, Voss gave public lectures on the scientific side of boat handling and sailing and explanations of his theories on the use of the sea anchor.[204]

BOUND FOR NEW ZEALAND

On February 9 they departed for Invercargill, New Zealand. Donner stayed with the vessel in spite of the usual warnings from bystanders who predicted disaster for the *Tilikum*. The heavy weather they encountered forced them to run under a storm sail. They secured everything on deck and inside, closing the cabin door so the vessel would be well secured. Voss attached two life-lines—one fastened to the mizzen-mast and one to a cleat on the deck. He was convinced that in this state the *Tilikum* could take a sea over her without much damage occurring. The noise from the sea and wind was ferocious, and at times it seemed the waves would go over the top of the mast. Voss was very careful to keep her stern in to the following sea. Despite taking on some spray, the *Tilikum* always rose to the occasion.

At 1700 Voss told Donner that he was going to keep her sailing until 1800 and then heave to under a sea anchor for the night. At 1730 their tea was ready. Donner had prepared fried potatoes with ham and eggs, and he opened the cabin door to hand Voss a cup of tea. Voss had just taken the cup when he heard the roar of a breaking sea coming up from behind. He shouted, "Close the door, quick!" and stood up in the cockpit. Steadied by the two lifelines, he kept one hand on the tiller with the cup of tea in the other, holding it as high as possible to keep the salt water out of it.

The sea was now close to the stern of the *Tilikum*, the boat standing on an angle of forty-five degrees with her stern up. She started to go along with the breaking sea at an astonishing speed, but the sea was moving faster and in a moment overtook the *Tilikum*. It broke over top of them with a colossal crash.

Running before a breaking sea is very dangerous. The overtaking wave tends to prevent the stern from rising and the sea usually runs faster than the vessel. It then breaks over the stern with tremendous force and often does damage. If this happens on a larger vessel the stern can rise so high that the rudder comes out of the water, gets into the breaking wave (which is the moving part of the body of water) and the rudder loses control. The wave smashed the *Tilikum*'s cabin door into pieces and filled the cabin with water. Voss recalled:

> I found the mate in the cabin up to his neck in water holding on to the pans and stove and shouting for help with the cabin filled with water up to the deck. Water was coming aboard almost as fast as we could bail it out with buckets, but slowly and surely we gained and in about two hours the water was nearly out of the boat. I found my watch in the bottom of the boat at least its pieces which had once been my chronometer. Everything on board was saturated with salt water. The stove broke up and we had no means to warm ourselves or to make a warm drink.[205]

The stove that heated the cabin, cooked their food and made hot tea was now ruined. Voss constructed a crude replacement stove out of a bucket and he soon had a contraption with some ballast sand in the bottom. He drove a few holes for a draft in the side. Once it was completed, Donner asked where they would get firewood as the old stove was a fuelled Primus stove. Voss took some of the cabin furniture—the bunk boards—and cut them up for fuel. In no time they had a warm cup of coffee. The next day with seas calmer, the mate took the stove up on deck and prepared what he called "Australian pancakes."

INVERCARGILL, NEW ZEALAND

On February 20 they passed Solander Island, at the western end of the Foveaux Strait in southern New Zealand. They dropped anchor at Invercargill on February 21, 1903, in the New River Estuary and stayed for eight days while they exhibited the *Tilikum* in Dee Street, next to the navy office. Ed Donner then resigned from the voyage. Voss took on an unnamed mate for the five-day passage from Invercargill to Dunedin.

After the exhibition, Voss transported the *Tilikum* to Bluff Harbour, the seaport for Invercargill. Before his departure, on Wednesday, March 4, he gave a public demonstration of his sea anchor while in tow of the large tug *Theresa War*, loaded with passengers, after which he sailed from Bluff Harbour toward Dunedin. He anchored at Port Chalmers in Deborah Bay on Saturday, March 7, and moved the *Tilikum* up to Dunedin on March 9.

TILIKUM NAMESAKES

By the time Voss reached Australia and New Zealand, the *Tilikum* was becoming well known and her reputation preceded her. In 1902 a racehorse named Tilikum was active in racing circles in Australia and New Zealand. The name was, no doubt, inspired by the news sensation created by the vessel's visits. An Australian cricket team in Ballarat became known as the Ballarat Tilikums, another name bestowed due to the influence of Voss and the *Tilikum* on Australian shores. A power launch in New Zealand was named the *Tilikum* and served in freshwater service for a number of years before the First World War.

DUNEDIN

The *Tilikum* was exhibited in the city at Hooper's Furniture Warehouse in the Octagon, an eight-sided plaza in the city centre, as an "amusement," and later in Dunedin's Forbury Park for the Floral Fete and Gymkhana—a benefit for the fallen soldiers of the Second Boer War (South African War).

It didn't take long for the temporary mate to have enough of bad weather and the *Tilikum*, and he resigned while they were in Dunedin. Voss again advertised for a new man. He interviewed several and engaged Mr. G. McDonald as mate for the leg of the trip to Port Lyttelton.

Top: The *Moerangi* with the *Tilikum* in tow at Otago, New Zealand.
The Otago Witness, *1903.*

**Bottom: The *Tilikum* wreathed in flowers for
Anniversary Day in Otago, New Zealand.**
Turnbull Library g2446_1.1.

At this time, Voss struck up a friendship with a Dunedin optometrist, George Chance, who would go on in later years to participate, with Voss, in the Talbot Clifton Expedition at Guayaquil, Ecuador.[206]

Two nights before sailing, the Otago Yacht Club held a "smoking concert" for Voss.[207] This men's gathering featured live music, drinking and smoking while participants engaged in lively discussions on current events. It was hosted at the Provincial Hotel by the club's commodore, Mr. Moller, and was very well attended by ticket buyers, with the house crowded to the doors.

On departure, the Dunedin yachtsmen set to sea and gradually the harbour filled with small boats under sail and decorated with flags. A number of boats from the Otago Yacht Club joined in the procession, and in the excitement two of the yachts collided (one was cut in half). The excursion steamboat *Onslow* accompanied the *Tilikum* down the river and the steamer *Moerangi* took her in tow.[208] After a couple of hours, Voss dropped the tow and sailed off to the echoes of three cheers from the passengers in the *Moerangi* and all the accompanying steamers blowing their whistles.

The operators of the *Onslow* capitalized on the arrival of the *Tilikum*, charging an inflated fee. This caught passengers by surprise; they learned of the raised rates only once the voyage was under way. Afterward, a "victim" complained angrily in the newspaper that he had been charged a premium without proper notice of the additional cost.

A SEA ANCHOR AT CHRISTCHURCH

On Friday, March 27, Voss and McDonald dropped anchor in Oamaru,[209] where they stayed for three days, exhibiting the *Tilikum* next to the D.I.C. department store premises. On March 30 the *Tilikum* departed to sail fifty miles to Timaru. A gale was blowing on the voyage, forcing Voss to shorten sail. He managed an average of almost nine knots for the transit, which he considered a record for the voyage.

He and the mate, McDonald, arrived in Timaru the next day and the *Tilikum* was placed on exhibit in Stafford Street. Mr. W. Arthur Donald, acting as the agent for Voss since Australia, handled the logistical arrangements and the promotion of the visit. The record is not clear, but we believe W. Arthur Donald was the

The crowd at Lyttelton, April 1903, waiting for the *Tilikum* to be lifted by a crane to be transported to its exhibition site.
Maritime Museum of British Columbia.

same person as Mr. McDonald, Voss's earlier manager at Glenelg, mentioned on page 143. It is uncertain which name is correct, but the same person appears to have turned up again when Voss reached London, England.

On April 6 they departed Timaru for Lyttelton, arriving on April 8. Here Voss put the *Tilikum* on a railcar and shipped her to Christchurch[210] for exhibition. He was running short of cash and expected this to be a prime opportunity to reach paying visitors.

While Voss was there, the Antarctic relief ship *Morning* was in port fresh from supporting Captain Robert Falcon Scott's expedition to the South Pole. The *Morning* was carrying an able seaman named Horace E. Buckridge. Voss was impressed by Buckridge, whom he described as having had "wonderful experiences," and lost no time in engaging him as his next mate.

Buckridge had left England as an apprentice boy in the ship *Invercargill*, in which he sailed to New Zealand. He left the ship and farmed there, later joining a surveying party in New Guinea. One report cited his service in the New Guinea Police. He did some pearling at Thursday Island but joined the army when war broke out. He later joined the New South Wales Imperial Light Horse as a volunteer for a year, advancing to sergeant major. He sailed out with them to fight in the Second Boer War. He served with General Buller, then was attached to Thornycroft's Mounted Infantry and Scott's Railway Guards, where he was again promoted to sergeant major. He served with Lord Methuen and was twice wounded at Spion Kop. Buckridge had met the team from the *Discovery* at Simon's Town, near Cape Town, and joined them to go to the South Pole as a laboratory assistant. He returned to Lyttelton on the *Morning* in March 1903. While serving on the *Tilikum*, he gave a number of lectures about his experiences in Antarctica.

Two days before Voss's arrival, a local Boer War veteran, George Spring, was drowned on the Sumner Bar when his launch was swamped while he attempted to cross this treacherous bar. Hearing of this accident, Voss was convinced that such incidents were preventable by use of a sea anchor, and he gave a public lecture on his experiences with handling the little vessel in storms. When he was challenged to prove his assertions, he responded by volunteering to give a demonstration by taking a 20-foot open rowing boat across the Sumner Bar. This was announced in the newspapers, and up to seven thousand onlookers arrived to witness the demonstration.

VOSS'S THEORIES OF SEAMANSHIP

Much to Captain Voss's chagrin, his voyages were frequently denounced as foolhardy —or worse. His voyages were certainly unusual for their time, but Voss was a master mariner with decades of successful deep-sea sailing experience. Whatever risks he took were fully calculated, drawn deeply from this first-hand knowledge.

He undertook at least four major blue-water voyages—each building on the cumulative experiences he gained. He developed and articulated his theories of small-craft management to dispel popular beliefs that voyages in small boats were inherently too

Captain Voss on the new *Tilikum II* at Yokohama, Japan.
John MacFarlane Collection.

risky to undertake and also to act as a rebuttal to the unkind and careless accusations made by those who had no knowledge of the preparations he undertook prior to his voyages. Voss believed that he was safe in a small vessel of which he had complete control and safer than those "who race across the briny deep in big greyhounds and have to entrust their lives to others!"[211] He stated that:

> Captain Slocum, who made a trip round the world in the Spray, a 12-ton yawl, was lost when attempting another long cruise in the same boat. The Pandora, a 10-ton yawl, left Australia on a cruise round the world, and after arriving in New York and having departed again, met with the same fate. Both these boats were considerably larger than mine, the Tilikum, and the two cases have been cited frequently as a sure proof that small vessels were not safe at sea.[212]

He also felt that single-handing a small sailing craft was tempting fate. He added:

> Captain Slocum sailed single-handed and therefore, was unable to watch his vessel night and day. The two men constituting the crew of the Pandora

have stated that both of them on repeated occasions went below, and like
Captain Slocum, left the vessel to look out for herself. A practice of this kind
may pass for a long time, but sooner or later it will revenge itself, for the dan-
gers are many if a vessel is not properly navigated and watched.[213]

The text of Voss's book contains eight pages of technical notes on seamanship in a small vessel that he felt would be of use to others. These included subjects such as the nature of waves, the frequency and height of waves, the dangers of a broken sea, how to ride out a storm while heaved to, sea anchor use, construction and design, and his table of sizes for sea anchors.

Captain Voss retains a reputation for being a superior seaman in small vessels. Even Luxton acknowledged this:

Voss knew the sea. He knew what to do at the right time and he did it.
He never took a chance and quit the sealing game in the Bering Sea for that
reason. As a sailor there was never anyone quite so wonderful; winds, weather,
water, currents, dead reckoning, he had no equal in his time.[214]

The *Tilikum* experienced extraordinary conditions that tested both the qualities of the vessel and the skills of her crew. Luxton recalled:

August 8th my diary says, having not touched it for three days, such con-
founded weather would take the heart out of anything ... This storm came up
fast ... This gale kept up for almost thirty-six hours, with waves quite thirty-five
feet high. It was one of the very few times I wished myself on land. It is a queer
sensation to be thirty-five feet below a wall of water, that looks just as if it were
going to fall right on top of you, when suddenly up goes the canoe and there is
a roar of water on each side of you that you can't see over, with a path through
the wall that the drag has made for the boat to go through. Then down once
more you go into the trough of the next wave.[215]

During his voyage in the *Sea Queen*, Voss established standing orders to govern the management of a vessel.[216] These were adapted from common practice in larger sailing vessels:

1. There would be three four-hour watches (there were three members of the crew) except for the period of 1600 to 2000, which was divided into two "dog watches."
2. Breakfast was served at 0700; lunch at noon; supper at 1730.
3. In the *Sea Queen*, he declared, "there is a place for everything, and everything must be kept in its place."
4. The man at the helm was responsible for keeping the boat either full and by or on her given course. He was prohibited from falling asleep under pain of a bucket of water thrown over his head by the man who caught him. He was not to leave the deck when on duty, but had to wait until relieved at the end of his watch. (This might be an oblique reference to Voss's claim that he had done this to his mate Norman Luxton in the *Tilikum*. Luxton claimed much later that this never occurred.)

Early on, Voss introduced logical systems of protocols for small vessels sailing in heavy weather that worked repeatedly well under his application. In *The Venturesome Voyages of Captain Voss*, several detailed principles of good seamanship are promoted.[217] These are the guiding protocols that Voss believed brought him home safely in all his small vessels (see Appendix II). Because boat designs, sailing expertise and equipment have improved, his methods no longer translate well to modern hull and rigging approaches. Modern yachtsmen are cautioned that they should not necessarily apply Voss's principles of seamanship to their voyages. Experience and technology have shown that there are safer and more effective approaches to seamanship.

The Sumner Bar is a sandbar where the estuary meets the sea and is notoriously dangerous to cross. In Voss's book, he incorrectly named this sandbar the "Sumno Bar."

The water over the Sumner Bar had always challenged unpowered boats needing to cross this dangerous stretch in order to reach the harbour. Waves rose stiffly and erratically, easily overwhelming oars and sails and sending boats and passengers to their destruction. Voss was accustomed to bringing the *Tilikum* through such rough patches with the use of the sea anchor.

After borrowing a small, non-powered rowing boat, Voss and Buckridge had a steamboat tow them out to the breakers. With the sea anchor in the water attached to the stern of the boat, Voss

Crowds filled with morbid curiosity gather at the Signal Station
(at top of hill on right) to watch Captain Voss cross and recross
the Sumner Bar, which had been the site of a recent drowning
tragedy. They anticipated seeing him killed in the process.
Canterbury Museum photo #10561.

was able to stop its headway and keep the stern straight in line
with the huge breakers. The stern rose to each breaking sea wave.
As each wave passed the middle of the boat, her stern would drop
down and Voss would pull on the sea anchor's tripping line. This
collapsed it and the boat could move forward under a pull on the
oars. This continued until the approach of the next wave, when
the tripping line was again relaxed and the sea anchor began its
function. It was slow but safe progress. They were able to cross
the bar without taking any water in the boat.

To make the impressive display even more memorable, Voss
related that Buckridge tied a rope around himself and "fell overboard." The crowds on shore shouted in alarm, the band quieted
their instruments mid-tune and the lifeboat made a valiant effort
to reach the stricken man. Before too much time was allowed to
pass, Voss "saved" Buckridge from the sea to resounding cheers

Captain Voss in the process of crossing the Sumner Bar in a small boat as part of a public demonstration of seamanship in extreme surf conditions.
Canterbury Museum photo #13020.

ashore. The exhibition was a great success, and Voss was presented with a cheque for fifty pounds.[218]

The *Tilikum* had modest impact on the local culture. While the crew was in town, the Christchurch Model Yacht Club opened their season by awarding a trophy for a race. Second place went to a Mr. Philpott for his model of the *Tilikum*. Voss had exhibited the *Tilikum* at Tattersall's Horse Bazaar in Cashel Street and given a public lecture on his voyage adventures, no doubt inspiring the model maker.[219]

On April 29 the *Tilikum* was returned to Lyttelton by rail, and the next day Voss departed for Wellington. The passage along the coast from Lyttelton to Cape Campbell Light was uneventful, and they passed the cape on May 3, after which it began to blow hard overnight.

WELLINGTON AND PALMERSTON

The *Tilikum* entered Wellington Harbour on May 4, 1903, and by May 6 she was on exhibition in the skating rink. Both Buckridge and Voss gave public lectures. It was estimated that three thousand people attended, producing large grosses at the gate. One of the prominent visitors was the Right Reverend Frederic Wallis, Bishop of Wellington. Wallis was appointed in 1895 to the colonial episcopate as Bishop of Wellington, a post he held for sixteen years before retirement in 1911. Voss and Buckridge remained in

Wellington until May 15, when the *Tilikum* was loaded on a train and taken overland to Palmerston. They stayed there four days, attending a Maori funeral and the feast afterward.

There is some evidence from newspaper reports that Dora Voss joined her husband at the New Zealand ports. However, Voss makes no mention of this in his manuscript or book; if true, it may have been the last time they were together. Voss's long absences must have created a great impediment to a happy marriage. As such, in 1905, Mrs. Voss divorced her husband. He makes no note of this in his book, either.

Local organizers put on an exhibit of sea anchors in which Voss took part. It is not clear why, but a local man, John W. Massey, sued Voss to recover ten pounds. The exhibit may not have been financially rewarding, and Massey may have been disappointed seeking return of his costs. Voss confidently responded to the suit, benefiting from his court experiences in Australia. Judgement was in favour of the defendant with costs.[220]

FEILDING AND WANGANUI

After the exhibition in Palmerston closed on May 18, Voss moved on to the town of Feilding on May 19.

The Feilding Drill Hall provided a one-day venue for the *Tilikum*, and a lecture by Voss and Buckridge was arranged by W. Arthur Donald, their self-described "sole manager." The lecture was billed in the newspaper as featuring "daring seamen, a plucky undertaking, thrilling lectures and quaint curiosities. Admission 3 shillings, 2 shillings, 1 shilling."[221]

TESTIMONIALS AND PRESS NOTICES

Voss made many friends at the *Tilikum*'s various venues, exhibiting a charm that was enjoyed by the public. In addition to press notices, testimonials were printed in newspapers in tribute to him. Below is a testimonial for the *Tilikum* in the "Letters to the Editor" section of an unknown New Zealand newspaper while Voss was there. This is typical of the great impression Voss and the *Tilikum* made on the public everywhere he landed:

THE TILIKUM; To the Editor, Sir: I have just been seeing The Tilikum canoe boat at the Drill Hall and was very much pleased and interested with the boat

Above: The *Tilikum* on display, fully rigged, in the Feilding Drill Hall.

Tilikum Fonds of the collection of the Maritime Museum of British Columbia.

Left: An advertisement for the *Tilikum* at Taranui, New Zealand.

Tilikum Fonds of the collection of the Maritime Museum of British Columbia (uncredited clipping from an unknown New Zealand newspaper).

and with Captain Voss's unassuming narrative of details and experiences. I was
sorry to see so few there this afternoon and would recommend all to go on Saturday who likes boats and adventure and get a description of boat sailing in a
seaway and other matters. I am, etc. John T. Stewart. Aramoho, May 22.[222]

Voss had many opportunities to take part in local culture. At Wanganui (also spelled *Whanganui*), he was particularly impressed while witnessing a Maori canoe hurdle race on the Wanganui River. He described how a small tree trunk, nine inches in diameter and the branches removed, was lashed to two piles across the river, about eight inches off the water. Three canoes, each carrying two men seated near the stern, left the starting point with their bows in the air. The canoes ran forward over the hurdle and when halfway over it, they stopped. Each crew rushed forward to tip the balance and race to the finish line. The race was also run separately by all-female crews.

On May 25 Voss was introduced to Richard Seddon, the prime minister of New Zealand.[223] After listening to Voss's description of his voyage, Seddon flattered him, advising him to abandon his trip and settle in New Zealand. Seddon said that New Zealand needed citizens with the sort of resolve and courage that Voss displayed.

In the afternoon, Voss travelled down the Wanganui River with Mr. and Mrs. Alf Mitchell "of the Hotel Metropole" and a Miss L. Imiss to the mouth of the river. A heavy breaking sea was present for a sailing demonstration of the *Tilikum*. Knowing the Wanganui Bar to be dangerous, a large throng of people travelled by tram to witness the demonstration from Shakespeare Cliff. Voss could see the high rollers crossing the bar and hitting the cliff; he knew it was high water and thus would be deep over the bar. Ordinarily he would have no difficulty crossing—he had the necessary skill—but with no wind he could not possibly sail across it.

Instead, he paid ten shillings for a man with a 35-foot launch to tow the *Tilikum* across the bar. Voss carried twelve passengers on board, charging them one shilling each. Voss suggested that his female passengers stay ashore as he thought there was a chance of shipping water and they might get wet. Mrs. Mitchell retorted that they were not afraid of getting wet, and the tow through the twenty-foot rollers began.

The tug went full speed and they were halfway across when the *Tilikum* met a large roller with a small break. It passed right over top of the *Tilikum*—Voss shouting for the women to hold on tight. He later wrote, "One of the ladies had a little paint washed off her face and it made a great difference in the looks of their white starched dresses as they stuck to their bodies like sticking plaster."[224]

Just as Voss was turning the canoe around to return, another roller broke in the middle of the bar close to the *Tilikum*. In spite of the steam launch going full speed, the *Tilikum* began to surf the roller and in a few seconds the tow line went slack. Travelling faster than the tug, she almost touched the stern of the steam launch. The breaking sea ran under the *Tilikum*, leaving her in the hollow, and picked up the launch, running her forward at speed with the slack 150-foot tow line. When the line was fully extended it broke, and as the sea had full control of the launch, it turned her sideways and the roller broke over the top of her, extinguishing the boiler fire. The owner got the boiler fire going again and headed straight for the river and safety. Just then a breeze began to blow, allowing Voss to raise the sails and bring the *Tilikum* under control.[225]

Before their departure, Voss and Buckridge were entertained at a celebration at the Wanganui Sailing Club.[226] According to Voss's book, on that same day, May 25, a train transported the *Tilikum* to Castlecliff, where Voss gave another sailing exhibition of crossing a sandbar using a sea anchor.

AT SEA AGAIN TO NEW PLYMOUTH

The voyage to New Plymouth was delayed by contrary winds until May 29, when a light wind allowed a late-evening departure over the bar. Rising winds in the Taranaki Bight forced them to sail off the lee shore. In the pitch-dark and stormy night, Voss and Buckridge shifted everything movable to the weather side of the boat to counteract the full suit of sails in use to keep the boat from swamping. Soon a gust carried away the storm staysail so they heaved to with the sea anchor until midnight, enduring high wind, rain and hailstones.

The southwest gale was slowly driving them onto the lee shore, so Voss raised a new staysail to drive the boat out to sea again. A lifeline was tied around Buckridge's waist and attached to the mast. (This was one of the few times that Voss acknowledged using any safety aids while at sea.) His mate crawled on his hands and knees over the cabin top to bend on the sail while Voss raised the mizzen. Voss held the lifeline in the darkness, unable to make himself heard over the howling of the wind. A pull on the lifeline provided no reply from Buckridge.

Moving forward, Voss found his mate with head and feet overboard and unresponsive, dangling at the end of his lifeline. Voss thought his mate had died of heart failure, but he took hold of the man, who weighed two hundred pounds, and lashed him to the mast. He pulled the sea anchor on board and set the storm sails, and the boat began making headway. The *Tilikum* steered herself under storm sails so Voss was able to turn his attention to his mate. Just then they took a huge sea over the vessel, but Buckridge was well secured and Voss hung onto the mast with all his might. The wave roused Buckridge, who shouted, "What the hell is this? I cannot move. I am tied down!"[227] As Voss dragged him back to the cockpit, he explained that Buckridge had struck his head on the mast. The two men wore oilskins and sea boots but the breaking waves and rain had drenched them to the skin, apparently causing Buckridge to slip. The squalls now laid the *Tilikum* down on her beam, but a small slackening of the sheets caused her to right herself.

At 0300, while Voss was in the cabin looking over a chart, the boat suddenly changed her motion from a heavy pitching to an easy rolling motion. In a second Voss was on deck, and to his surprise found her heading northeast rather than the southeast course on which he had left her. He kept the boat on the new course and carried on until 1800, when he was assured that they were out of danger. Needing a rest, they took in the sails, put out the sea anchor and retired to the cabin for a hot cup of coffee. They turned in and slept until 1000 the next day.

The wind had moderated and Mount Egmont was bearing due north about thirty miles distant. Taking up the sea anchor they made for New Plymouth harbour, dropping anchor at 0300 on June 1, 1903, after a harrowing and exhausting voyage.

NEW PLYMOUTH

On June 4 Voss exhibited the *Tilikum* in a tent on an empty lot on Devon Street East, next to McEwan's Boat Shop where he gave a public lecture. On June 5 a brawl between two hired men diverted attention away from the *Tilikum*. The defeated man insulted Voss and damaged the tent. Voss, brooking no foolishness, responded with a walking stick, using it to drive the man from the tent.

This event was reported in the newspapers and caused a minor public relations problem. To restore their image, Voss and Buckridge addressed St. Mary's School in a charity benefit, donating 25 per cent of the proceeds to the organ fund. This wasn't the first venue, however, where Voss conducted specific presentations for schoolchildren and their teachers.

The *Tilikum* on the ways at New Plymouth, New Zealand.
Marine ways are ramps, often equipped with rails, used to
pull vessels out of the water for painting or repairs.
Maritime Museum of British Columbia.

Voss found New Plymouth "a very nice little city" in "splendid farming and grazing country."[228] He met Maori people there who intrigued him with tales of their people voyaging by canoes from the Cook Islands hundreds of years before. The Maoris were apparently equally fascinated by the *Tilikum* and gathered to see her in most of Voss's New Zealand ports of call.

A delegation of Maori people later visited Voss:

> During my stay in New Zealand I put my boat on exhibition. The Maoris came in to see what was going on. When they saw that the *Tilikum* was a canoe like their own and was built on the other side of the world by people a good deal like themselves and had come to their country by sailing across the ocean it strengthened their ideas concerning their forefathers coming to New Zealand in canoes.
>
> They were pleased to meet a man who had done as much as their forefathers had done. They offered me a Maori welcome. I had no idea what to expect but a couple of days later when I was standing alongside my boat in came about 50 Maoris (men and women). Without saying a word to me they lined up alongside the boat and sang a song which lasted for some time. After this the Chief gave me an introduction.
>
> After they had a good look at the boat inside and outside I gave them a small explanation of what the *Tilikum* had gone through and they expressed their surprise. The Chief gave me an invitation to his house. They all shook my hand, said "Kia Ora" (a greeting in the Maori language) and left the place.[229]

NELSON

On June 9 they departed for Nelson, rounding Cape Egmont and crossing the Cook Strait. On June 11 they sighted Nelson Light. When the wind dropped, they drifted much of the day until a power launch came out and asked if they wanted a tow. Voss inquired after the cost but the launch skipper, John G. Glasgow, who turned out to be the commodore of the Nelson Yacht Club, merely asked Voss to share some refreshment with him once they had arrived. This delighted Voss and Buckridge, and they were greeted ashore by a cheering crowd. The *Tilikum* was taken

The *Tilikum* at the Nelson Yachting Club in Nelson, New Zealand.
(Note J.C. Voss signature on the mat of the image.)
Tilikum *Fonds of the collection of the Maritime Museum of British Columbia.*

to the Railway Wharf, lifted ashore and exhibited in Collingwood Street next to the Panama Hotel.

Voss and his mate spent eleven days in Nelson. While they were there, the Nelson Yacht Club, New Zealand's oldest yacht club, established in 1857, elected Voss as an honorary member. Commodore Glasgow and vice-commodore Phil Moore hosted a banquet that included Nelson mayor Henry Baigent, a timber miller and city councillor before his mayoralty. Afterward Voss was described in the newspaper as "a real live Viking" and he was eulogized for "his dogged pluck and perseverance."[230]

While he was in Nelson an elderly lady, Mrs. Webster, came to see Voss to ask if he would be good enough to take a parcel containing a fruitcake and letter for her son, who was employed as a radio officer with the Eastern Extension Cable Company on the Cocos (Keeling) Islands, a remote territory of Australia in the Indian Ocean. She wished it to arrive for his birthday. Voss told her that he would be pleased to do so and sure enough, shortly before he sailed, a large square tin was delivered to the boat. Although the package would take up valuable space in the forepeak, Voss promised to take the best care of it and deliver it when he arrived.

On June 23 Mr. Glasgow towed them back out to sea with his launch, the *Charles Edward*. They let go close to the Nelson Bar, on course for the French Pass, a notoriously dangerous channel used by ships travelling between Wellington and Nelson. The tide was set in the same direction as the course of the *Tilikum*, and they flew through the passage. As they got to the other side of the pass, however, the wind dropped and the *Tilikum* was taken under siege by a whirlpool, turning her around a dozen times in five minutes before releasing her from the grip of the current.

Although they were on course to Napier, the light winds forced them to anchor early near a farm on the shore of French Pass. As soon as they anchored, George W. Webber, who was a postmaster, boarding-house keeper and farmer, came out in a small boat and introduced himself. Webber said he had been following the voyage in the newspapers with great interest. He asked them to come ashore and stay a few days at his farm to enjoy fishing, hunting, riding or driving. Voss explained that they had a long way to go yet and not much time to lose but that they would stay one day.[231]

The house reminded Voss of a city mansion. Soon after they arrived, Mrs. Ethel Webber set the table with mutton chops and bread, supplying the two men with a good breakfast. Afterward they took a gun and walked the hills. But this turned out to be hard on Voss's legs, which were weakened by lack of use, so they returned home.

At noon a steamer stopped in the pass with freight for Webber's farm. Webber and Voss boarded the steamer and while Webber attended to his business, Voss noticed all the passengers were looking over the starboard side, watching a large, snow-white "fish" alongside the steamer. It was none other than Pelorus Jack, a Risso's dolphin that was famous for meeting and escorting ships through a stretch of water in Cook Strait between 1888 and 1912.[232] Pelorus Jack was usually spotted in Admiralty Bay between Cape Francis and Collinet Point, near the French

Pass. The dolphin had once been shot at from a passing ship and was later protected by a 1904 New Zealand law. A passenger told Voss it was widely believed that Jack had a special understanding of humans and accompanied every steamer transiting the pass. For many years, the famous dolphin was popular with mariners, and it made a big impression on Voss.

ON TO NAPIER AND AUCKLAND

After passing through Cook Strait, Voss and Buckridge arrived at Napier on July 4. Again the *Tilikum* was exhibited, this time at Mr. Cohen's rooms on Hastings Street. They departed from Napier on July 13, arriving at Auckland on July 18. They were hailed as having "the distinction of being the smallest overseas ship that ever visited Auckland."[233]

Voss exhibited the *Tilikum* on Wellesley Street East (opposite the art gallery) daily from 1100 to 2200. This was a most profitable arrangement for Voss, with large crowds attending. After his departure, the Auckland papers reported that he had earned between six hundred and eight hundred pounds (a small fortune to someone like Voss). He also addressed schoolchildren and teachers in Auckland at a special event.

The *Tilikum* in Auckland, New Zealand.
Tilikum *Fonds of the collection of the Maritime Museum of British Columbia.*

Voss must have had an impressive cash flow from all the exhibitions he initiated. But what happened to all this money? By the time he arrived in South Africa he was broke—and had to go through the exhibition process again. Though possessing endless entrepreneurial drive, he seems to have lacked a businessman's skill.

While Voss retold his adventurous stories of crossing the Pacific, Buckridge lectured publicly about his experiences in Antarctica while serving with Scott and Shackleton.

The *Tilikum* stayed in Auckland for thirty-two days, receiving a thorough overhaul for the long run to South Africa. Voss was entertained by Charles P. Murdock, the commodore of the Royal New Zealand Yacht Squadron, New Zealand's senior yacht club, which had recently been established in 1901.[234] His hosts took Voss out in a launch to tour the harbour, but most local yachts were out of the water for repair and cleaning as it was then wintertime in the southern hemisphere. Some enthusiastic yachtsmen presented Voss with a set of wire rigging and all new running gear. The Northern Roller Milling Company presented him with enough rolled oats, rolled wheat and cereal to take him all the way to London![235]

With a new coat of paint inside and out and a new set of rigging, the *Tilikum* was once more put into salt water. After stowing the ballast and five months of provisions on board, she was ready for the long voyage around the north coast of Australia.

SPAWNING IMITATORS

The successful public lectures Voss gave inspired a number of imitators. Voss himself had been motivated by Joshua Slocum's voyage in the *Spray*. Several others would in turn follow Voss as a new breed of mariner—the record-breaking cruiser—inspired by long voyages in small boats.

In New Zealand, Felix Tanner of Wakefield designed his *Ark No. 3* (nicknamed *Tanner's Ark*), a barrel-shaped vessel built to challenge Voss in his voyage to England. She was divided into three compartments, the centre one consisting of the cabin fitted with lockers for stores. She was ballasted with water and had just one mast carrying thirty yards of sail. Her bow was shaped like a swan's head and was fitted with an electric light—one eye showing red and one green. Tanner exhibited the craft before its launch and announced that Horace Buckridge (one of Voss's mates, who had recently left the *Tilikum*) would join him as mate.[236] The *Ark No. 3* appears to have been the third in Tanner's series of at least four experimental vessels. The first two were unsuccessful designs. The second, just 18 feet in length, was ill fated, sinking at her mooring in New Plymouth. The *Nelson Evening Mail* referred to this plan as "Another Fool Voyage."[237] The *Ark No. 3* departed Auckland in 1903 to race against Voss but almost immediately had to be rescued by the harbour board dredge. The *Feilding Star* was less charitable, referring to them as "Another Crank."[238] In May 1904 *Ark No. 3* was driven ashore by the wind at Terawhiti, New Zealand, ending the voyage. Tanner and Buckridge swam ashore. Tanner then dropped his interest in boats and moved on to "aerial navigation."

Buckridge designed the purpose-built *Kia Ora*. Leaving Voss and the *Tilikum* abruptly in Auckland, he announced that Bailey and Lowe Shipbuilders would construct the small craft resembling a lifeboat of about two-and-a-half tons. Originally he had intended to sail to New York and then exhibit at the 1904 world's fair at St. Louis, Missouri, but later he decided to race Voss around Cape Horn to England and try to best Voss's record.

It was reported in a South African newspaper that Charles Russell, also formerly a mate in the *Tilikum*, had designed the *Intoihili*, based on a Norwegian whaleboat. His mate was Mr. Toomey. He expected to sail to England from New Zealand, and then on to New York. Russell believed that New York was Voss's ultimate destination and he intended to reach there before Voss.[239] There is no record of what came from this challenge.

Buckridge, the reliable mate who had sailed with him around the coast of New Zealand, resigned at almost the last minute. The positive newspaper coverage they received may have had some influence on Buckridge's decision to initiate his own expedition to London in a head-on challenge to Voss and the *Tilikum*.

This was initially awkward for Voss, but he had no difficulty replacing Buckridge with another good man who promised to go all the way to London. The new mate was the Reverend Mr. Charles Russell but sometimes lived under the name of Herbert "Mac" McMillan. Russell was the brother of Herbert Russell, who was fourth officer in a nitrate carrier. He was an Irishman who was variously reported as being an electrician and a clergyman from Croydon, Surrey, in England. But Voss himself claimed Russell was born in Ireland and was twenty-five years old when they met in Auckland. This mate, like so many of the previous ones, was a landsman who had very little experience serving in a boat as small as the *Tilikum*, especially at sea during a gale. However, Russell declared he would stay with her as long as Voss could keep her afloat.

On August 19 an Auckland Harbour ferry named the *Eagle*, with about four hundred passengers on board to see the *Tilikum* depart, gave them a tow line. As thousands of people on the wharves gave cheers, the *Tilikum* was slowly towed out of the harbour.

At Rangitoto Island the steamer blew three whistles, the signal to raise the sails and drop the tow line. But unfavourable conditions forced the *Tilikum* to anchor in the lee of Rangitoto Reef, giving the impression to onlookers on the ferry that they had been stranded. This incorrect news was widely reported in the newspapers and relayed around the world as a wreck. They were finally able to get underway at sundown, passing the Tiritiri Lighthouse and exchanging messages with the lightkeepers. (The Tiritiri Lighthouse was just the third to be built in New Zealand, first lit on January 1, 1865.)

The long transit to South Africa had begun.

11

SOUTH AFRICA

For the final legs of his Pacific Ocean voyage, Voss's original intention had been to shape a course via Norfolk Island through the Coral Sea to the south end of the Great Barrier Reef. But the wind shifted, and he was obliged to stay on the port tack until he entered the southeast trade winds on August 29. The wind died and shifted again, and a southern island of the New Hebrides was in nearly a straight line from their position to Torres Strait. Voss set a course instead for Aneityum Island. Ocean currents and shifting winds often forced Voss to take alternate routes. He had little ability in the *Tilikum* to sail against either. For the *Tilikum* the shortest route was often not a straight line.

AT SEA AGAIN
Once under way, the *Tilikum* encountered a large patch of floating volcanic pumice that covered the ocean as far as the eye could see. Voss's newly acquired mate, Charles Russell, initially thought they had run aground. Some of the pieces were as large

Travels of the *Tilikum*

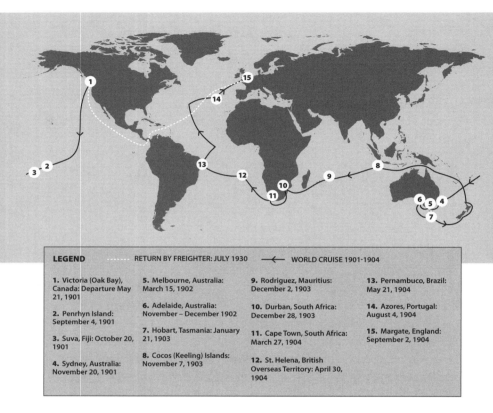

LEGEND ········· RETURN BY FREIGHTER: JULY 1930 ←— WORLD CRUISE 1901-1904

1. Victoria (Oak Bay), Canada: Departure May 21, 1901

2. Penrhyn Island: September 4, 1901

3. Suva, Fiji: October 20, 1901

4. Sydney, Australia: November 20, 1901

5. Melbourne, Australia: March 15, 1902

6. Adelaide, Australia: November – December 1902

7. Hobart, Tasmania: January 21, 1903

8. Cocos (Keeling) Islands: November 7, 1903

9. Rodriguez, Mauritius: December 2, 1903

10. Durban, South Africa: December 28, 1903

11. Cape Town, South Africa: March 27, 1904

12. St. Helena, British Overseas Territory: April 30, 1904

13. Pernambuco, Brazil: May 21, 1904

14. Azores, Portugal: August 4, 1904

15. Margate, England: September 2, 1904

as "a cabbage head and as light as a feather..." Voss formed the idea that an underwater explosion must have occurred to account for such a tremendous amount of debris. It was so thick it almost stopped the *Tilikum*'s progress. The next day they passed out of the zone of floating material.

There were also large numbers of flying fish, a welcome potential source of fresh food, but not one fish landed on board. Once it became dark, Voss tried a scheme he had seen used at Manihiki Island to catch the fish by attracting them with a light. Shortly after sundown he put out a bright lantern and pulled the boom of the mainsail down to the deck. While he was still busy preparing things, a large flying fish struck him square in the face, which he recalled "made me see the American flag..." Using this method, they gathered twenty-three fish between six and eleven inches long in just a half-hour.

ANEITYUM ISLAND, NEW HEBRIDES (VANUATU)
They sighted Aneityum, the southernmost island of what is now Vanuatu (the New Hebrides Islands) on September 6. As they approached, they saw Indigenous people running in large numbers on the beach. Still worried about rumours of cannibals, Voss changed his mind, not wanting to risk a landing. As he sailed up the coast the islanders followed, making motions to come ashore. They did not have canoes, so Voss anticipated he would be safe as long as they stayed offshore. They anchored but kept all the sails set.

As soon as the anchor went down some of the islanders swam out to the boat. A fire was lit onshore, and it slowly occurred to Voss that to avoid any difficulties they should depart just as the swimmers were alongside. Voss and Russell pointed firearms at them, motioning a warning not to touch the boat. The islanders quickly turned back to the shore, apparently recognizing the threat the vessel posed. Voss hauled up the anchor and continued along the coast of the east and north side of the island, and at dark they set a course for Tanna Island.

TANNA ISLAND
On September 9 they sailed overnight to Tanna Island in what is now Vanuatu, about forty miles from Aneityum Island. There was no mistaking the signs of recent eruptions of a volcano. The volcano's lightning flashes grew brighter as they approached the coast, so they heaved to near the south end of the island to await daylight. The wind died and the current carried the *Tilikum* back out to sea. When the wind rose again they sailed up close to the coast, looking for an anchorage where there was no house or village in sight. In the bright flashes in the ash plume of the volcano, they could see lots of coconuts and other fruit trees. They sailed in, but with guns ready for action. It was now very late at night, so Voss turned the boat about and stood off the coast to wait for daylight.

The wind died again, and at that moment they sighted a boat coming directly toward them from the inner end of the inlet. There appeared to be a great number of men in the boat, which was approaching quickly under oars. The *Tilikum* was in a flat calm and unable to make way. With guns at the ready, Voss hollered to the advancing boat to stop and put up their hands. It stopped about two hundred feet away, but the occupants did not put up their hands. Once again Voss gave them the order. Instead they all stood up, watching the *Tilikum*.

Unexpectedly, the man in the stern hailed the *Tilikum* and asked clearly, "Are you afraid, Captain?" Voss answered, "No!" but secretly he was fraught with concern about cannibals. He queried the men, wanting to know what they were after. The reply was that the local missionary had sent them out to invite the *Tilikum* into their harbour, and to tow her in. Suspicious of a trap, Voss asked where the missionary's house was located, because as a rule it would be prominently visible, close to the water. The leader of the group pointed to the shore and sure enough, there was a mission house, quelling Voss's thoughts of a trick.[240]

Still somewhat skeptical, he permitted the boat to come alongside and they all shook hands, the speaker introducing himself as the chief of his tribe. When Voss asked how he had come to speak English, the chief revealed that, years before, a labour schooner had called at the island and captured him. He was put aboard the schooner and taken to Queensland, Australia, to a sugar plantation where he was forced to work. Over a number of years there, he had learned English quite well. The chief then ordered his crew to take the *Tilikum* in tow up the harbour.

Voss and Russell met Mr. Watt, the missionary, and his assistant and a trader. They were welcoming, and Voss and Russell spent a pleasant evening in the mission house. Mrs. Watt made a little dinner, and afterward Mr. Watt told them something of his thirty-five years of experience among the people of the New Hebrides.

After a sound sleep in the *Tilikum*, in the morning Voss and Russell went ashore for breakfast. In addition to his mission house, Mr. Watt had a cottage on the bank of the harbour. There was a cleared area of about two acres with a large breadfruit tree in the centre. This area was fenced in and used as a playground for young and old. The night before, villagers had competed to knock breadfruit out of the tree by throwing sticks and stones at it. Outside the fence was the village of the Indigenous people, which consisted of about a dozen small huts made of round sticks and covered with palm leaves.

Voss called on the trader, who had a small, sparsely furnished wooden cottage with two rooms. The goods in his store consisted of a large box of tobacco with twenty-eight pieces to the pound. He traded this to the locals principally for coconuts and generated a 200 per cent profit. He also had guns and ammunition, a box of biscuits, some calico and a few other sundries. The haphazard nature of his supplies reflected the method of trade in these waters. A vessel called at the village once a month and the trader ordered what he wanted from the inventory on board. His supplies were then landed by the ship's boats and in return, the trader's merchandise—the coconuts—was sold. He stated he cleared about $100 per month and sometimes better. As well, Mr. Watt made occasional trips to New Zealand and Australia to give benefit lectures and raise money for the local inhabitants, and he was often presented with all kinds of goods for his congregation. When he got back to the island, he would sell the goods to the locals for a lower price than the trader. This occasionally created friction between the trader and the mission.

On September 5, when the time came for the *Tilikum* to depart, the locals brought fruit. Some villagers rowed a boat out carrying Mr. Watt to accompany the *Tilikum*, headed now toward the Torres Straits.

An attempt to land at Erromango, the fourth-largest island in the Vanuatu archipelago, was unsuccessful. Fear again overtook Voss, who recalled that the landing area was poor and the locals had murdered five missionaries. Erromango was the target of "blackbirders" who would kidnap islanders into slavery for sale to farmers for agricultural work in Queensland or in South America. The crew decided to press on to the Great Barrier Reef.

BEYOND THE GREAT BARRIER REEF

With a fresh easterly breeze, they soon left the islands of the New Hebrides. On September 23 they steered into Raine Island Passage to cross the Great Barrier Reef, and on the evening of September 25 they were successfully across and dropped anchor to await daylight. In the morning they shaped a course for Cape York but anchored again in the evening as Voss considered nighttime navigation too risky.

Soon after they anchored they sighted a schooner and sailed up to her. The men on board were Japanese and could not speak a word of English. Voss went on board to look around. The captain gave him his telescope and pointed over to a small island where four boats with naked divers were harvesting *bêche-de-mer*—sea cucumbers. (These marine invertebrates are used in fresh or dried form in various cuisines. In some cultures the sea cucumber is thought to have medicinal value. Most cultures in East and Southeast Asia regard them as a delicacy.) While the divers were harvesting, the captain was drying and smoking the *bêche-de-mer* on the vessel. These sea cucumbers had a market value of around C$500 a ton at the time.

The following day they sailed on to Cape York and then to Thursday Island.

THURSDAY ISLAND ON A SUNDAY

Voss and Russell anchored at Thursday Island on September 27, 1903. Voss came ashore after clearing pratique with the collector of customs, Alex Rose. Voss was carrying a letter to the mayor of the island, Mr. T.J. Farquhar, from Farquhar's sister in Auckland. The mayor introduced Voss to the local notables, including the Honorable John Douglas, the government resident and magistrate who had for a period been the premier of Queensland.

Pearling was the island's primary industry at the time the *Tilikum* visited. Voss observed a huge pearling schooner fleet with most of its vessels built by Japanese shipwrights. He noted that a complete outfit for a season of pearling cost nearly $3,500.[241] Indigenous locals and ethnic Japanese did the diving.

On October 1 they stocked up with fresh provisions and filled the water tanks. In a light easterly breeze they entered the Arafura Sea. Voss began to experience pain in his stomach. By the evening he was unable to eat and the pain grew worse. He was hardly able to sit up but was still standing a watch and navigating. He changed course to the Wessel Islands, a group belonging to the Northern Territory of Australia. He hoped to find a doctor there who could provide medical assistance. He reckoned it would take the *Tilikum* three days to reach there, and he had taken all the medicine on board to no effect.

The pain became excruciating, and Voss thought he might die before they arrived. They could not get back to Thursday Island as both the current and the wind were against them. Voss grittily determined that they must keep heading toward to the Wessel Islands, giving instructions to Russell on what to do should he die before they arrived. Finally on October 5 they sighted the Wessel Islands late in the day.

They could see breakers but no lights on shore. They sailed around, looking for a shelter where they could anchor for the night. At the end of the island they saw what looked like a cut. Voss, desperate to get to shore, decided to risk the shallow water to get shelter. They entered at four feet of water (the *Tilikum* was drawing only two feet) and finally anchored in two-and-a-half feet. All they could see was the faint suggestion of a white sand beach. Voss wanted to wade ashore but the fear of sharks kept them in their bunks for the night.

The boat began to list to port as the tide ebbed. The *Tilikum* stuck on a rock. Voss and Russell went into the water to try to move her off but to no avail. The splash of a shark forced them quickly back on board. Finally, the canoe fell over on her beam end and at the same time slipped off the rock, leaving her high and dry. By late afternoon she was again afloat, but Voss felt he

Captain Voss portrayed lying on the beach on an unnamed island, expecting to die.
World Wide Magazine, 1904.

would soon be dead. They could find no habitation so they went ashore, where Voss spread a blanket under a scrub tree and lay down, not expecting to get up again. After a time, however, he decided he didn't want to die in such a place, so he got Russell to help him back on board.

He wanted to head toward Darwin on the Australian northern coast, where there would be a hospital. But Russell decided it was time for desperate measures, telling Voss he could make a medicine that, if it did not kill him, would certainly cure him. Voss demanded that he try it. Russell boiled a half pint of water and added Colman's mustard, stirring it well. He told Voss to drink it and hold it. Voss took the whole dose and almost immediately felt "an explosion in the stomach." For a moment he thought his mate had killed him, but suddenly he began to vomit, after which the pain disappeared. Voss felt like a new man.[242]

On October 11 they set to sea again, passing the Wessel Islands in the northwest of the Northern Territory. They were now on the Timor Sea, which is part of the Indian Ocean, sailing toward the Mermaid Shoal. Voss was anxious to see one of the mermaids rumoured to live in these waters so he sailed to the shoal and they dropped anchor. They erected an awning over the cockpit, and after breakfast they prepared their fishing gear. Voss reckoned he could catch a mermaid with a baited hook. But no fish were interested in the bait despite the crew seeing lots of them in the water.

One afternoon, the heat and the boredom of seemingly endless glassy water caused the two men to conjure an apparition. Seeing splashing in the water, they pulled up the anchor and used the oars to row closer. As they approached, a long arm appeared to come out of the water, so they stopped the boat and got their guns ready. The arm belonged to a massive octopus. Voss's wild imagination interpreted this as a sea serpent with a young mermaid fastened to its suckers. He imagined he saw a mother mermaid fighting the octopus to release her child.

Voss recalled, "It looked to be a very cruel affair and as the maid was getting the worst of it I took a shot at the Octopus' arm when he brought it up to trash the old lady. The shot must have gone through his arm as it doubled up like it had broken in two. The struggle continued for about five minutes more after which they all disappeared."[243]

In the Arafura Sea, they saw hundreds of sea snakes moving across the surface of the water, which was so smooth and clear they could see sharks below. The deck of the *Tilikum* was very low to the water, and it was unsettling to be in such proximity to the curious sharks as they came alongside the *Tilikum*. On one occasion a large shark bumped the boat and Voss wondered if it wasn't trying to turn the boat over. They were glad when they left the Arafura Sea and entered the waters of the Indian Ocean.

IN THE INDIAN OCEAN
On October 27, 1903, they passed the spot where Lady Anna Brassey, a celebrated English traveller and writer, died at sea of malaria. Her bestselling book, *A Voyage in the Sunbeam, our Home on the Ocean for Eleven Months,* was published in 1878. Voss was impressed by the stories he had heard about this woman and was sad about the circumstances of her death. He wanted to do something to mark her memory; having no flowers, he lowered their Canadian flag to half-mast.[244]

With the wind running in the southeast, Voss set a course for the Cocos (Keeling) Islands. He wanted to call there to get fresh water and deliver the cake that had been entrusted to him in New Zealand. In the heat of the Arafura Sea they had consumed more water than their allowance, thinking they could easily make Cocos (Keeling) with the water remaining in the tanks.

"TELL CAPTAIN VOSS TO SEND THAT CAKE"
At noon on November 7 Voss reckoned they were thirty miles east of the Cocos (Keeling) Islands, and he lay down for his afternoon rest. At 1430 his mate called out that a low-lying island was only eight miles ahead. It was one of the islands in the Cocos (Keeling) archipelago. With the wind still fresh, it at first looked to be an easy landfall.

Voss had a shave and dressed in better clothes to be ready to go ashore as soon as they arrived. He estimated they would be there in two hours. When he came up on deck they were within four miles of land, but as they approached the wind dropped, a heavy cloud settled over the island and it disappeared from sight. All through the cloudy night they did not see the land again.

In the morning the weather cleared. They had drifted with a

strong westerly current by the south end of the island and it was almost out of sight. The wind then picked up from the east, and the *Tilikum* now had both wind and current against her if they decided to make a landing on the island.

They had only eight gallons of water left and over 2,200 miles to go before reaching Rodrigues Island. The previous 2,200 miles had taken thirty-seven days. To make two thousand miles with only eight gallons of water was almost out of the question, but Voss doubted he could sail back against the current and headwind, so he decided they had to skip the Cocos (Keeling) Islands and press on for Rodrigues. He hoped to make the island in fifteen days, and to ensure they would not run out of water altogether, they cut their daily water allowance to one pint a day. At that rate they should have had enough water for thirty-two days.

On November 9 Voss took two bottles and put a pint of water in each, keeping one for himself and giving the other to Russell. He fitted a yard on the mast (which up till then had been stored on deck) and a square sail on the foremast. This made the *Tilikum* look like a barquentine, and with this rig she flew along.

The warm weather made them very thirsty. At noon they made coffee, which they put into their water bottles. Using salt on food was out of the question. They ate tinned meat and had a small drink of the coffee. In the early evening, they took the last drink of cold coffee, knowing they could not have another drink until the next morning. The weather continued to grow hotter and the crew thirstier.

Voss had the idea that the rolled oats they had been given in New Zealand could be moistened with a little water, and when chewed it offered them some relief. On the fifth day Voss saw heavy clouds so they rigged rain sails over the deck to catch water, but the clouds passed over, leaving not even a drop. More clouds arrived, and in the early afternoon it started to sprinkle but not enough to gather water. However, they got some relief standing with their mouths wide open and inhaling the moist air. At last, at 1500 it began to rain, and within an hour they had gathered sixty gallons of good water.

They were able to brew afternoon coffee. Voss instructed Russell to fetch a square tin. In a few minutes the mate returned with the tin in his hands. After Voss removed the paper wrapping, a fine fruitcake was staring them in the face. His mate looked at the cake and then at Voss. "No wonder we missed Cocos Island!" he exclaimed. They ate the cake and celebrated the "good old New Zealand lady" and her son's birthday. Voss recalled that he had never enjoyed a coffee and cake so much as he did that afternoon. (Later, when they reached Rodrigues Island, the manager of the British cable station would present Voss with a cable that read, "Tell Captain Voss to send that cake." He had been sent to get retribution for the missing cake, but Voss's usual charm worked its magic, and all was settled with a hearty laugh.)[245]

The rain kept pouring down in torrents, but a strong wind came with it so they went under sail again. Voss remembered their prayers for rain and thought perhaps they had prayed too much. The rain continued for seven days. This continued until November 22, when the wind moderated and became very light. On November 27 the sea was alive with flying fish chased by dolphins. Voss harpooned a dolphin and hauled it aboard.

After a dolphin breakfast, they both became ill with bad headaches and in a short time were obliged to lower the sails and lie down. They used a Colman's mustard emetic, and once they had vomited they felt much better. Dolphins followed the boat and Voss observed them eating barnacles from the hull. He surmised that the dolphin they'd consumed had not only barnacles but copper paint in its system, which had poisoned it—and then them.

RODRIGUES ISLAND

Early on the morning of December 2, they sighted Rodrigues Island. They followed a fishing boat through a passage in the reef into the lagoon where they anchored among a dozen fishboats near a fishing village. They had a fish dinner and slept on the boat.

The next day they sailed for the village of Port Mathurin, the capital of the island of Rodrigues (a dependency of Mauritius), where the port medical officer visited them. He was not satisfied with their bill of health and would not allow them to land, saying he had to report their case to the magistrate. They were given a permit to go alongside a small wharf in the village where they met the magistrate, George Rouillard. Rouillard told Voss that if they had arrived a little sooner, they would have experienced a devastating hurricane that swept over the island. It had done a lot of damage, including lifting a boat out of the water and into the coconut trees. Trees were uprooted and houses damaged.

On December 4 they set sail for Durban, South Africa, with a clean bill of health. They set all their sails for extra speed so they could celebrate Christmas in Durban. On December 7 they sighted Mauritius. On December 9 they sailed south of Réunion Island, where they met a large, full-rigged ship that passed very close by. Voss wrote:

> The ship's Master shouted out to us in a very coarse voice "What ship is that?" "The *Tilikum*" I answered. "What is your cargo?" he shouted back. He knew very well my vessel was not a cargo vessel and too small to carry cargo. Very often square-rigged captains, as they are called in San Francisco are actually masters of fore and aft ships (schooners) and this captain was trying to have a little fun with me. I think that the square rig man was quite satisfied when I told him that I had my boat loaded with postholes!
>
> On December 15 we sighted Madagascar sighting land in South Africa on December 22 north of Durban. We were running before a strong Northeast wind and I wanted to make sure that we were in that night so we could have our Christmas turkey on shore.[246]

But as Voss recalled, "Sometimes poor wind jammers have to figure twice."[247] When they were only thirty miles from Durban, a storm came upon them very quickly and they were forced to remain at sea for four more days in a southerly blow, running under storm sails and a sea anchor. Their provisions ran short, and instead of turkey they ate a half-pound of corned beef with hard biscuits for their Christmas dinner.

DURBAN, SOUTH AFRICA

Voss and Russell anchored at the entrance to Durban Harbour on December 28, 1903, a total of 131 days at sea from Auckland. They were met first by a harbour tug whose master asked where they had come from and marvelled at their "nerve" in undertaking such a voyage. The master declined to tow the *Tilikum*, saying that at his standard rate of sixpence a ton he wouldn't make enough to pay for a whisky and soda. He steamed away, leaving them at the harbour approaches.

The port medical health doctor and the customs officials paid a visit and offered a tow. Although they passed pratique, Voss recalled, "To tell the truth, I was nearly busted. I had sent my clothes by steamer from Auckland and some other things which I had used for exhibition purposes in New Zealand. This stuff had not arrived so there was no money."[248]

Russell wanted some money so he could go ashore, so Voss told him he would make some arrangements for cash. Although Voss knew no one in Durban, the newspapers were full of stories about their trip, so news of their pending arrival had preceded them.

Ashore, Voss met Mr. D. Taylor, a member of the Parliament of South Africa and the commodore of the Royal Natal Yacht Club (formed in 1891 from two predecessor yacht clubs). Voss laid his case before him, and Mr. Taylor arranged for Voss to exhibit the *Tilikum*. The newspapers reported that "thousands" of people attended the exhibit at the Volunteer Hall.[249] Within ten days Voss had cash again, but by that time Charles Russell had left the voyage to chase his dream of becoming a mining millionaire, having "contracted the gold and diamond fever."

About this time, Voss learned that one of his New Zealand mates, Horace Buckridge, had made a second start on his own voyage to London. In a letter back to New Zealand, Voss wished his former mate every success in his voyage. Tragically, Buckridge's expedition hopes had already ended in failure; it was reported that Buckridge and his mate got as far as the Chatham Islands when, in bad weather, Buckridge was thrown overboard and was lost.[250]

In Durban, waterfront skeptics again challenged Voss, expressing doubt about the origin of his voyage. South African Ervin Ray vouched for Captain Voss to all those who claimed Voss was a fraud. Ray had been in Victoria, BC, in 1901 when Voss departed on his epic voyage. He worked for the South African Railways in Pretoria and invited Voss to travel with the *Tilikum* to Pietermaritzburg and up into the province of Transvaal.

PIETERMARITZBURG AND COLENSO

Voss put the *Tilikum* on a railway flatcar and took a trip to Pieter-maritzburg, where he stayed for a few days. He shipped the *Tili-kum* to Johannesburg while he went for a visit to Colenso, located on the southern bank of the Tugela River. Colenso was the site of an engagement during the Second Boer War, and Voss wanted to see the spot where Lieutenant the Honourable Frederick Rob-erts, the only son of Field Marshal Lord Roberts, was killed in action. He had quite an interest in the Second Boer War. He also wanted to see where Boer forces wrecked an armoured train.

JOHANNESBURG

Voss then travelled to Ladysmith and from there to Johannes-burg, where the *Tilikum* was stored. He was particularly pleased that the canoe had set an unexpected world record for the high-est altitude reached by any deep-sea vessel. (This record was not surpassed until 1973, when Tristan Jones took his *Sea Dart* on the bed of a truck up fifteen thousand feet to sail on Lake Titicaca in South America.)

He stayed ten days, during which he met a number of Brit-ish Columbians at various gentlemen's clubs, many of whom had mobilized for the Second Boer War only to stay on for business. The *Tilikum* was exhibited at the Wanderers sport grounds and attracted large crowds.

PRETORIA

Voss travelled on to Pretoria by rail, while the *Tilikum* was again shipped as freight. When he went to the freight office to claim his vessel, he was dismayed to learn that a horse had been alarmed by the figurehead and had begun to buck, kicking off the deco-ration in its frenzy. The railway provided a carpenter to carve a replacement—one that "looked a little more civilized."[251]

THE FIGUREHEAD

Luxton takes credit for carving the original figurehead for the *Tilikum*.[252] There is no description of the condition of the dugout when Voss and Luxton acquired her, but as a whaling canoe, her slender bowsprit would rise from the stem and finish with a notch, almost resembling ears. Here harpoon shafts and the unstepped mast for a

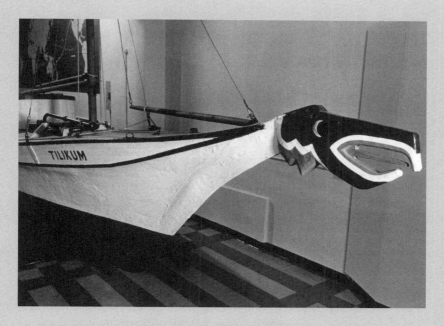

The figurehead of the *Tilikum* now in possession of the Maritime Museum of BC (detail as it currently appears on the vessel).
John MacFarlane collection.

sail would be stowed while under way. Luxton likely copied his crude figurehead from those he saw on other canoes.

Norman Luxton wrote, rather hyperbolically, "While I was not helping to re-model the canoe and when work had become stale, I was no means idle. Through my carving and imagination the figurehead on the bowsprit came into being which even among the native American Indians was a source of wonder. All through the South Seas the lagoon folks still talk of the boat with the head whose mother was a sea serpent and whose father was a bird, and carried in its pit the heads of dead men on which to feed."[253]

Decades later, Eleanor Luxton visited the *Tilikum* at the Maritime Museum of British Columbia, noting the difference in the figurehead. She wrote, "The vessel as she may be seen at the present time, is not exactly as she was when Voss and Luxton sailed her in the South Pacific. The figurehead, which Norman Luxton carved, was kicked in by a horse in Pretoria, South Africa, and was broken. It was replaced by a new and slightly different one. When she was abandoned on Canvey Island the stem rotted and once again the figurehead was lost. One of wood and metal was part of the restoration carried out by the Thermopylae Club."

In fact, the figurehead on the hull of the *Tilikum* has been replaced several times over the years:

- The original, carved by Luxton.
- A replacement carved in South Africa (the original was reportedly kicked off by a frightened horse and replaced by railway workers). This one was lost at Canvey Island.
- A replacement probably carved by Victor Jacobsen in 1937 of tin and plywood.
- Another added at the Maritime Museum of British Columbia after she was moved into its Bastion Square building in Victoria but before 1972 by an unnamed "Provincial First Nations carver"; this is the one that is currently fitted.[254]

Voss was introduced to the Second Boer War veteran General Louis Botha, who took a great interest in his voyage. Botha opined that he "would rather go through another South African war than attempt to cross the Atlantic in the *Tilikum*."[255] Botha had commanded and led the Boer forces impressively at Colenso and Spion Kop. In a notable footnote to history, on November 15, 1899, Botha captured Winston Churchill (who was serving in South Africa) when a British armoured train was ambushed.

Christian W. Becker, a native of Victoria, BC, met with Voss and acted as Voss's host while he was in Pretoria. It was also in Pretoria that Voss met his next mate, Mr. C.L. "Harry" Harrison[256] (in Voss's published version the name is E. Harrison[257]), who had a position with the South African Railway. Harrison came from the city of Sale in Victoria, Australia. His only seamanship experience was in coming from Australia to South Africa as a first-class passenger. Aside from a Canadian named Cairns, Harrison would prove to be the last of the series of mates in the *Tilikum*, and he was suffering from either consumption or tuberculosis when Voss engaged him. Harrison quit his job at the railway office in Pretoria and joined Voss in Cape Town. He would travel throughout the last leg of the voyage, via Brazil, to Margate, England. Although he was very ill for the first half of the trip, his health improved markedly for the duration of the voyage and he developed a voracious appetite, prematurely reducing their provisions

**The *Tilikum* lying alongside the steamer *Hermione*
at East London, South Africa.**
World Wide Magazine, *1904.*

to near starvation levels. He was reputed to be from Gippsland, Australia, and was apparently later killed in the First World War.

EAST LONDON

Once again, Voss shipped the *Tilikum* on a flatcar by rail, this time to East London, South Africa, a two-day trip. There she was overhauled and once again painted inside and out before being launched and made ready for sea. In East London Voss found a temporary mate in a Canadian named Cairns, who declared that he was willing to sail the short hop around the Cape of Good Hope to reach Cape Town.

A Captain Harrison (no relation to the new mate, C.L. Harrison), who was the East London manager for the Union-Castle

Line shipping company, took the *Tilikum* in tow and they departed for sea. After crossing the bar outside the harbour, Voss let go of the tow line. On a fresh eastern breeze they sailed for twenty-three hours to Port Elizabeth.

PORT ELIZABETH

Voss dropped anchor in the harbour at Port Elizabeth, which he likened to a "ship boneyard." He counted more than twenty large sailing vessels pulled up on the beach in front of the city. Port Elizabeth had an open harbour, and easterly winds blew directly in to throw up a heavy surf. Anchored vessels were always at risk. Voss departed on March 18, 1904, with westerly winds that made progress very slow.

He stopped over at Mossel Bay, a harbour town on the Southern Cape, for two days to respond to a request from people there for a lecture on the voyage. The mayor chaired the presentation in the town hall. On March 23 the *Tilikum* sailed for Cape Town.

Getting around the cape was difficult for Voss, as many yachtsmen have similarly experienced. He had to anchor under Cape Agulhas to repair the rigging. The keeper at the Cape Agulhas Lighthouse sent them some fresh vegetables and also word that they had anchored in a very dangerous place for an easterly wind. The sea was calm so they ignored the warning and put up a light on deck before turning in. But at midnight the sea kicked up, and they were obliged to raise the anchor to set sail with the ballast trimmed to the portside. Once they picked up the easterly wind, they flew along toward the Cape of Good Hope, the southernmost extremity of the continent of Africa.

Voss reflected later that he should have heaved to in such dangerous seas but he was anxious to make Cape Town by the next nightfall. He put the sea anchor over the stern, towed it with a tripping line and kept running under the small sails. This stopped her headway for every breaking sea. The large seas ran in groups of three or four, running three to ten minutes apart, and at times they broke very heavily.

The lighthouse at the Cape of Good Hope was supposed to be visible for thirty-five miles out to sea. The night was stormy and cloudy but not foggy, but Voss passed within two miles of the light and never saw a glimpse. The wind died down with the current setting to the south, and by the following evening they were very near the cape again.

CAPE TOWN

A fishing steamer, *The Star of the South*, bound for Cape Town, gave a friendly tow and the *Tilikum* came alongside the wharf on March 27. The following day Voss moved the *Tilikum* into Filisse's Circus and exhibited at this municipal facility. The crowds—all paying visitors—were huge. Filisse's Circus was described by Voss as a large "circus building" owned by the City of Cape Town. The *Tilikum* was publicly exhibited there for three weeks.

Voss again gave the boat an overhaul, fitted new rigging, and painted her inside and out. It was here that Voss encountered the marine writer and publisher Weston Martyr, who was skeptical of Voss's claims of his adventures and origins, which seemed entirely outlandish to him. Martyr recalled, "As I object to having my leg pulled, I looked knowing and left that place. And as I went away I said to myself, 'That's only a very small man, but by Jove,

The *Tilikum* in 1904 at Cape Town, on the beach at Table Bay. The *Tilikum* is sporting the new figurehead carved at Pretoria by the railway carpenter.

Image B-09352 courtesy of the Royal BC Museum and Archives.

Christian W. Becker (standing) and Captain John C. Voss (seated), photograph taken in Pretoria, South Africa.
Image A-00855 courtesy of the Royal BC Museum and Archives.

he's certainly a most monumental liar!' "[258] Years later, he recalled this episode when, as Voss's publisher, he put Voss's book into a popular edition that has remained available for purchase for over one hundred years.

C.L. Harrison, the new mate from Pretoria, arrived and was ready to go on board. On April 11 they put her in the water with enough provisions for the voyage through the South Atlantic to South America.

On April 14, 1904, a large crowd gathered to witness the departure. It took Voss considerable time to shake everyone's hands. When he managed to get on board, a number of small steamers and launches crowded with passengers swarmed the *Tilikum* to see them off. One of the steamers took them in tow until outside Table Bay, where they set all the sails and let go the tow line.

Harrison, like many other of Voss's mates, discovered the motion of the *Tilikum* was difficult to endure. But Voss left him on the tiller and went below to square away the gear. Inside he found many parcels of food, each one with a note saying that the sender wished them to enjoy the contents. There was a still-warm

The *Tilikum* berthed alongside a 6,000-ton Union-Castle Line freighter.
Captain J.C. Voss in the first edition (1913) of The Venturesome Voyages of Captain Voss.

roast duck, two warm turkeys and many other edibles. By 1800 the boat was dancing about and Harrison had no appetite for tea. Voss did not feel well either so both agreed they would take no evening meal on that day.

Early the next morning, they anchored at the north end of Robben Island and had a small breakfast of tea. Soon the wind was coming from the north and they got under sail.

At noon Voss asked Harrison, who was down in the cabin, to pass him one of the roasted ducks. He told him to look beneath where he was sitting to find a box of knives and forks and to pass out a set. Harrison reported that the box was there but it was empty. "There was a note in the box," the mate said, "that will explain what became of your knives and forks." He passed it out to Voss, who read:

Dear Captain Voss: My father, mother, and all my sisters and brothers are taking a great interest in your most wonderful voyage. My father has killed the two very best turkeys we had around the house and my mother roasted the same to send on board the *Tilikum* for your benefit. I hope that you will enjoy the same. My sister Carry and myself took them on your boat and as you or nobody else was on board we put the parcel in the cabin and got a souvenir for each of our family. We have taken the liberty to help ourselves to your knives and forks by which we will always remember the *Tilikum* and her Captain. Wishing you a Bon Voyage and hoping to hear from you again. (Signed) I remain yours very sincerely C.W. Walker, Cape Town.[259]

"That settled the knives and forks," wrote Voss, "and I did not care about crossing the South Atlantic without knives and forks. I asked my Mate what he thought of it and he said if he did not feel better than what he did at that moment he would not need any."

As luck would have it, when they were ten miles north of Robben Island, the wind was from the north, so Voss went back to anchor at Robben Village. He went ashore to meet Mr. Pearson, the governor of the island. The whole island was government property, used as a penal colony, but Voss was able to get the supplies he needed. (Robben Island is perhaps best known later in its history for its most famous political prisoner, future South African president Nelson Mandela.)

Voss charted a course from Robben Island with good winds but his new mate still could not get used to the motion of the *Tilikum*. Voss's intention was to go straight through to South America, but as Harrison grew worse from day to day, he changed course to the island of St. Helena. They made it in fifteen days.

ST. HELENA

It was evening when they anchored offshore at St. Helena, South Africa, on April 30, and nobody on shore knew they were there. They needed to pass their pratique before they could go ashore, so they made a lot of noise to attract attention from the port officials.

Voss went ashore in the morning to send postcards describing his progress to the yacht clubs that had hosted him in Australia and New Zealand. The arrival of these cards made local news in the papers at each of their locations. He participated in some typical tourist activities at St. Helena, including climbing the 699 steps of Jacob's Ladder. At the top Voss wished that he was down again!

The next day he hired a horse and rode out to see the house where Napoleon spent his last days. He also visited the site where Boer prisoners had been interned and where there were still resident ex-prisoners who had become British subjects and stayed on as businessmen. The visit was busy but brief. On May 4, despite the fact that Harrison was still ill, the *Tilikum* set sail for Pernambuco, Brazil, with a fresh southerly trade wind.

12

BRAZIL AND UP THE ATLANTIC TO ENGLAND

PERNAMBUCO

As Voss and Harrison approached the coast of Brazil, after sixteen days at sea, the winds became variable with occasional heavy rain squalls. The mate had been quite ill during the three-week passage but finally, on May 20, 1904, they were becalmed just fifty miles from Pernambuco. The following morning they got their first glimpses of the port.

The British consul, Mr. Williams, and some leading citizens entertained both Voss and Harrison. They were given a free railway pass, arranged by the consul, and took a trip through the sugar cane district observing the cane fields and sugar mills along the line.

The consul treated Voss royally except for one minor conflict. Williams ordered Voss to take down the little Canadian flag the *Tilikum* always flew—since her departure from Victoria, BC, to every port of call along the voyage. Consul Williams, writing a formal letter to Voss, apologized over the enforcement of this regulation but wrote that it was required under British law. Voss complied, though grudgingly. The letter, in part, reads:

> Sir, I have to call your attention to the paragraph of the Merchant Shipping Act 1894 viz (1) a ship belonging to a British subject shall hoist the proper National colours … If default is made on board any such ship in complying with this section, the Master of the ship shall for each offence be liable to a fine not exceeding one hundred pounds … It is therefore my duty to request you to show me your authority for carrying a flag with a distinctive addition in the National colours and in the event of having no authority you will haul the flag now flying and deliver it up to me. I have the honour Sir, your most obedient humble servant, Williams.[260]

The night before their departure, the British people of Pernambuco honoured the crew with a banquet held in the hall of the British Cable Station. More than two hundred people attended. On June 2 they began the run toward the North Atlantic. Two steamers loaded with passengers came out to see them sail away. One of the boats took the *Tilikum* in tow while the other followed.

Before leaving port, Voss tallied all the days spent on his voyage and concluded that the *Tilikum* had completed a *double* world record: not only as the smallest vessel to cross the three great oceans but also as the only canoe to do so. Voss and the *Tilikum* had been voyaging for nearly three years. To be exact, the tally was two years, eleven months, twenty-nine days and twenty-two-and-a-half hours.

Predictably, once outside the harbour Harrison became sick again, with this bout worse than before. To his credit, he never failed to complete his duties though it was obviously difficult for him at times. There was little Voss could do to improve their comfort.

The Southern Cross dipped lower and lower on the horizon. On June 4 they crossed the equator. Harrison was still ill, so Voss overlooked the fact it was his mate's first equatorial crossing. "Neptune had pity and did not trouble him."[261]

Astonishingly, the *Tilikum* had sailed two thousand miles without either man touching the tiller, a feat reminiscent of Joshua Slocum's *Spray*. Voss merely trimmed the sails by the wind for three weeks. This spritely voyage came to an end once the westerlies of the North Atlantic played out.

They were becalmed for over a week and though no headway was made, covering a mere twenty miles, Harrison's condition improved remarkably during the lull. Unfortunately, just as he was recovering from his seasickness, Voss became ill with indigestion serious enough to keep him in misery for some days.

AT SEA IN THE SOUTH ATLANTIC

By this time they were forty-one days out of port and had covered only twenty-five hundred miles. Voss knew that if the light airs kept up they would run short of provisions long before they reached London. On July 24 they sighted a becalmed sailing vessel some distance away. The weather was clear, allowing them to see just the sails on her topmasts above the horizon. Voss and Harrison rowed as hard as they could, making slow progress, until the *Tilikum* was alongside.

Voss went on board the barque *Port Sonachan* out of Glasgow, under the command of Captain Sainty. Clifford Claude Sainty was qualified as a master mariner and went to sea in full-rigged ships. He served as a master in New Zealand from 1880 to 1886 and from 1896 to 1907. In 1900 he became master of the *Port Sonachan*, on which he encountered Captain Voss in the *Tilikum* in the North Atlantic. Sainty would arrive in Victoria, BC, in 1908 in the full-rigged ship *Port Patrick*. In 1934 he would be elected as a member of the Thermopylae Club in Victoria.

The *Port Sonachan* had been out for 142 days from Costa Rica with a cargo of dye wood for Dunkirk. Sainty gave Voss and Harrison a warm welcome, inviting them to stay on board during the calm, an offer enthusiastically accepted. A crew was placed on board the *Tilikum* to keep her clear of the ship's side for two days. When a fresh breeze sprang up from the northwest, it was time to part company and cast off. Captain Sainty ordered his men to fill the *Tilikum*'s water tank, but he could not spare any provisions.[262]

Voss and Harrison were desperately short of food stores. On board the *Tilikum* there were exactly two tins of salmon—and one of those with a suspiciously swelled lid. They had to sail the remaining fifteen hundred miles to London with a stock of one tin of salmon. The *Tilikum* turned east to head to Ponta Delgada in the Azores.

PONTA DELGADA

On August 3 they saw a flash of light and reckoned their position to be thirty miles from the west end of São Miguel Island. The next day they sighted the Ponta Delgada harbour lighthouse. As they approached the west end of the island, a heavy squall struck that split the foresail, amazingly the only occurrence of a split sail during the entire voyage.

In the harbour, the pilot boat from Ponta Delgada met them. Voss declined the offer of the pilot's services and carried on into harbour, dropping anchor. Soon after, another launch approached with the port doctor aboard. He and his interpreter grabbed hold of the *Tilikum* to steady their vessel alongside it, and then proceeded to interview Voss, asking for his bill of health from their last port of call. When Voss informed them that he had no such papers—the British consul at Pernambuco assured him there would be no need of such documents—the doctor and his interpreter hastily let go of the *Tilikum* as though it were "a hot brick."[263]

Voss was told to move to the quarantine anchorage. They did so but with slight protest, indicating they only wished to take on provisions and would then leave immediately. By this time, they must have been weak with hunger. Shortly after transferring their anchorage, a small boat arrived and, to Voss's amazement, they received porterhouse steaks, mutton chops, eggs, new potatoes, fresh bread and butter, all slung over to them in a basket dangling from a boat hook. The generous provisions were left without hesitation and no payment was taken! Voss and Harrison wasted no time in making a feast of breakfast.

Many more boats carried potential visitors but Voss had to wave each of them off because of the problem with his missing bill of health. Unable to board, visitors would pass over baskets containing beer, wine and fancy cakes proffered at the end of a boat hook. It made for a very pleasant day for the undernourished crew.

Arrangements were made to submit the *Tilikum* and her

crew to a thorough fumigation. Voss reluctantly accepted this condition, as he wanted to go ashore for a day or two. He also wanted to clean the boat. When the doctor and his interpreter returned, they had good news. The government in Lisbon had been contacted for direction on how to handle the *Tilikum*'s case, and it was decided that they posed no risk and were now free to come and go as they pleased. Visitors immediately came on board including Ponta Delgada's mayor, Alfredo da Camero, who was also the commodore of the Ponta Delgada Yacht Club. Voss showed him the ship's papers and the interior of the boat as well as letters from the different yacht clubs that he had visited. Voss and Harrison dined with the mayor. With a yachtsman's curiosity, he inquired what work Voss wanted done with the *Tilikum*. Voss explained she needed cleaning, scraping, painting and her sails repaired. Because he was still feeling ill, he and Harrison stayed in a hotel while the *Tilikum* was towed up the harbour to a shipyard.

The following morning a doctor tended to Voss and ordered him to rest. The interpreter visited every afternoon and kindly drove Voss to the shipyard to inspect the progress of the work: some of the men were painting, some were scraping and others were repairing the sails. Voss worried that he would not have enough money to pay the bill.

On Sunday Voss heard a brass band playing outside the hotel. The mayor arrived in a car with his interpreter. Voss and Harrison were invited to accompany the mayor to march ahead of the band along with the people of the city. They marched down to the harbour and found the *Tilikum* launched and ready for sea.

Two days before sailing, the mayor helped Voss buy provisions. Voss was surprised and delighted to learn that these were intended as a gift, as were the hotel rooms, his medical care and the work on the canoe. On August 11 the *Tilikum* set sail, in company with the yachting fleet of the Ponta Delgada Yacht Club, on the final leg of her voyage. As the fleet returned to harbour, they dipped their flags in salute to the *Tilikum*. Voss "answered from the mizzen" and then charted a course for London.

ARRIVAL AT MARGATE TO CHEERS AND CHAMPAGNE

Early one morning, when they were about four hundred miles southwest of the English Channel, they sighted a sail of the British four-masted barque *Colonial Empire* en route from Antwerp with a cargo of merchandise for San Francisco under command of Captain Simson.[264] As they drew alongside, the captain gave the orders to stop their headway. He invited Voss and Hamilton to come aboard for lunch, enticing them with an offer of plum pudding for dessert and indicating that he knew all about the *Tilikum*. After lunch they enjoyed a cigar as they discussed the voyage. Then, with a refreshing breeze in the air, Voss and Harrison left the southbound barque to continue on their way.

An anecdote concerning their arrival at Margate was recorded in the local paper:

> Eventually the English coast was made, and the appearance in the Channel of the *Tilikum* was signalled from Lloyd's stations. There was signalling all along the coast for the vessel to put into Southampton, but having no code-book with him, Captain Voss could not interpret the signals, and all he could do was to dip his flag in salute. Captain Voss, after a pleasing run up Channel, ended his memorable run at Margate, where he met with a most enthusiastic reception. The *Tilikum* will be taken to London, where it will be exhibited.[265]

W. Arthur Donald, in a letter to J.E. Smith of Melbourne,[266] wrote to say he had travelled ahead of the *Tilikum* to London by steamship as Voss's manager to make preparations for their arrival. Donald would arrange for the papers to dispatch a tug to meet the *Tilikum*. He stated that London's *Daily Mail* and the *Daily Mirror* newspapers had exclusive rights to report the epic story Voss would tell on arrival. The London Hippodrome was booked for exhibiting the *Tilikum*, with Donald eagerly anticipating a gross of 100 to 150 pounds per week. Voss also carried a letter of introduction given to him by the British consul at Pernambuco to present to Sir Alfred Harmsworth, proprietor of the *Daily Mail*.[267]

On September 2, 1904, the *Tilikum* sailed around the end of the jetty at Margate, a seaside town on the coast of Kent. Instead of a ship sent by the newspaper, they were greeted by a man in a boat who shouted, "Hello, Captain, how are you? When we met in Sydney I told you that I would be the first to welcome you to England!" It was Mr. E. Myers, who owned a wholesale tobacco company in London. No doubt he was pleased with himself for holding to his promise.

The end of the jetty was crowded with onlookers. The crew was immediately accosted with shouts from the curious throng.

"What ship is that?" they called out.

"This is the *Tilikum* from Victoria, British Columbia," Voss answered.

"How long have you been out?"

"Three years, three months, and twelve days" he answered.

"How many miles have you sailed in your boat?"

The *Tilikum* about to enter Margate Harbour at the end of her voyage, her sails patched and worn.

Maritime Museum of British Columbia.

"Forty thousand miles," was his last answer.[268]

The onlookers began cheering and kept it up until the *Tilikum* was made fast alongside a fishing schooner called the *Sunbeam*. When Voss got ashore, so many people clustered around him that it was almost impossible for him to get through—everyone wanted to shake his hand. Suddenly he felt himself going up in the air and the next moment dropped in a carriage to be taken to a hotel where champagne was opened—bottle after bottle—to mark the end of the voyage.

Voss's progress was still being closely followed by readers of Victoria's *Daily Colonist* newspaper: "When Captain J.C. Voss, at one time proprietor of the Queen's Hotel, started from Victoria on May 21, 1901, to sail around the world in a three-ton Indian canoe, rigged as a yacht, few Victorians realized the wealth of advertisement he would bring to the city." The paper also tells of his lectures on his exploits, under the headline of "Round the World in a Canoe":

The extraordinary voyage of Captain J.C. Voss, a mariner of British Columbia, in an Indian canoe dug out of a single tree, was told in interesting fashion at the Townhall, West Hampstead, last night, by the explorer himself. Hitherto the record small-boat voyage round the universe was held by an American vessel, the Spree (Spray) of 13 ½ tons, but Captain Voss easily lowered that distinction by doing the same distance in his little *Tilikum* (Indian for Friend) a sailing boat of only 2 ½ tons. The time occupied no less than three years and a half.

The Hon. J.H. Turner, ex-Premier and Minister of Finance, now Agent-General for British Columbia, presided. He said that he came from Vancouver to London in thirteen days, but Captain Voss had more adventures. His voyage took three years and four months, he covered 40,000 miles on sea, and 2,000 miles by land, with little but a watch and a compass. His first land was 5,000 miles off, and he made the extensive journey in his frail craft with a single companion. He was a worthy descendant of the Vikings.

Captain Voss, with a slight American accent, told his audience that any boat would float in any sea provided it was properly handled. However he had an additional security in his patent sea anchor, which would prevent almost any vessel from sinking. His boat was hewn out of a cedar tree about 43-years ago, and he put three small masts in her carrying thirty-eight square yards of canvas. One day they sailed 177 miles.

They took arms and ammunition for hunting and defensive purposes, some of the islands where they proposed to land having a very bad reputation. They first touched land fifty-eight days from Victoria B.C. and were overwhelmed by the Natives with fruit and coconuts. At one savage island they had pork and pancakes, indeed they met the greatest hospitality everywhere. After leaving the Fiji Islands, his companion was washed overboard, and he navigated the canoe alone 1,200 miles to Sydney. Another day he lost one of the masts, which was blown overboard, and he had six large waterspouts all around him. He was twenty-three days in the boat without assistance.

The lecturer went on to describe the manners, customs and religion of the cannibal Pacific Islanders and then treated of the distinguishing features of Australia, Tasmania and New Zealand. The Indian Ocean was also explored, and the Atlantic Islands were visited. In every clime the sea anchor proved a veritable lifesaving apparatus. The lecture was extremely entertaining. It was profusely illustrated by lantern slides.

Captain Voss is understood to have been invited to give a lecture on the scientific side of his remarkable voyage before the Royal Geographical Society.[269]

LONDON, ENGLAND

Voss evidently stayed on in the United Kingdom for about eighteen months after he ended his voyage. The first project he undertook was to arrange for the *Tilikum* to be exhibited. The agent-general reported in the gossip column of the *Daily Colonist* on June 10, 1905, that Captain Voss "of *Tilikum* fame" would be showing her at Earl's Court (in the Naval, Shipping and Fisheries Exhibition) and that he hoped "Voss would make a success of it." However, other newspaper accounts suggest that this venture was not a success

Exhibiting Earls Court, 1905.   Tilikum Sailed round the World.

MARGATE HARBOUR TILIKUM

**Contemporary postcard showing the *Tilikum* beached
at low tide, Margate Harbour, 1904.**
John MacFarlane collection.

for Voss. The *Tilikum* was described as "neglected," and indeed Voss appeared to have been losing interest in his little ship.

He addressed a number of scholarly bodies, recounting his adventures while on the voyage and sharing his theories of small-craft handling. Those institutions included the Royal Geographical Society and the Geographical Institute in Newcastle, where the famous author C.S. Forester introduced him. In December 1904 he addressed the Royal Scottish Geographical Society centres in Edinburgh and Glasgow, where his presentations were well received. Lieutenant Ernest Shackleton (later to become the famous Antarctic explorer) introduced him at the presentation in Edinburgh.[270]

After the Naval, Shipping and Fisheries Exhibition, the *Tilikum* was removed from display and put back in the water. Shortly afterward she was sold, ending any speculation that Voss would continue the voyage and return to Victoria with her. That was the end of his original plan to sail her around the world. At that time, he became interested in the group sea-voyage touring business, but there is no evidence his proposed scheme actually proceeded.

Voss gave no clues as to the reason he cut his round-the-world plans short, but it is likely he was disappointed with low financial return from the exhibitions. Interest in his voyage was waning, and perhaps he could not see the point of continuing—or could simply not afford to continue. Voss may have hoped the *Tilikum* would be acquired by the British Museum for permanent display as a reason for leaving the trip "unfinished" in England.[271] The *Tilikum* would not complete the journey around the world until she arrived back in Victoria in the cargo hold of a freighter more than twenty years later.

As for Voss's feelings towards the sturdy little craft that delivered him safely time and again over more than three years of voyaging, little is written in his account except for this one endearment, added near the end of his journal:

Who will wonder that the little vessel by that time had become to me something more than inanimate wood, constructed to be run down and then replaced without difficulty by another? No, she was worth more to me, having proved a trustworthy friend on many occasions, as her name implied. I never felt this more than on that day, when, starting out for a final run, and, patting her side, I said, "*Tilikum*, after all the ups and downs you have experienced in surveying the three oceans you have taken it cheerfully, and it was to you like a picnic ... here you are, looking as well as ever, and working diligently your way over the salt waves towards your final destination."[272]

13

REPATRIATION TO VICTORIA

THE *TILIKUM*'S TRIALS IN ENGLAND

In 1905 W. Arthur Donald, Voss's advance agent since Australia, was reported in the press to have been a "part owner" of the *Tilikum*.[273] He took her up the Thames and she was anchored off the Houses of Parliament.

In 1906 the *Tilikum* was acquired by Harold Ingersoll, not as seasoned a mariner as Voss but who had spent eighteen months as a cadet on a 3,000-ton windjammer. Ingersoll converted the *Tilikum* to a motor yacht at a boatyard named Benfleet after spotting her in a factory yard at Harlesden. He had the hull painted green, fitted her with a seven-horsepower, single-cylinder engine and rebuilt the cabin. Under Ingersoll's care, the *Tilikum* had many misadventures, the first of which was the attempt to put her back into the water—from a very narrow street to the launch at Putney—after fitting her with the motor. A wheel on the cart hauling her to water let go, blocking the main road until a repair could be made. Back in the water after two years on exhibit she began to leak excessively but "once remedied" she was sailed on the quiet waters of the Thames near Putney and down to Westminster. At some point a miscalculation with a bridge span caused her figurehead to be "knocked off in a complicated episode that followed the engineers thinking his motor in neutral when it wasn't" and a replacement was fashioned in order to take the headsail. Over the next two years trouble with masts, sails, rigging and even the anchor caused Ingersoll and the *Tilikum* to be rescued by local boaters several times including a bad entanglement with a barge that sent her back to Benfleet for repair. Near the end of Ingersoll's ownership, he had a mishap with the Primus stove after a harrowing night of dragging anchor across the channel. While attempting to return to her proper berth, trouble with the fuel started a fire. Ingersoll and his mate were briefly "trapped in the cabin while flames raged between [us] and

The *Tilikum* anchored to the right at Pin Mill.
Maritime Museum of British Columbia.

the door" but the two men escaped via the fore-hatch and were able to extinguish the fire by bucketing water over it. The *Tilikum* was laid up in Pin Mill.[274]

Until 1911 she was a familiar sight working on the River Orwell off Pin Mill near Ipswich. Frank F.G. Carr, a young boy at the time, reported that his boatman, Harry Ward Sr., looked after her during this period and that he kept the damaged figurehead in his boatshed until the 1930s, when, rotten beyond repair, it was burned in a bonfire. Carr was the director of England's National Maritime Museum from 1947 to 1966. It was he who preserved the *Cutty Sark* and the *Gipsy Moth IV* at Greenwich. Later he visited Victoria in 1961 and viewed the *Tilikum* at Thunderbird Park.

In 1911 the *Tilikum* was laid up and abandoned on land owned by Mr. Price-Powell on Canvey Island, an island of seven square miles on the south coast of Essex in the Thames Estuary. She gradually filled up with river mud that preserved her from rotting until a friend of the next owner discovered her.

The *Tilikum* derelict in Small Gains Creek, Canvey Island, as found by Leslie Bentley during the First World War.
Maritime Museum of British Columbia.

By 1916 she was owned by Leslie Bentley, who found her lying on her side at Oyster River (also known as Gains or Small Gains Creek) on the north side of Canvey Island. She was rudderless and carried no rigging. After the removal of several tons of mud, he righted the vessel and hired a team of horses to drag her up onto dry land to restore and paint the *Tilikum*'s hull as well as replace the hatch covers. He named her *Benlaric* (not *Bentaric* as is often reported) after his friend, merchant navy officer Archie Wallace, and fixed the nameplate to the bow. Wallace's father was the Commodore of the Ben Line of ships registered at Leith, Scotland and each vessel in the line was named for a mountain in Scotland, *Benlaric* being the one "of which my friend was particularly associated with."[275]

As this period was during the First World War, Bentley applied for permission to have the boat towed to Benfleet for overhaul, but this request was denied. Despite this, Bentley enjoyed his time with the *Tilikum*. "My chief interest was in restoring the hull and I did not have the means to rig her but enjoyed 'messing about in boats' and got much pleasure from this."[276]

Bentley mentioned in his correspondence with the Maritime

Leslie Bentley reclining on the bowsprit of *Benlaric/Tilikum*.
Tilikum *Fonds of the collection of the Maritime Museum of British Columbia.*

Museum of British Columbia in the early 1980s that the vessel had been towed up the Seine River and exhibited in Paris before he acquired her. He often wondered about her fate when he was no longer able to get to Canvey Island. The *Tilikum* languished again until the Byford brothers obtained her.[277]

By 1920 Bentley had abandoned the vessel at Bugby's Hole near East Greenwich. Around 1924 she was owned by two brothers, W.E. Byford and A. Byford, who were yachtsmen at Greenwich. The Byford brothers were both members of the Thames Sailing Club. Founded in 1870 it is the United Kingdom's oldest river sailing club. It is located between Surbiton and Kingston on the Surrey bank of the river.

Ultimately they too found the *Tilikum* unsuitable for use as a yacht.

The exact story of the rediscovery of the *Tilikum* along the banks of the Thames is uncertain, but it seems to have started with a 1924 story, "Derelict Yachts in the Thames Estuary," featured in *Yachting Monthly* magazine.

In one version of events, a Royal Navy officer from Sheerness who had read the *Yachting Monthly* story wrote to Harry T. Barnes, the manager of Rithet's Consolidated Company in Victoria, BC, to tell him about the location of the *Tilikum* and the desirability of repatriating her to Victoria. This was around the time that Voss's book was becoming popular after publication in the United Kingdom.

In another version of events, yachtsman H. Stone contacted Captain J.A. Phillipsen, then master of the Thermopylae Club in Victoria and an associate of Stone's from Yokohama, about the location and perilous condition of the boat. Stone had been one of the partners with Voss in the 1912 voyage of the *Sea Queen* (he is referred to as "F. Stone" in Voss's account) as well as a member of the Yokohama Yacht Club. An uncredited newspaper article attempted to sort out the sequence of events:

> Stone, a yachtsman of Yokohama, who knew Voss well, had done some sailing with him on the Japan coast and in fact, possessed the log of Tilikum ... turned up in Victoria and met Captain J.A. Phillipsen ... told [him] about Tilikum and urged that it should

The *Tilikum* in 1924, laid up at Charlton-on-Thames.
Tilikum *Fonds of the collection of the Maritime Museum of British Columbia.*

be brought back to its port of origin and preserved. Stone and Phillipsen got in touch with H.T. Barnes, local yachtsman, who passed on the word to George I. Warren of the local publicity bureau ... who in turn got in touch with W.G. McAdam, then secretary of the Agent-General for British Columbia in London.[278]

REPATRIATION TO VICTORIA

Captain Phillipsen then contacted Harry T. Barnes, manager of the Victoria Publicity Bureau,[279] asking him to write to George I. Warren, commissioner of the Victoria and Island Publicity Bureau and director of the Victoria Chamber of Commerce. Warren then wrote to W.G. McAdam, the British Columbia agent-general in London,[280] asking him to investigate. McAdam placed an advertisement in the *Yachting Times* asking for further information. In answer to the ad, the Byford brothers offered the *Tilikum* to the City of Victoria as a gift, provided she would not be exhibited for financial gain and that the city would assume the expenses of returning her to Victoria.

Donald A. New of Galiano Island arranged for R. Ree of the Greenwich Yacht Club to crate the vessel. Ted King, of shipping agents King Brothers, organized through Captain H.F. Harrison, the Vancouver manager of Furness, Withy and Company to carry the *Tilikum* "freight free as arranged."

In June 1930, the hull of the *Tilikum* was carried to Victoria through the Panama Canal. She was stored in the number-two cargo hold on the maiden voyage of the Furness Withy Line's freighter *Pacific Reliance* at the expense of the company. The Port of London waived the usual loading charges.

HOME AGAIN — ON DISPLAY IN VICTORIA

When the *Tilikum* arrived at the Rithet's Consolidated Company wharf in Victoria, it was realized that no one had thought to arrange for a place to store and display the vessel. The Victoria Chamber of Commerce debated over the most appropriate place to display her. The provincial government refused to have her on the Legislature grounds. The manager of the Empress Hotel did not want her on the grounds of the hotel but eventually offered a site beside the Crystal Gardens for her display. Local lumber companies donated the material needed to build a shelter. The Victoria Chamber of Commerce undertook some basic repairs on the boat, and on August 7, 1930, she was put on public display.

By 1936 she had again become "pitiful through neglect." Captain Alexander McDonald, a Cape Horner with twenty-six transits who was also a master of Victoria's Thermopylae Club, led a public crusade to raise $200 for the necessary restorations. After newspaper articles and public lectures, the Thermopylae Club had managed to raise only $90.

In 1937 the Thermopylae Club undertook the restoration project. Captain Victor Jacobsen, one of Voss's fur-sealing colleagues in Japan and by then a retired sealing schooner master, undertook the work of shipwright on the project. Jacobsen had apprenticed in a shipyard at Helsinki. He came to the Pacific coast about 1880, working mainly as a sealer. He was elected as a member of the Thermopylae Club in 1934.

By this time the club had raised $150 for the restoration by passing a hat at a meeting of the British Columbia Historical Society at which Captain McDonald had presented a talk on the significance of the *Tilikum*. Their minutes record that "his graphic description was gripping from first to last."[281]

The crew of the sailing yacht *Tai-Mo-Shan*, transiting from Hong Kong to London before the start of the Second World War, also decried the neglected condition in which they found the vessel on their visit to Victoria. (The *Tai-Mo-Shan* was a Hong Kong–built sailing yacht navigated by young Royal Navy officers across the Pacific on their way to the United Kingdom.) Their visit to Victoria is commemorated by a plaque on the seawall at the Inner Harbour. In his book, *The Voyage of the Tai-Mo-Shan*, Martyn Sherwood wrote:

> At Victoria can be seen the remnants of the old *Tillicum* [sic] on a grass-plot at the back of the Empress Hotel. I think it is a pity that so remarkable a vessel cannot be preserved in a better condition, for she is rapidly falling into a sad state of decay. However, for all that, she is well worth a visit. This *Tillicum* was an Indian canoe, thirty feet in length, in which Captain Voss, after

Captain A. McDonald (left) and Captain Victor Jacobsen
at work on the restoration of the *Tilikum*.
Vancouver City Archives item AM54-S4-: Bo P349.1.

many remarkable adventures, achieved an ocean passage of 40,000 miles. I believe that her owner ended his days in California, where he was a taxi-driver.[282]

The *Tilikum* story was featured in one of the *Ripley's Believe It or Not!* syndicated newspaper columns on April 28, 1942. This would have appeared in hundreds of newspapers throughout North America.

When Thunderbird Park was established in Victoria in 1941, Mr. E.G. Rowebotham, the deputy minister of trade and industry, gave permission for the *Tilikum* to be displayed there. The *Tilikum* was moved to the park and placed under the care of the British Columbia Provincial Museum (now the site of the Royal British Columbia Museum). She was set on a concrete foundation and given an overhead shelter.

Three years later, in 1943, Mr. Justice Sydney Smith, in an address to the British Columbia Historical Society,[283] extolled the virtues and value of the *Tilikum*, while lamenting her decrepit condition. He stated, "Now it is being scrawled over by people with little weight and less manners. It should be better looked after."

In 1944 the British Columbia Historical Society and the Thermopylae Club implored the provincial government to put a railing around her. By this time the vessel's rudder had been stolen, the tongue of the replacement figurehead had been torn out and the vessel herself vandalized.

Captain Maximillian Edmund Lohbrunner was born in New York in 1887. He served as a master in several sealing schooners and owned the Deepsea Fish Company in Victoria. He was elected as a member of Victoria's Thermopylae Club, and in 1958 undertook a survey of the *Tilikum*'s hull, discovering dry rot. He reported the situation to the Thermopylae Club, whose members provided him with lumber and paint for the hull. This was probably part of the upwelling of pride that came with the 1958 centennial celebrations of the British Columbia Gold Rush. On several occasions, members of the Thermopylae Club painted the canoe at their own expense.

By 1965 the government of British Columbia was looking for a new home for the *Tilikum*. Dr. Clifford Carl, then the director of the British Columbia Provincial Museum, wrote to Colonel John

W.D. Symons, asking the Maritime Museum of British Columbia to display the *Tilikum* in the main gallery of the museum building in Victoria's Bastion Square. The museum enthusiastically accepted this addition to their collection.[284] Symons had been appointed as the director of the Maritime Museum of British Columbia in 1961.

The fact that the museum charged an entry fee prompted

The *Tilikum* during her 1965 move to the Maritime Museum of British Columbia building in the old courthouse in Bastion Square, Victoria. Workers are swiftly opening up the wall to slip the vessel inside before a potential protest might materialize.

Maritime Museum of British Columbia.

some members of the public to object to the transfer of ownership and location. A Victoria tour bus driver, George "Rebel" Mowat, who had included the openly displayed *Tilikum* on his route, claimed the City of Victoria owned the vessel and that it had not been consulted about the move. Mowat presented a petition with thirteen hundred signatures on it protesting the transfer to the museum.

There ensued a debate on the subject of ownership of the vessel at a Victoria city council meeting. Heated questions were asked and bold statements were made in the provincial legislature. Frank Calder,[285] a Nisga'a MLA, declared that his people regarded the vessel as a form of Indigenous art and insisted on a "free display of such items."

Mowat even threatened to press charges of theft or piracy against the Victoria Van and Storage Company, the trucking company that carried the *Tilikum* to her new quarters from Thunderbird Park. The headline in the Victoria *Daily Times* read, "Legal Squall Hits *Tilikum*; Rebel at the Helm."

The *Tilikum* during her 1965 move to the Maritime Museum of British Columbia building. Note the door and bricks of the structure have been removed to allow the *Tilikum* to enter through the back of the building.
Maritime Museum of British Columbia.

By the time it was determined that the Byford Brothers of London, England, had given the boat to the Victoria Visitors' Bureau, the fate of the vessel was literally sealed. In March 1965, the north door of the Maritime Museum of British Columbia was removed and part of the wall demolished in order to allow the vessel to enter the building. The wall was immediately bricked

The *Tilikum* finally on display in the main gallery of the Maritime Museum of British Columbia in Bastion Square, Victoria, in 1967 where she remained until her removal to storage in 2015.

Tilikum *Fonds of the collection of the Maritime Museum of British Columbia 993.117.0007.*

up again and when the "mortar was hard and dry" the *Tilikum* was safe at last. The museum was able to tell her amazing story to visitors while protecting her from vandals and the weather.

The Victoria Visitors' Bureau, the British Columbia Provincial Museum, the Thermopylae Club and Victoria's city council all declared their support for the museum's solution for the issue. Public concern subsided and the *Tilikum* remained undisturbed and admired until 2015.

In 1965 Captain Voss's daughter, Caroline Kuhn, wrote to the museum from Portland, Oregon, to say that she had recently visited and was delighted to see her father's canoe on display. She volunteered to pay for renovations and offered the museum a portrait of her father.[286] Then in February 1969 Norman Luxton's daughter, Eleanor, wrote from Banff, offering to pay the cost of completing the renovations to the *Tilikum*. The museum was able to install rigging, deck fittings and masts. The height of the gallery's ceiling forced a concession of shortening the masts to fit.

The museum undertook yet another restoration in 1970 and displayed the vessel on a cradle in the main gallery with rigging and fittings resembling those in the photographic record. Regrettably, no notes were kept of the approach taken to conserve and restore the vessel.

In 1976 the museum participated in the release of a new edition of *The Venturesome Voyages of Captain Voss* by Gray's Publishing in Sidney, BC. The remainders of this edition were acquired and put up for sale in the museum's gift shop for many decades afterward. They are still actively sought on the antiquarian book market.

PUBLICATION OF *THE VENTURESOME VOYAGES OF CAPTAIN VOSS*

Norman Luxton stated that in the original agreement between himself and Voss, Luxton would write the story of the voyage, publish it and make their fortune. Having left the voyage early and breaking with Voss, he was unable to fulfill his part of the bargain.

Voss began work on his manuscript in late 1904. He wrote to Luxton in Banff, telling him that the voyage was successfully concluded and asking him if he would send the images he had taken from the first leg of the trip. He also asked if Luxton would like to have his picture in the book. There is no record of Luxton answering the request – and tellingly there is no picture of Luxton in his book.

The title of Voss's original account derives from story headlines reported in New Zealand newspapers referring to the "venturesome voyages of Captain Voss." The original text of the book, written phonetically as one imagines Voss to have actually spoken, was recorded in a number of school notebooks ("scribblers") found in R.T. Rithet's vaults on Wharf Street in Victoria, BC. These scribblers were given by a sailor friend of Captain Voss (likely H. or F. Stone from Yokohama and the *Sea Queen* adventures) to Harry T. Barnes of Victoria for safekeeping, then were loaned to Luxton. Sadly, these original notebooks are now lost, but before their loss they were faithfully typed out for Barnes. That manuscript was a verbatim copy of the original, both in spelling and grammar. This manuscript copy is held in the British Columbia Archives.

Voss's writing apparently did not capture the dramatic vitality of the stories as they had been recounted personally, so his editor in Japan acted as a ghostwriter and embellished the text to make it more commercially marketable. In the process unchecked errors entered the text that have never been corrected.

The manuscript was published twelve years after the start of the voyage; perhaps the sole motivation was to derive revenue from it. We do not know who the original editor in Japan was. The book was published privately in Japan and, initially at least, it was directly marketed by Voss, who sent out advertising circulars around the world by mail. Orders were mailed out from Siberia, presumably because postal service to Europe was quicker and more reliable than if mailing the books from Japan.

Voss handled the sales and distribution himself. After he left on the voyage of the *Tilikum II* in 1914, his agents in Yokohama handled sales. It is thought that most of the copies of the book were destroyed in the Great Kanto earthquake in 1923.

After *Venturesome Voyages* was published, Luxton wrote his own account in 1927, but it languished on a shelf for forty-four years before a publisher looked at it. Eleanor Luxton seemed to have acquired the resentment her father held toward Voss and was easily persuaded to publish Luxton's story, convinced her father had been defrauded by a villainous ex-partner. She therefore intended to publicize what she felt was the truth. She stated, "Luxton had ... insisted on an agreement signed before a notary that he should have all publishing rights. Then Voss went back on his word and drafted an account, subsequently published under the title of *The Venturesome Voyages of Captain Voss*. Because Voss's account was not wholly accurate Luxton wrote a journal based on his day-to-day diary."

W.S.Draycott Esq.,Hon.Librarian of the
    Royal Cruising Club,LONDON.

Dear Sir,
           Thanking you for your kind order of
June 29th I took much pleasure in sending you
per bookpost registered via Siberia 4 copies
of my book"Venturesome Voyages". Please excuse
the delay caused through the difficulties of
printing in Japan and remit £ 1.4.- (price
including postage and reg.fee) to my Agents
Messrs.VEHLING & CO.,92 Settlement,Yokohama.
          Thanking you again,I am,dear Sir,
                yours very truly

Yokohama,6th December 1913   J. C. Voss

A postcard mailed by Captain Voss via Siberia to one of the customers of the book in England, requesting payment. Apparently postage via this method was cheaper and faster than by sea voyage directly from Japan.
John MacFarlane collection.

In his personal copy of Voss's book, Luxton wrote, "Captain Voss got things badly mixed up and where his memory failed him he made fiction. He also took a lot of the experiences from Vancouver to Fiji and put them in his later voyages. He missed two wrecks we had, one a very bad one."[287] It appears that Luxton got his own facts confused—and perhaps embellished or even invented some stories in his memoir, since he had no intention of publishing his account.

It is true that Voss erased Luxton's memory from the telling of some of his own stories where Luxton had been present. On the other hand, Luxton claims to tell about events for which there is no evidence—including the so-called shipwrecks Luxton has happening in a time frame too tight for them to have occurred. Perhaps storms or close calls with reefs became actual shipwrecks in Luxton's memory.

Interestingly Luxton's printing company (which produced the *Crag and Canyon* newspaper) could easily have printed his version of the trip at any time. The fact that he did not have them do so, even after Voss published his book, suggests perhaps that he knew his account would be unsupported.

(See Appendix I for a list of editions of *The Venturesome Voyages of Captain Voss* and *Luxton's Pacific Crossing*.)

Likely as a result of the book publication and renewed interest in Voss's voyage, a request from two men associated with the us Coast Guard to "restore *Tilikum* to her seaworthy condition … and actually sail her on a complete circumnavigation" was received in December 1977.[288] The correspondence indicated a desire to take the *Tilikum* back to the ocean to complete a true circumnavigation and that preparations would need to start immediately to meet the proposed launch date of May 1981—the eightieth anniversary of the *Tilikum*'s departure from Victoria. No doubt they were disappointed with the reply from the museum: "The *Tilikum* is our only legacy of Captain Voss … and the principal attraction at our museum and people come from far and wide to see her … you will appreciate our reasons for wanting to secure *Tilikum*'s future as a cultural asset."[289]

The *Tilikum* was placed in a new display setting in 1998 when the lower floor displays were completely refurbished. In 2001 the museum reworked her rigging and steering controls and applied a new coat of paint on her hull.

The *Tilikum* is trucked away to storage in a warehouse from the Maritime Museum in 2015 past the Parliament Buildings, where her future had been debated fifty years earlier.
John West photograph.

The closure of the Maritime Museum of British Columbia's Bastion Square location in 2015 forced the museum to put the *Tilikum* in storage at the passenger terminal at the Outer Harbour wharf at Ogden Point. Although her situation is not now as secure as it once was, the museum anticipates funding that will assist them to replace the masts and sails and create an exhibit to be enjoyed by arriving cruise ship passengers. It is hoped the sturdy little canoe, now almost a century-and-a-half old, can be properly displayed, cared for and appreciated just as she was when Voss took this craft on her incredible forty-thousand-mile adventure, departing from the shores of Victoria in 1901.

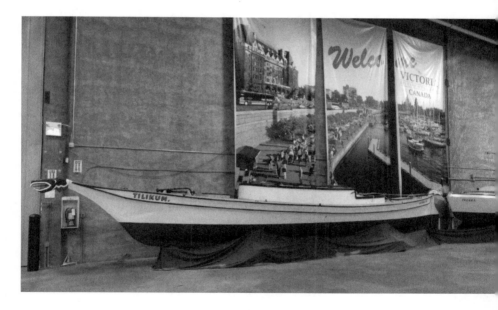

The *Tilikum* in storage at the Ogden Point passenger terminal at the Outer Harbour wharf, Victoria, BC. Note John Guzzwell's *Trekka* (see sidebar, page 46) astern. The *Tilikum* is now unrigged and exposed to casual handling under less than ideal conditions.
John MacFarlane photograph.

14

THE *SEA QUEEN*, THE *TILIKUM II* AND VOSS'S LAST YEARS

THE *SEA QUEEN*

In 1911 the introduction of the North Pacific Fur Sealing Convention, created to address and end the dramatic overhunting of fur seals, put Voss and other hunters out of business. Compensation was offered to vessel owners who were no longer able to exploit the valuable but diminishing trade supply of fur seals. Voss was waiting for the payout promised by the Japanese government, living ashore in Japan with no immediate prospects.

The North Pacific Fur Seal Convention, formally known as the Convention between the United States and Other Powers Providing for the Preservation and Protection of Fur Seals, was an international treaty signed on July 7, 1911. It was designed to manage the commercial harvest of fur-bearing mammals, such as Northern fur seals and sea otters, in the Pribilof Islands of the Bering Sea.[290]

Top: The crew of the *Sea Queen* in Japan. F.J.H. Stone (left) and S.A. Vincent (right) with Captain Voss in the centre.
Captain J.C. Voss, in the first edition (1913) of The Venturesome Voyages of Captain Voss.

Bottom: The yawl *Sea Queen* under sail in Tokyo Bay, Japan, in 1912.
Captain J.C. Voss, in the first edition (1913) of The Venturesome Voyages of Captain Voss.

In 1912 two young yachtsmen approached Voss with a proposal for a small-craft sailing voyage. Voss was well known to
yachtsmen in Japan. Two of them, F.J.H. Stone and S.A. Vincent,
who were members of the Yokohama Yacht Club, were building
a yawl named the *Sea Queen*. She was based on the sturdy design
of the 25½-foot *Sea Bird*.

The *Sea Queen* was a wooden-hulled yawl 25 feet in length
with a beam of 8 feet, drawing a shallow 3½ feet and carrying 400
square feet of sail. She was launched on July 1, 1912, and fully
provisioned by July 26. She carried 130 gallons of fresh water,
provisions for three months, two rifles, one revolver and ammunition. She also carried a Kodak camera, a gramophone and navigation instruments.

The Victoria papers reported the announcement of Captain
Voss's adventure:

Captain Voss on Daring Cruise—Former Victorian Who Made Voyage in *Tilikum* Leaves Japan to Round World in Small Yacht

Mr. C. Julian [Charles Otis Julian who, in 1906, donated the
C.O. Julian Trophy to the Royal Vancouver Yacht Club] of Vancouver, a yachtsman who returned by steamer *Empress of Japan*
from the Orient, reports seeing Capt. J.C. Voss, formerly of this
City, who was preparing to start on another cruise similar to that
made ten years ago from Victoria in the little *Tilikum*, an Indian
canoe decked over and converted into a yacht. Capt. Voss told
Mr. Julian to whom he showed his little craft, that he would start
from Yokohama on July 27 and complete a three-year cruise at
Victoria. He will be accompanied by S.A. Vincent and F. Stone.
The vessel, which will carry the adventurous trio, is the *Sea
Queen*. She is a craft of small proportions. Her length overall is
but 25 feet, 8 inches; her waterline 13 feet; beam 8 feet 3 inches;
draft 3 feet 6 inches and sail area 400 square feet.

The first stop will be made at the Marshall Islands, about
twenty days from Yokohama. From the Marshall Islands the sail-
boat will proceed to the New Hebrides taking about 30 or 40 days
in which to reach Brisbane, and stopping at many island spots on
the journey. It is calculated to stop at Sydney and Melbourne and
then cross to Hobart, Tasmania, after which it is expected that a

call will be made at New Zealand, before the long trip through the Torres Straits is commenced, the goal of which is India.

On the latter leg of the journey the boat is scheduled to call at Timor and Sumatra. Crossing the Indian Ocean the *Sea Queen* is to proceed toward the Suez Canal, seeking a tow through the channel from some steamship. After leaving the canal the boat is to skirt the North African coast as far as Gibraltar, turning north and making for Southampton and London from there, and from the latter city laying a course for Hamburg and Baltic Sea ports, before retracing to cross the Atlantic.

Arrived off the North American coast, the *Sea Queen* will journey coastwise to Panama, with the expectation of coming into the Pacific Ocean through the Panama Canal in 1914. It is then expected that a trip up the west coast of America will be made, the Panama–Pacific Exposition [a world's fair held in San Francisco from February 20 to December 4, 1915] visited, and the journey continued to Victoria from where the voyage across the Pacific may be attempted. Three years is the estimated length of the cruise. The *Sea Queen* will be able to carry 150 gallons of water and enough food to last about two months.[291]

On July 27, 1912, the adventurous trio embarked on their voyage, towed out of Tokyo Bay by a steam launch. Their first anchorage was at Uraga, Japan, for the night. Here they made arrangements for restowing their gear and all the parting gifts they had received from well-wishers.

At sea they passed the *Chicago Maru*, a passenger ship. In *The Venturesome Voyages of Captain Voss*, Voss wrote:

At about nine o'clock we sighted smoke to the north-eastward, and by looking through our glasses we could see two masts and the top of a smokestack rising gradually out of the water. It was apparently a large steamer steering to the south-west, and an hour later, when the steamer was about a mile and a half ahead of us, she turned and stood towards us, and coming alongside proved to be the Japanese steamship *Chicago Maru* from Seattle, bound for Yokohama.

The *Sea Queen* under tow leaving Yokohama Harbour.
Captain J.C. Voss, in the first edition (1913) of The Venturesome Voyages of Captain Voss.

"What are you people doing round here in that boat? Have you been blown away from the land? Are you lost?" the Japanese captain shouted. "Come alongside, and I will hoist you on my davits and you can go with me to Yokohama."

We thanked the captain for the trouble he had taken for us, and for his kind offer to take us on board, and after a short explanation of our doings, the captain gave us his longitude, and we parted the best of friends. In less than an hour the steamer was out of sight and we were left to ourselves again.[292]

The *Chicago Maru* was owned by the Osaka Shosen Line. On October 15, 1943, she was torpedoed by the submarine uss *Tullibee* (SS-284) off the west coast of Formosa.

On August 1 the wind lightened and they released the reefs in the sail, but later in the day the weather freshened, gradually becoming stormy. The *Sea Queen*, without a sea anchor, apparently behaved in the same way as the *Xora* and the *Tilikum*, lying sideways to the sea. They eventually heaved to under a sea anchor, and Voss recalled that once the little mizzen was hoisted and the sheet hauled in the vessel swung head to sea and she rode every sea steadily and calmly. In a pattern, she rose on the crests of large seas and then gently sank again in the troughs.

Voss pragmatically expected his crew to be seasick for a few days, which "would have been hard luck on them, but it would have saved the provisions." But there was no such malady affecting the two crewmen. They were always ready to do their duty at meal hours, and sometimes between meal hours too. "I was soon convinced that my hopes were vain, and it made me think very seriously as to how I could manage to reduce their appetites by about two-thirds." That night they heaved to, their dinner consisting of four fried eggs each, four large slices of bacon, apples, bread, butter, cheese, tea and stewed fruit. They spent the evening smoking, chatting and listening to the gramophone.

The winds persisted in spite of relatively clear weather. On August 5 they were hit by a large breaking wave on the port quarter that almost turned the boat on its beam end. Voss and Stone were on deck, barely hanging on. Vincent was thrown clear of his bunk against the opposite side of the cabin. Crockery was broken, a box of eggs overturned, and the rifles, ammunition and camera were all doused with seawater. Vincent felt the dozen broken eggs were too good to throw away so they were scraped together and fried up to be eaten with the afternoon coffee.

With the wind now a heavy gale, the seas increased in size and began breaking. The vessel drifted astern at an unusually fast rate. The next morning they noticed the vessel had sprung a leak. After hauling in the sea anchor, they found the bottom torn—damage they attributed to a shark.

Voss wanted to turn back to Japan to address the leak in the hull. His crew members were very much opposed to this idea; they offered to bail night and day, if necessary. Voss agreed, provided the situation did not get worse. But the leak worsened and Voss worried that it was gradually loosening the fastenings in the boat's frames. He convinced the crew to make for the Bonin Islands. But their drift put them farther north than they anticipated, and with the leak increasing, they altered course for Ayukawa, five hundred miles away. Voss reflected that he had never before been forced to turn back due to a leaky boat and felt the turn of events was an omen of bad luck.

Ayukawa was the site of a whaling station near Kinkasen Island. On arrival they discovered there were no marine ways (ramps) to pull the boat from the water, but the manager of the whaling company, a Mr. Kurogane, helped them get the *Sea Queen* up on the beach. An inspection showed that the leak had resulted from a poor caulking job, and once it was rectified the *Sea Queen* was "tight as a bottle." They departed Ayukawa on August 22 and set course for the Marshall Islands.

Their early progress was slow in light airs. A week later the breeze and swell picked up from the southeast. Voss was uneasy as he noted the darkening sky. A "heavy-looking ring of varied fiery colours formed around the sun. The atmosphere became very sultry, and the appearance of a dense bank of clouds of threatening appearance on the horizon" convinced Voss that a typhoon was at hand.

The barometer began to drop steadily, and with the increasing swell Voss was sure the approaching typhoon was not far off. They reefed the mizzen and hoisted a storm staysail. They were riding under control of the sea anchor and a riding sail. The barometer continued to drop and the wind increased in intensity accompanied by breaking seas and heavy rain squalls.

The crew rigged two oil bags over the side, which were changed every hour as the oil seeped from them into the adjacent water, calming the turbulence of the sea against the boat. They were pleased with the results. By 2000 hours that evening, Voss wrote, "It was blowing so hard that I did not think it possible for the wind and sea to increase. I told my shipmates that the little vessel would weather the typhoon without much trouble; and I am certain she would have done so had our storm gear been stronger. After making the cruises in the *Xora* and the *Tilikum*, I thought I knew all about the sea and what was required to manage a small vessel through a heavy gale."[293]

At 2100 the wind blew so hard that it was impossible to stand on deck and they were forced to lie out flat in the cockpit and hang on for dear life. Up to this point the oil bags had served their purpose, but in these conditions they had no effect. "The spray was flying over the boat like a heavy snow storm." Yet no seas came on board.

Shortly after 2100 the boat fell sideways into the sea and the mizzen sheet parted. Voss ordered, "All hands on deck!" Crawling over the deck with seas now breaking on them, the crew secured the mizzen sail. The sea anchor was lost but they rigged one using the cabin ladder and a metal anchor, all done while lying flat on the deck. But the new one was too light to be effective and by 2300 it too parted company with the *Sea Queen*.

The two mates were in the cabin and Voss was in the cockpit when a huge sea struck the boat. On her beam end, the *Sea Queen* quivered before turning turtle. Voss let go and was in the water. For a moment he considered giving up, but he suddenly thought of his two shipmates in the cabin unable to get out and he wished to see them one more time to say goodbye.

Grabbing hold of the stern, he managed to climb over it. Another enormous sea broke over him, and Voss hung on with his nails dug into the wood of the hull. The weight of the iron on the keel slowly but surely brought her right side up again. Voss was then able to climb into the cockpit just as the draining water allowed his two shipmates to emerge from the cabin. Voss recalled:

> In spite of being on a small craft which was broadside on to the worst storm and largest sea that I ever experienced in all my years at sea, and all three of us lying down in the cockpit and hanging on for dear life, our meeting after the incident was quite joyous, and if the boat got smashed up in the typhoon, it would have given us a chance to say good-bye to each other.

It was impossible for them to open the cabin door while they were lying on the starboard tack and they were unable to bail her out. If the ingress of water continued they would founder so Voss was forced to change tack. As they turned, a breaking sea went over top of them and broke the main boom. Stone and Vincent were strong swimmers and elected to stay in the cockpit and bail. Voss, not a swimmer, crawled into the cabin through the now open door to bail.

The water dislodged the gear that had been so carefully stowed, and now it floated in the ocean, mixing with the fish oil they used for the oil bags. The smell and the rolling of the boat almost made Voss seasick. He used a sugar tin as a bailer, tossing water out of the port light scuttle.

During the bailing, Stone was washed overboard and then washed right back again. It took three hours before enough water was removed to make the boat more stable. Stone was washed overboard a second time as they approached the eye of the typhoon. After his retrieval, all three waited in the cabin with the port lights and hatch closed up tightly. The barometer read 1003 millibars—a very low reading, suggesting terrible weather.

When they reached the dead calm of the eye, they emerged from the cabin. Both masts and all the deck gear had gone overboard. They worked furiously to retrieve what they could see in the water. Although the wind ceased to blow the seas were still mountainous. The *Sea Queen* bobbed up and down like a cork. They took advantage of the situation to clean up some of the mess in the cabin. The only dry item was the matches kept sealed in a bottle.

In a short time they had water boiling and made hot coffee, which lifted their spirits. But within half an hour the wind of the typhoon picked up again. The barometer began to rise and the dismasted vessel rode out the rest of the storm. The heavy seas prevented any further jury-rigging.

The *Sea Queen* riding at her sea anchor.

Captain J.C. Voss in the first edition (1913) of The Venturesome Voyages of Captain Voss.

On September 2 the winds abated to moderate, but there were still large westerly swells to contend with. The crew managed to step (remount) a piece of the broken mizzen-mast and a spinnaker boom and rigged a storm staysail. Incredibly, they were sailing again. They estimated their position now to be 350 miles from Yokohama.

They turned their attention to the main mast, which was broken in three places. With nailed-on wood and lashings, the main mast was made whole again and re-stepped. They rigged shear legs to coax the mast into the step and upright again. They charted a course for Yokohama and managed to cook and eat a modest meal.

Sailing without a chronometer, the men were unsure of their longitude. On September 4 the sun emerged and Voss estimated they were now 240 miles from Yokohama. On September 9 they sighted Oshima Island (about sixty miles west of Tokyo Bay). They made a stop at Habu to rest before sailing on. On their arrival at Yokohama, the three friends enjoyed a champagne dinner to celebrate their good fortune in surviving the ordeal.

History has lost track of what became of the *Sea Queen* and her intrepid crew. It is unlikely she carried on with the ambitious plan to sail around the world. No mention of her arriving at any ports can be found and Voss himself leaves no record beyond the harrowing tale of survival in the *Sea Queen* during the typhoon. Perhaps the close rub with death discouraged him or simply made him more aware of his own mortality.

THE *TILIKUM II*

Little known is the fact that Captain Voss attempted a repeat of his voyage to England, this time starting in Yokohama, Japan, two years after the voyage of the *Sea Queen*. Voss designed the *Tilikum II*, translating all the features and advantages that he had experienced in his years of cruising small craft around the world into the design.

She was built of wood, 35 feet in length with an 8-foot beam and 4 feet of freeboard, decked in and rigged as a three-masted schooner-yawl with a "sharp stern." She was launched on December 30, 1913, and registered in Germany. This made sense as she was built for a German, W.G. Vied, who had lived in Yokohama for the previous six years.

Left: Captain Voss's published description of the voyage undertaken by the *Tilikum II* with W.G. Vied.
John MacFarlane collection.

Right: The *Tilikum II* in Yokohama Harbour in 1914.
John MacFarlane collection.

Vied proposed this cruise, having helped to compile John Murray's famous *Handbook for Travellers in Japan*. Vied also drew the illustrations and maps in the first edition of *The Venturesome Voyages of Captain Voss* printed in Japan. (We wonder if he was the mysterious editor who compiled the text of the book from Voss's manuscript.)

On this expedition, Voss would act as sailing master, with Vied serving as mate. They sailed on January 24, 1914, bound for the islands of the South Pacific. Arriving on February 8 in the Bonin Islands, they encountered a new island of volcanic origin and ascertained its position. They estimated it to be one mile in diameter and seven hundred feet in height.[294]

They carried on to the Mariana Islands and Saipan. When Vied broke his arm, they were forced to seek medical assistance at Guam. They then sailed on to the Caroline Islands and Rabaul (New Britain). Almost all their ports of call were German possessions in the South Pacific.

Voss and Vied intended to sail down the Australian coast to Cooktown, Cairns and Townsville. They arrived in Brisbane on May 25, and then in Samarai, Papua, on May 27 before moving on to Port Moresby.[295] Vied left the voyage at this point, apparently because of his broken arm. Voss bought the boat from his mate and turned her over to a Captain Small, who took charge of the vessel when Voss went on to Brisbane on business. Small had been master of a vessel called the *Kia Ora* (owned by the Whitten Brothers).[296] It was announced that they would depart in September for Java, where the vessel would be placed on exhibition. This plan fell through and the *Tilikum II* was sold in Townsville to Smith and Agnew, local contractors, for two hundred pounds.[297]

On July 16, 1914, at Townsville, the *Tilikum II* was stolen by two young men intent on getting to Darwin. The pair rowed her out of her river moorage late at night and then sailed out toward Thursday Island. When the crime was discovered, there was a sensation in the Australian press.[298] The harbour master left in the steamer *Woy Woy* to investigate reports that the *Tilikum II* had been sighted at Eclipse Island in the Hinchinbrook Channel south of the Palm Islands Group. The steamer was carrying Inspector McGrath as a police presence.

The commissioner of police at Cairns sent a telegram announcing the arrest of John Campbell and Michael Stevens near Thursday Island. They admitted to the theft since the boat was found in their possession at the time of their arrest. The men were in bad shape from hunger and had been surviving for an extended period on a diet of beans, yet they declared they had not intended to dispose of the boat when they arrived at Darwin.

Arrangements were made by the *Tilikum II*'s owners to bring her back to Townsville, and she eventually arrived in Cairns[299] from Cooktown in November 1914. The subsequent fate of the *Tilikum II* is not known, but with the outbreak of the First World War, a yacht voyage around the world would have little chance of exciting public interest.

By 1915 Voss had relocated to the United States. His nephew Carl Voss Kinkel recalls meeting his uncle at the San Francisco World's Fair. "He was living with a shipmate in a hotel on Mission Street. The Captain was a fine person."[300] By 1918 he had moved to Tracy, California, approximately one hundred kilometres inland from San Francisco, where he settled among relatives. Driving a jitney, he charged a nickel a ride. While visiting a friend's ranch on the outskirts of Tracy, he contracted pneumonia and died shortly after on February 27, 1922. His final port, his grave, is marked with a plain headstone inscribed with the dates of his birth and death and crowned with a single word: "Father."

* * *

In this age of computers and instant communications, it may be difficult to comprehend the tremendous curiosity that was piqued by the epic voyage of the *Tilikum*. The turnout of spectators to see the captain and his foreign canoe was recorded in great numbers wherever they went, generating much excitement among the onlookers and providing columns and columns of editorials, in local papers as well as abroad.

People tracked Voss's progress through to England with keen interest and marked the occasion of their first encounter with Voss and the *Tilikum* in a variety of unique ways. Model makers were likely the most prolific, building scale models faithfully from photographs and from memory. Many other manifestations also appeared.

The impact the *Tilikum* had during her voyage may be little appreciated today, but on her epic transit around the world, she sparked imagination and motivated others to embark on adventure in the face of naysayers and doubters. The *Tilikum* and Voss inspired others to reach beyond their comfortable lives and take up the challenge—to push their own limitations as well as seek a place in history. That is the true legacy of the *Tilikum*.

ACKNOWLEDGEMENTS

Alf Beeching, historian, Margate, England
Astrid Bell, Eleanor Luxton Historical Foundation, Banff, AB
Robert Bell, research assistant, Maritime Museum of British Columbia
Nicolas Boigelot, Canterbury Museum, New Zealand
Peter Costolloe, Classic Yacht Association of Australia
Christopher Cole, British Columbia Nautical History Facebook Group
George Duddy, British Columbia Nautical History Facebook Group
Angelika Eirisch, CPA, business manager, Buffalo Nations Luxton Museum
Andrew Evans, solo sailing expert, Victoria, BC
Derek Fairbridge, copy editor
Edith Fry, Australiana research librarian, city of Ballarat
Tony Gooch, record-setting solo circumnavigator and vice-commodore of the Ocean Cruising Club
Tony Grove, master shipwright, Victoria, BC
Colin Henthorne, master mariner, Canadian Coast Guard, Victoria, BC
Rona Hollingsworth, curator, Maritime Museum of Tasmania
Lynn Hurras, manager, Historic Luxton Home Museum, Banff, AB
Tracy Hudson, secretary, River Canoe Club of New South Wales, Australia
Elizabeth Kundert-Cameron, head librarian, Archives of the Canadian Rockies
Gary Luke, River Canoe Club of New South Wales, Australia
Catherine MacFarlane, heritage interpreter, Qualicum Beach, BC
Arlene Prunkl, editor, PenUltimate Editorial Services, Kelowna, BC
David C. Retter, research librarian, Alexander Turnbull Library, National Library of New Zealand
Ian Rose, Classic Yacht Association of Australia
Tad Roberts, naval architect/wooden boat expert, Gabriola Island, BC
Dan Salmon, the Nauticapedia Project, Courtenay, BC
Jeanne Socrates, record-setting solo circumnavigator, Victoria, BC
Lindsay Stokalko, reference archivist/librarian, Archives of the Canadian Rockies
Judy Thompson, librarian, Maritime Museum of British Columbia
Christopher Thornhill, archivist, Royal Cruising Club
Brittany Vis, associate director, Maritime Museum of British Columbia
Nicol Warn, marine artist and wooden boat specialist, Sechelt, BC
Jamie Webb, former master of the Thermopylae Club, Victoria, BC
John West, Maritime Museum of British Columbia
P.W. Win, historian, Nelson Yacht Club, Nelson, New Zealand

APPENDIX I

THE BOOKS

EDITIONS OF *THE VENTURESOME VOYAGES OF CAPTAIN VOSS*

1. *The Venturesome Voyages of Captain Voss*, 1st ed. Tokyo (Kanda), Geiser & Gilbert Ltd. (Yokohama: Japan Herald Press, 1913).
2. *The Venturesome Voyages of Captain Voss*, 2nd ed. (London, UK: Martin Hopkinson and Co. Ltd., 1926). Introduction by Weston Martyr.
3. *The Venturesome Voyages of Captain Voss*, 1st cheap ed. (London, UK: Martin Hopkinson and Co. Ltd., 1930).
4. *The Venturesome Voyages of Captain Voss* (Boston, MA: Charles E. Lauriat Co., 1931).
5. *The Venturesome Voyages of Captain Voss*, reprint (Boston, MA: Charles E. Lauriat Co., 1934).
6. *The Venturesome Voyages of Captain Voss*, reprint (Boston, MA: Charles E. Lauriat Co., 1941).
7. *The Venturesome Voyages of Captain Voss* (New York: Dodd, Mead & Co., 1941).
8. *The Venturesome Voyages of Captain Voss* (London, UK: Mariner's Library, 1949). Introduction by Richard Hughes.
9. *The Venturesome Voyages of Captain Voss*, 2nd impression, by arrangement with John Lane (London, UK: The Bodley Head Ltd., 1950).
10. *The Venturesome Voyages of Captain Voss* (London, UK: The Travel Book Club, 1950). Introduction by Richard Hughes.
11. *The Venturesome Voyages of Captain Voss* (New York: Dodd, Mead & Co., 1950). Introduction by Weston Martyr.
12. *The Venturesome Voyages of Captain Voss* (London, UK: Rupert Hart-Davis, 1955).
13. *The Venturesome Voyages of Captain Voss: Around the World in the Tilikum, 1901* (Sidney, BC: Gray's Publishing Ltd., 1976). Introduction by Frederick E. Grubb.

The voyage of the *Tilikum* is mainly remembered through the text of Voss's book. Editions of the book have been published in English, French, German, Spanish and Russian. The book has been in print for over one hundred years since its first publication in Japan in 1913. Like the voyage itself, the story has global dimensions. The book is still popular to a wide demographic of readers around the world.

EDITIONS OF *LUXTON'S PACIFIC CROSSING*

1. *Luxton's Pacific Crossing: Being the Journal of Norman Kenny Luxton, Mate of the Tilikum, May 20, 1901, Victoria B.C. to October 18, 1901, Suva, Fiji,* ed. Eleanor Georgina Luxton (Sidney, BC: Gray's Publishing Ltd., 1971). Foreword by George F.G. Stanley.

2. *Luxton's Pacific Crossing,* ed. Eleanor Georgina Luxton (Toronto: Key Porter Books, 2002). The Eleanor Luxton Foundation updated and reprinted the book. It is still available at the Luxton House Museum in Banff, AB.

Norman Luxton was a prolific storyteller and the many adventures of his early life, as well as his years spent building and investing in Banff, would produce volumes of interesting reading. His manuscript was written twenty-seven years after the voyage; by then he was working from memory and photographs. It is an engaging personal story of adventure, intrigue and fortitude. He can perhaps be forgiven for putting a heroic spin on a venture that, in the end, turned out to cost him more money than he ever earned.

APPENDIX II

VOSS'S PRINCIPLES OF GOOD SEAMANSHIP

In his book, *The Venturesome Voyages of Captain Voss*, Voss promoted the following principles of good seamanship, which we address here in light of modern understanding and knowledge:[301]

1. **In what size of vessel is it safe to heave to under sail in bad weather?**

   Based on his experience in the little sealing schooner *Ella G.* (49 feet, 18 tons), Voss concluded that it was safe for a vessel of 50 feet or more to heave to without a sea anchor. He weathered four heavy gales in the North Pacific under a storm trysail hoisted on the main mast. With this she swung about, sideways to the sea and wind, as much as eight points without shipping a sea.

2. **What is the proper time to heave to when running before a strong wind and sea?**

   Any vessel can get into difficulty with a bad "pooping sea" (i.e., a sea breaking over the stern when running). Voss recommended taking early action—to heave to once the waves commence breaking. He explained that all that is necessary is to let the boat come into the wind with her sails set. If the seas are running strongly, he suggested watching for a brief lull in the seas and then to put the helm hard down and let the vessel come up into the wind. In an extreme situation, take the sails down and come up into the wind with bare poles. Set a storm sail afterward. Modern circumnavigators and blue-water sailors now accept that heaving to can actually be dangerous, and experts usually give general advice not to do it. Circumnavigation expert Tony Gooch states that, "current practice has evolved into better solutions for sailing in heavy weather than what Voss employed."

3. **What storm sails should be carried in a gale, and how should they be set?**

   Voss advises masters to make trials of their vessel to learn the weak points of their rig. Trying combinations of reduced sail to determine what works is the way to have the knowledge ahead of an emergency. Modern rigging styles are quite different from those in Voss's day. Tony Gooch suggests that, "it is through trial and error that the master learns what works best."

4. **What signs assure the master that his ship is properly hove to in a gale and thus safe from shipping seas?**

   Voss wrote that if the vessel lies four to five points from the wind and makes nearly a square drift, she is safe.

5. **How should a small vessel of about 25 to 50 feet in length, under storm sails in a moderate gale, heave to?**

   In the sloop *Xora*, Voss rigged a small storm staysail tack over the stem with the sheet to windward and the mainsail closely reefed. He kept the sheet well in and the helm half down. In the yawl *Sea Queen*, he set a storm jib with the sheet to windward, a single-reefed mizzen and the helm a little down.

6. **Why should small vessels heave to under sea anchor and riding sail in a heavy gale?**

   Voss felt that the deployment of a sea anchor and riding sail enabled the crew to get a night's rest while being out of danger from shipping seas. Modern practice has evolved into better and safer techniques.

7. **What is the best kind of cable for the sea anchor with regard to material and length and how to fasten the same?**

   Time and technological innovation have made Voss's advice on this subject somewhat dated. He recommended manila rope. The size specified varied with the size of the boat. For vessels of 20 feet at waterline, he suggested using a 2½-inch circumference; for 30 feet, 3 inches; for 40 feet, 4 inches; for 50 feet, 5 inches. He cautioned that chafing was a concern, particularly over time. To counteract this he recommended splicing in a chain to the upper end and fastening this to the foremast and lead clear of the headgear.

8. **How should a small vessel lie under a sea anchor and riding sail, in a heavy gale, so as to keep dry and comfortable?**
   Voss recommended keeping the vessel straight ahead to the sea. The sea anchor should be out about 150 feet and kept about 15 feet below the surface under a cork buoy. The riding sail should be set over the stern with the sheet hauled flat.

9. **How should the rudder be secured when heaved to under sea anchor and riding sail?**
   When a small vessel is hove to under a sea anchor, she will have sternway. Seas breaking against the stern will be hard on the rudder. Voss's remedy was to fasten two heel ropes to the upper back of the rudder blade, one to each side, and to haul them up and over the quarter, then place the rudder amidships, haul the heel ropes tight and fasten on deck. He recommended leaving the tiller unlashed.

10. **How will a small vessel drift when heaved to under sea anchor and riding sail?**
    Voss stated that the drift of a small vessel will be opposite to the direction of the wind. He stated categorically that the rate of drift would be about one-and-a-quarter miles per hour out at sea.

11. **What is the best way to cross surf breakers in a boat or launch?**
    Voss recommended deploying a sea anchor behind the stern, then approaching the shore straight on and slowly. He claimed this would work regardless of the propulsion of the vessel. He said that the stern will rise to meet the waves. He was able to publicly demonstrate this on a number of occasions.

12. **What gear should be carried in lifeboats aboard ships for the safety of "shipwrecked persons"?**
    Lifeboats are now the subject of international standards, but in Voss's day vessel masters were very lax about what should be included in their equipment. In those days crews setting to sea in boats could expect a long period on their own before rescue—there were no radio or emergency beacons. Voss managed the lifeboat on the west coast of Vancouver Island after his return to Victoria and formed strong positions on how it should be equipped and managed.

13. **How should a small boat be handled in a typhoon?**
    While sailing the *Sea Queen* in 1912, Voss encountered a typhoon at sea in the North Pacific. He recommended to a vessel master that if a typhoon is approaching, early preparation is essential.

These precautions include setting the sea anchor, unbending all sails except the riding sail, removing all gear on deck, unreeving the running gear, and lashing gaffs and booms to the deck. Since very few vessels now carry this type of gear, his recommendations are mostly no longer relevant.

14. **Is there any effect of oil on breaking seas in heavy gales, and what kind may be expected to give the best relief?**

The use of oil on heavy seas is a very controversial topic today. Obviously, deliberate dumping of contaminants at sea is unacceptable practice. Voss found that kerosene was too light and in small quantities was ineffective. A heavier fish oil, he found, was much more effective, even in small quantities. As soon as the oil hit the water, it spread over a large area and a breaking sea would crawl under the oil and lose its breaking top.

15. **Other miscellaneous principles that appear randomly in Voss's writings include the following:**[302]

Through experimentation, Voss found that when being towed across a bar, a sea anchor over the stern of the boat being towed, rowed or sailed will keep both the boat and the tug in control.[303]

Voss was opposed to undertaking a long voyage in a boat with a leak, large or small.

He recommended that the master of a small vessel must take early action to interpret the indication of an approaching storm and to position the vessel safely.

He recommended that a ketch, schooner-ketch, yawl or schooner-yawl are the best vessels in which to make an ocean cruise because they all carry a mizzen sail that eliminates the necessity of setting an extra riding sail when hove to.

Voss found that breaking wind waves in the open ocean become dangerous only when the vessel is driven through the water, and the faster she is travelling the more damage a sea is likely to inflict. Pooping seas are the most dangerous.

Captain John C. Voss, 1913.

Captain J.C. Voss in the first edition (1913) of The Venturesome Voyages of Captain Voss.

ENDNOTES

1   Letter from Norbert Schafer-Juhl to the Maritime Museum of British Columbia, January 10, 2005, *Tilikum* Fonds, Maritime Museum of British Columbia, Victoria, BC.

2   Letter from Karl Voss Kinkel to the Maritime Museum of British Columbia, September 6, 1979, *Tilikum* Fonds, Maritime Museum of British Columbia, Victoria, BC.

3   Norman Kenny Luxton, typescript of "Pacific Episode: An account of my part in the world-circling cruise of the canoe *Tilikum*," Luxton Fonds, Lux II/B.1.a/5, Archives of the Canadian Rockies, Banff, AB, 3.

4   John C. Voss, *The Venturesome Voyages of Captain Voss*, Sidney BC: Gray's Publishing Ltd., 1976, 210.

5   *Daily Colonist*, January 13 and 31, 1894.

6   *Daily Colonist*, January 18, 1895, 4.

7   Lillian Gustafson, *Memory of the Chemainus Valley: A History of People*, Recollections of Mrs. E. Ankel Jones, Chemainus BC: Chemainus Valley Historical Society, 1978, 195.

8   Lillian Gustafson, *Memory of the Chemainus Valley: A History of People*, Recollections of Mr. B.M. Cryer, Chemainus BC: Chemainus Valley Historical Society, 1978, 232.

9   Victoria Directory, 1904.

10   Letter from Dora Voss to John Voss, n.d., Luxton Fonds, Archives of the Canadian Rockies, Banff, AB

11   *The Victorian*, May 24, 1972.

12   *Daily Colonist*, October 1, 1905, 14.

13   *Daily Colonist*, March 4, 1906, 1.

14   Ibid., 2.

15   Joshua Slocum Society International website, "Slocum Awards," http://www.joshuaslocumsocietyintl.org/awards.htm#Voss, accessed July 8, 2018.

16   *Daily Colonist*, February 9, 1907.

17   *Daily Colonist*, October 9, 1906.

18   *Daily Colonist*, July 1, 1906.

19   *Daily Colonist*, July 7, 1906.

20   *Daily Colonist*, October 12, 1906.

21   *Daily Colonist*, October 9, 1906.

22   *Daily Colonist*, October 23, 1906.

23   *Daily Colonist*, October 9, 1906.

24   *Daily Colonist*, May 7, 1906, 7.

25   Tyne Built Ships: A History of Tyne Shipbuilders and the Ships That They Built, http://www.tynebuiltships.co.uk/M-Ships/miltonstuart1892.html, accessed July 8, 2018.

26   *Venturesome Voyages*, 262.

27   *Venturesome Voyages*, illustrations.

28 Letter from John Voss to Royal Geographical Society, July 25, 1914, *Tilikum* Fonds, Maritime Museum of British Columbia, Victoria, BC.

29 Death certificate for John C. Voss, in the Fonds of British Columbia Archives, B-07816.

30 Eleanor G. Luxton, ed., *Luxton's Pacific Crossing*, Gray's Publishing Ltd., Sidney, BC, 1971, 29.

31 John C. Voss, *The Venturesome Voyages of Captain Voss*, 1st ed., Tokyo (Kanda), Geiser & Gilbert Ltd. (Yokohama: Japan Herald Press, 1913), 296.

32 *Venturesome Voyages*, 6.

33 Ibid., 7.

34 *Daily Colonist*, July 13, 1899.

35 *Daily Colonist*, January 9, 1900.

36 *Winnipeg Free Press* history, www.winnipegfreepress.com/history/history.html, accessed June 18, 2018.

37 James A. Burns. "Edward Darbey, Taxidermy, and the Last Buffaloes," *Manitoba History* No. 63 (Spring 2010), www.mhs.mb.ca/docs/mb_history/63/lastbuffaloes.shtml.

38 *Luxton's Pacific Crossing*, 11.

39 Ibid., 19.

40 Ibid., 11.

41 Brett Bilyk, Montanna Mills, and Alex Weller, "The Crowd of Crazy Fools: The Gold Rush in British Columbia and the Yukon," Canadian Museum of Immigration at Pier 21, n.d., www.pier21.ca/research/immigration-history/the-gold-rush-in-british-columbia-and-the-yukon, accessed July 8, 2018.

42 *Luxton's Pacific Crossing*, 12.

43 Ibid., 52, footnote 15.

44 Ibid., 61.

45 Luxton, Letter from Village Island, BC, to his mother July 2, 1901, Luxton Fonds, LUX/I/A-Z, Archives of the Canadian Rockies, Banff, AB.

46 *Luxton's Pacific Crossing*, 23–24.

47 Luxton, Letter from Apia, Samoa, to father and mother, October 3, 1901, Luxton Fonds, LUX/I/A-Z, Archives of the Canadian Rockies, Banff, AB.

48 Luxton, Letter from Apia, Samoa, to father and mother, October 3, 1901, Luxton Fonds, LUX/I/A-Z, Archives of the Canadian Rockies, Banff, AB.

49 *Daily Colonist*, March 21, 1902, 3.

50 *Daily Colonist*, March 25, 1902, 3.

51 *Luxton's Pacific Crossing*, 17.

52 Ibid., 16–19.

53 Ibid., note inside the dust jacket; attributed to a conversation with the future publisher.

54 Luxton, *10,000 Miles in a Canoe*, Luxton Fonds, Lux/I/B1.7, Archives of the Canadian Rockies, Banff, AB.

55 Letter from John Voss to Norman Luxton, October 1, 1904, *Tilikum* Fonds, Maritime Museum of British Columbia, Victoria, BC.

56 *Luxton's Pacific Crossing*, 159.

57 Ibid., 13.

58 Norman Kenny Luxton, "Pacific Episode: An account of my part in the world-circling cruise of the canoe *Tilikum*," Luxton Fonds, Lux II/B.1.a/5, Archives of the Canadian Rockies, Banff, AB.

59 *Venturesome Voyages*, 47.

60 Voss manuscript (the original text of Voss's account), *Tilikum* Fonds, Maritime Museum of British Columbia, Victoria, BC, 1.

61 "Pacific Episode," 4.

62 Luxton, Letter Archives of the Canadian Rockies, Banff, AB. Letter to parents from the SS *Birksgate*, Suva, Fiji, October 26, 1901, Luxton Fonds, LUX/I/A-5, Archives of the Canadian Rockies, Banff, AB.

63 *Brisbane Telegraph*, Saturday, November 23, 1901.

64 *Sydney Daily Telegraph*, Wednesday, November 20, 1901, 7.

65 David Neel, *The Great Canoes: Reviving a Northwest Coast Tradition* (Vancouver, Canada: Douglas & McIntyre Ltd., 1995).

66 Nicol Warn, "Tilikum the Dugout Canoe," *The Resolution: Journal of the Maritime Museum of British Columbia*, no. 52 (Spring 2001).

67 *Venturesome Voyages*, 47.

68 *Luxton's Pacific Crossing*, 30.

69 Communication between Tad Roberts and John MacFarlane, October 16, 2017, Gabriola Island, BC.

70 Jack Fleetwood, "The *Tilikum*: excerpts from my diary," handwritten manuscript fragment, n.d., *Tilikum* Fonds, Maritime Museum of British Columbia, Victoria, BC.

71 Colonel J.W.D. Symonds, "Notes on Building of the *Tilikum*," 1965, *Tilikum* Fonds, Maritime Museum of British Columbia, Victoria, BC.

72 A.J. Helmcken, 1979, Notes from the Victoria City Archives, *Tilikum* Fonds, Maritime Museum of British Columbia, Victoria, BC.

73 Letter from Kelvin Dodson to the Maritime Museum of British Columbia, 1980, *Tilikum* Fonds, Maritime Museum of British Columbia, Victoria, BC.

74 Freeman, B.J.S., ed., *A Gulf Islands Patchwork: Some Early Events on the Islands*, recollections from Nellie Aitken Georgeson, Gulf Islands Branch BC Historical Association, 1961, 26.

75 *Daily Colonist*, July 8, 1951, 11.

76 Letter from the Maritime Museum of British Columbia to the Vancouver Maritime Museum, June 19, 1974, *Tilikum* Fonds, Maritime Museum of British Columbia, Victoria, BC.

77 Letter from Lottie Vollmer to the Maritime Museum of British Columbia, December 1, 1966, *Tilikum* Fonds, Maritime Museum of British Columbia, Victoria, BC.

78 *Luxton's Pacific Crossing*, 30.

79 Klaus Muenter, "Down by the Old Millstream," *Daily Free Press*, September 19, 1982 (Nanaimo), *Tilikum* Fonds, Maritime Museum of British Columbia, Victoria, BC.

80 Letter from A.C. Thorpe to *Daily Colonist* November 26, 1978, *Tilikum* Fonds, Maritime Museum of British Columbia, Victoria, BC.

81 Letter to Maritime Museum of BC, May 11, 1979, *Tilikum* Fonds, Maritime Museum of British Columbia, Victoria, BC.

82 Letter from A.C. Thorpe to *Daily Colonist* November 26, 1978, *Tilikum* Fonds, Maritime Museum of British Columbia, Victoria, BC.

83 Richard Henderson, *Singlehanded Sailing: The Experiences and Techniques of the Lone Voyagers* (Camden, me: International Marine Publishing Co., 1976), 143.

84 *Luxton's Pacific Crossing*, 31.

85 Manuscript fragment. *Tilikum* Fonds, Maritime Museum of British Columbia, Victoria.

86 Personal communication between Tad Roberts and John MacFarlane, October 28, 2017.

87 Voss manuscript (the original text of Voss's account), *Tilikum* Fonds, Maritime Museum of British Columbia, Victoria, BC, 1.

88 Letter from E.R. Hosking to Norman Luxton, St. Paul, MN, May 4, 1901, Luxton Fonds, LUX/I/A-Z, Archives of the Canadian Rockies, Banff, AB.

89 Luxton, *10,000 Miles in a Canoe*, Luxton Fonds, Lux/I/B1.7, Archives of the Canadian Rockies, Banff, AB.

90 Voss manuscript (original text), 1.

91 *Luxton's Pacific Crossing*, 32.

92 Ibid., 148.

93 Ibid., 23.

94 Ibid., 52.

95 Ibid., 36.

96 Ibid., 35, footnote 4.

97 *Daily Colonist*, June 6, 1901, 3.

98 *Luxton's Pacific Crossing*, 38.

99 Voss manuscript (original text), 2.

100 Ibid., 5.

101 *Luxton's Pacific Crossing*, 51.

102 *Daily Colonist*, June 13, 1901, 6.

103 *Luxton's Pacific Crossing*, 81.

104 Voss manuscript (original text), 163.

105 Voss manuscript (original text), 163-164.

106 Richard Henderson, *Singlehanded Sailing: The Experiences and Techniques of the Lone Voyagers* (Camden, ME: International Marine Publishing Co., 1976), 298.

107 *Luxton's Pacific Crossing*, 63-64.

108 *Luxton's Pacific Crossing*, 68.

109 The *Marine Digest*, June 28, 1941, 2.

110 *Venturesome Voyages*, 71.

111 *Luxton's Pacific Crossing*, 85.

112 Charles Wilkes. *Narrative of the United States Exploring Expedition During the Years 1838, 1839, 1840, 1841, 1842.* https://books.google.ca/books/about/ Narrative_of_the_United_States_Exploring.html?id=lbMNAAAAQAAJ&redir_ esc=y. Website viewed March 1, 2019.

113 *Venturesome Voyages*, 78.

114 Ibid.

115 "A.B. Donald Ltd.'s Last Trading Schooner: Tiare Taporo," https://www.imagesandwords.co.nz/tiare-taporo, accessed July 8, 2018.

116 Peter Benchley, "One of a Kind: Tahiti; Maison James Norman Hall," *New York Times Magazine*, May 2, 2004, http://www.nytimes.com/2004/05/02/magazine/one-of-a-kind-tahiti-maison-james-norman-hall.html

117 Voss manuscript (original text), 19.

118 Ibid.

119 Ibid., 26–28.

120 Note from Stan Raynor, September 3, 1984, *Tilikum* Fonds, Maritime Museum of British Columbia, Victoria, BC.

121 *Luxton's Pacific Crossing*, 135–137.

122 *Venturesome Voyages*, 96.

123 "SMS *Adler*, 1883 Kanonenboot," https://www.deutsche-schutzgebiete.de/sms_adler.htm, accessed July 17, 2018.

124 Voss manuscript (original text), 39.

125 Ibid., 41.

126 Flowers, Charles, Affidavit, October 14, 1901, Luxton Fonds, Archives of the Canadian Rockies, Banff, AB.

127 *Luxton's Pacific Crossing*, 148.

128 *Venturesome Voyages*, 100.

129 *Luxton's Pacific Crossing*, 150–153.

130 Voss manuscript (original text), 49.

131 *Luxton's Pacific Crossing*, 153–154.

132 *Venturesome Voyages*, 103.

133 *Daily Colonist*, November 11, 1901, 5.

134 Norman Kenny Luxton, Letter to mother and father from the S.S. *Birksgate*, Suva, Fiji, Luxton Fonds, Lux/I/A-5, Archives of the Canadian Rockies, Banff, AB.

135 *Luxton's Pacific Crossing*, 154.

136 Lars Bruzelius, "Hawaiian Isles," 1997, http://www.bruzelius.info/Nautica/Ships/Fourmast_ships/Hawaiian_Isles(1892).html. Accessed 2018.

137 Voss manuscript (original text), 51.

138 Ibid., 52.

139 Ibid.

140 Ibid., 53.

141 Telephone interviews between Tony Gooch and Jeanne Socrates with John MacFarlane, conducted in April 2018, Victoria, BC.

142 Voss manuscript (original text), 54–57.

143 Ibid.

144 Ibid., 57.

145 *Luxton's Pacific Crossing*, 155, footnote 70.

146 "Pacific Episode."

147 *Luxton's Pacific Crossing*, 145.

148 *Venturesome Voyages*, 145.

149 *Luxton's Pacific Crossing*, 155, footnote 70.

150 Ibid., 13.

151 Ibid., 62.

152 Letter from John Voss to Norman Luxton, October 1, 1904, *Tilikum* Fonds, Maritime Museum of British Columbia, Victoria, BC.

153 Voss manuscript (original text), 54.

154 Ibid., 55.

155 Ibid., 54.

156 Ibid., 1.

157 *Wagga Wagga Advertiser*, Wagga Wagga, NSW, March 15, 1902.

158 *Luxton's Pacific Crossing*, 158.

159 *Venturesome Voyages*, 116.

160 Voss manuscript (original text), 61.

161 The *Brisbane Telegraph*, Saturday, November 23, 1901.

162 Voss manuscript (original text), 64.

163 *Brisbane Telegraph*, Saturday, November 23, 1901.

164 Voss manuscript (original text), 65.

165 Ibid.

166 The *Launceston Examiner*, Monday, November 25, 1901.

167 *Luxton's Pacific Crossing*, 155.

168 Memorandum from the shipping master to Captain John Voss. Luxton Fonds, Archives of the Canadian Rockies.

169 *Daily Colonist*, November 30, 1901, 5.

170 *Venturesome Voyages*, 117.

171 Ibid., 117–118.

172 Norman Kenny Luxton, Letter to "Roy" from Sydney, NSW, Luxton Fonds, Lux/I/A-6, Archives of the Canadian Rockies, Banff, AB.

173 *Luxton's Pacific Crossing*, 156.

174 *Sydney Morning Herald*, December 28, 1901, 7.

175 Voss manuscript (original text), 72.

176 *Sydney Morning Herald*, December 12, 1901.

177 Voss manuscript (original text), 71.

178 J.C. Voss, Letter from Newcastle, NSW, to Norman K. Luxton, Sydney, NSW, Luxton Fonds, Lux/I/A-8, Archives of the Canadian Rockies, Banff, AB.

179 Voss manuscript (original text), 74.

180 Ibid.

181 Ibid., 77.

182 *Australian Star*, Sydney, NSW, Tuesday, March 11, 1902, 7.

183 Pilkington, *Memories of Sandy Point*, 1952, 160–164. *Tilikum* Fonds, Maritime Museum of British Columbia, Victoria, BC.

184 Ibid.

185 *Wagga Wagga Advertiser*, Wagga Wagga, NSW, March 15, 1902.

186 *Sydney and New South Wales Advertiser*, Saturday, May 20, 1902.

187 Voss manuscript (original text), 84.

188 *Sydney Morning Herald*, June 24, 1902.

189 *Daily Colonist*, June 12, 1902, 2.

190 *Ballarat Star*, Tuesday, July 1, 1902.

191 Voss manuscript (original text), 87.

192 *Melbourne Age*, Friday, November 21, 1902, 8.

193 Voss manuscript (original text), 88.

194 Ibid., 91.

195 *Adelaide Express and Telegraph*, January 7, 1903, 4.

196 *Adelaide Register*, Wednesday, January 7, 1903, 3.

197 *Adelaide Evening Journal,* Wednesday, December 17, 1902.

198 Voss manuscript (original text), 94.

199 Ibid.

200 *Adelaide Register*, December 29, 1902.

201 Voss manuscript (original text), 94.

202 Ibid., 96.

203 Ibid.

204 *Hobart Mercury*, Saturday, February 7, 1903, 4.

205 Voss manuscript (original text), 100.

206 In 1920 Chance purchased a first edition of Voss's book in Yokohama, which is now in the possession of John MacFarlane.

207 Voss manuscript (original text), 100, 104.

208 *Otago Witness*, no. 2560, April 8, 1903.

209 Voss manuscript (original text), 104.

210 Ibid., 105.

211 *Venturesome Voyages*, 296.

212 Ibid.

213 Ibid., 297.

214 *Luxton's Pacific Crossing*, 22.

215 Ibid., 76–77.

216 *Venturesome Voyages*, 265–266.

217 Ibid., 299–322.

218 Ibid., 161.

219 *Wellington Press*, vol. LX, no. 11558, April 15, 1903.

220 *Wellington Press*, no. 11590, May 22, 1903.

221 *Feilding Star*, May 16, 1903.

222 *Wanganui Chronicle*, Volume XXXXVII, no. 11953, May 23, 1903.

223 Voss manuscript (original text), 109.

224 Ibid.

225 Ibid., 111.

226 *Wanganui Chronicle* XXXXVII, no. 11976, June 20, 1903.

227 Voss manuscript (original text), 113.

228 Ibid., 115.

229 Ibid.

230 *Nelson Colonist*, Saturday, June 20, 1903.

231 Hilary Stace, "Webber, George William Wallace," *Dictionary of New Zealand Biography*, 1996, Te Ara: The Encyclopedia of New Zealand, https://teara.govt.nz/en/biographies/3w6/webber-george-william-wallace. Accessed June 18, 2018.

232 "The Story of Pelorus Jack," *The Encyclopedia of New Zealand*, https://teara.govt.nz/en/photograph/4696/the-story-of-pelorus-jack. Accessed July 18, 2018.

233 *New Zealand Herald*, Monday, July 20, 1903.

234 Royal New Zealand Yacht Squadron, "Past Commodores," http://www.rnzys.org.nz/the-squadron/past-commodores/. Accessed June 18, 2018.

235 Letter to Voss from Northern Roller Milling Company, July 25, 1903, MS2228, Collection of the British Columbia Archives, Victoria, BC.

236 *Taranaki Herald*, volume L, no. 12341, August 25, 1903.

237 *Nelson Evening Mail*, Vol XXXVIII, no. 66, March 31, 1904.

238 *Feilding Star*, Vol. XXV, no. 242, March 31, 1904.

239 *Wanganui Chronicle* XXXXVII, no. 12231, June 18, 1904.

240 *Venturesome Voyages*, 194.

241 Voss used several methods of reporting currency. We have presumed he was thinking of either Canadian dollars or English pounds, but in some cases the currency he is referring to is not clear.

242 *Venturesome Voyages*, 203.

243 Voss manuscript (original text), 130.

244 Ibid., 132.

245 *Venturesome Voyages*, 218.

246 Voss manuscript (original text), 137.

247 Ibid., 138.

248 Ibid., 139.

249 *Sydney Daily Telegraph*, Friday, January 29, 1904.

250 Webber, George, *The History of French Pass*, 1962, 9, *Tilikum* Fonds, Maritime Museum of British Columbia, Victoria, BC.

251 *Quarterly Bulletin of the South African Library* 49, no. 4, June 1995.

252 *Luxton's Pacific Crossing*, 26.

253 Ibid., 32.

254 Notes Maritime Museum of BC, June 30, 1972, *Tilikum* Fonds, Maritime Museum of British Columbia, Victoria, BC.

255 *Venturesome Voyages*, 236.

256 Voss manuscript (original text), 140.

257 *Venturesome Voyages*, 236.

258 *Luxton's Pacific Crossing*, 21.

259 Voss manuscript (original text), 144.

260 M. Williams, Letter to John Voss, May 23, 1904, MS2228, Collection of the British Columbia Archives, Victoria, BC.

261 *Venturesome Voyages*, 248.

262 Ibid., 250.

263 Ibid.

264 *Revelstoke Herald*, November 18, 1904.

265 *Keble's Margate and Ramsgate Gazette*, Saturday, September 10, 1904.

266 *Melbourne Leader*, Saturday, September 24, 1904, 22.

267 *Venturesome Voyages*, 260.

268 Voss manuscript (original text), 156.

269 *Daily Colonist*, February 19, 1905.

270 *Scotsman* and *Daily Record and Mail*, December 13–14, 1904.

271 *Islander*, June 22, 1980.

272 *Venturesome Voyages*, 247.

273 *Adelaide Express and Telegraph*, Thursday, January 28, 1904.

274 *Yachting Monthly*, 1908 and the *Daily Colonist*, June 13, 1971.

275 Letter from Leslie Bentley to the Maritime Museum of British Columbia, May 3, 1982, *Tilikum* Fonds, Maritime Museum of British Columbia, Victoria, BC.

276 Letter from Leslie Bentley to the Maritime Museum of British Columbia, June 1981.

277 Letter from Leslie Bentley to the Maritime Museum of British Columbia, September 1981.

278 Uncredited newspaper article clipping, n.d., *Tilikum* Fonds, Maritime Museum of British Columbia, Victoria, BC.

279 Harry T. Barnes appears to have held several positions over the considerable time he was involved with Captain Voss: manager of Rithet's Consolidated Co., manager of the Victoria Publicity Bureau and keeper of Voss's transcript. It is not clear whether these positions were consecutive or simultaneous.

280 *Daily Colonist*, April 30, 1942, 8.

281 *British Columbia Historical Quarterly,* ed. W. Kaye Lamb, April 1937, http://www.library.ubc.ca/archives/pdfs/bchf/bchq_1937_2. pdf#search=%22tillicum%20illicum%22.

282 Martyn Sherwood, *The Voyage of the Tai-Mo-Shan* (London, UK: Geoffrey Bles, 1935), 91.

283 *British Columbia Historical Quarterly*, October 1943, 299. http://www.library. ubc.ca/archives/pdfs/bchf/bchq_1943_4.pdf.

284 Letter from G.C. Carl to J.W.D. Symons, January 29, 1965, *Tilikum* Fonds, Maritime Museum of British Columbia, Victoria, BC.

285 Honouring Our Past – Dr. Frank Calder, http://www.nisgaanation.ca/news/ honouring-our-past-dr-frank-calder. Accessed August 10, 2018.

286 Letter from Caroline Kuhn (née Voss) to the Maritime Museum of British Columbia, February 6, 1966, *Tilikum* Fonds, Maritime Museum of British Columbia, Victoria, BC.

287 *Luxton's Pacific Crossing*, 15.

288 Letter from USCG to Maritime Museum of BC, December 17, 1977, *Tilikum* Fonds, Maritime Museum of British Columbia, Victoria, BC.

289 Letter from Maritime Museum of BC to USCG, January 6, 1978, *Tilikum* Fonds, Maritime Museum of British Columbia, Victoria, BC.

290 *Venturesome Voyages*, 232.

291 *Daily Colonist*, August 4, 1912.

292 *Venturesome Voyages*, 272–273.

293 Ibid., 278.

294 *Brisbane Courier*, Saturday, June 6, 1914.

295 *Brisbane Courier*, Tuesday, May 26, 1914.

296 *Cairns Post*, Monday, June 29, 1914, 4.

297 *Brisbane Courier*, Saturday, July 11, 1914.

298 *Brisbane Daily Standard*, Monday, July 20, 1914, 5.

299 *Cairns Post*, Wednesday, November 4, 1914, 2.

300 Letter from Carl Voss Kinkel to the Maritime Museum of British Columbia, September 6, 1979, *Tilikum* Fonds, Maritime Museum of British Columbia, Victoria, BC.

301 *Venturesome Voyages*, 299–322.

302 Voss manuscript (original text), 157-163.

303 Ibid., 106.

304 The distance of 12,300 miles in this title refers to the distance Voss had travelled up to that point, not the total distance of his voyage.

305 Letter from A.C. Thorpe to *Daily Colonist* November 26, 1978, *Tilikum* Fonds, Maritime Museum of British Columbia, Victoria, BC.

GLOSSARY

binnacle
> The stand that houses a compass. In the *Tilikum* it would have been made of wood so as not to affect the accuracy of the compass, and would have contained a small oil lamp so the compass could be read at night. In a small sailing vessel, it is portable for moving into positions useful to the helmsman.

boom
> A spar, joined with a hinge to the mast, to which the lower part of a sail is attached.

captain
> A rank in the navy; also, a position in a civilian vessel. More formally, it is the master of the vessel, who would be qualified as a master mariner. While holding this position in a ship, this person is addressed as "Captain."

cockpit
> The area at the stern of the vessel where the helmsman and the crew are normally located while operating a yacht sailing vessel.

drogue
> A piece of ship's gear that attaches to the stern whose drag is used to slow the boat in heavy weather to keep the hull perpendicular to the waves. It prevents a vessel from broaching or going end over end in large waves.

gimbals
> A pivoted support that allows a compass or a table (for example) to swing free and level in spite of the motion of a ship.

heave to
> To stop progress through the water either by turning into the wind or by lowering sails.

into the wind
> When a vessel is pointing directly into the wind it does not make forward progress and can stop or even go backwards.

jib
> A small triangular sail closest to the bow.

knot
> A rate of speed measured in nautical miles per hour. Travelling one nautical mile in an hour is equal to a knot.

laid to
> Another term to describe heaving to.

main sail
> The sail closest to the rudder. Often the largest sail, but in the *Tilikum* all three were of equal size.

master mariner
> A qualification achieved through a combination of service and examination.

mate
> The second in command of a vessel. In a crew of two the mate is automatically the person who is not the master or captain.

nautical mile
> A nautical mile is equal to 1.852 kilometres.

oil bag
> A canvas bag permeated with oil and dragged in the sea. It is thought that oil is useful to smooth the effect of heavy seas by reducing breaking waves. The oil weighs down the water, keeping the wind from building up the size of the waves.

pratique
> A licence given to a ship to enter port on the assurance given from the captain to the port authorities that she is free from contagious disease.

schooner
> A two- or three- (or more) masted vessel whose sails are all aligned fore and aft (no sails carried on yardarms). Usually the after-mast is taller than the foremast. The *Tilikum* was rigged as a three-masted schooner with all masts the same height.

sea anchor
> A cone-shaped device that is towed (usually from the bow) in the water. The drag created by a sea anchor keeps a vessel from drifting too quickly. For a more detailed description of Voss's patented sea anchor, see page 75.

sextant
> A navigational instrument used to measure the angle between the horizon and the sun, moon or stars. For many centuries it was the chief tool for navigation at sea.

sloop
> A small, single-masted vessel, usually a sailing yacht.

storm jib
> A small version of the triangular sail carried on the bow. It is smaller because it is safer to carry in the high winds of a storm.

tack (of a sail)
The place on a sail where the boom and mast connect.
tacking
Tacking a boat is making a change of direction that moves the bow from one side through the eye of the wind to the other side to go in a new direction.
to turn turtle
When a vessel has flipped upside down in the water.

REFERENCES

BOOKS

Compton, Nic. *Notable Boats: Small Craft, Many Adventures.* New York: Rizzoli, 2017. With illustrations by Peter Scott.

Freeman, B.J.S., ed. *A Gulf Islands Patchwork: Some Early Events on the Islands,* Gulf Islands Branch BC Historical Association, 1961.

Gustafson, Lillian. *Memory of the Chemainus Valley: A History of People.* Chemainus, BC: Chemainus Valley Historical Society, 1978.

Henderson, Richard. *Singlehanded Sailing: The Experiences and Techniques of the Lone Voyagers.* Camden, ME: International Marine Publishing Co., 1976.

Jupp, Ursula, ed. *Deep Sea Stories from the Thermopylae Club.* Victoria, BC: Jupp, 1971.

----- ed. *Home Port Victoria.* Victoria, BC: Jupp, 1967.

Neel, David. *The Great Canoes: Reviving a Northwest Coast Tradition.* Vancouver, BC: Douglas & McIntyre; University of Washington Press, 1995.

Sherwood, Martyn. *The Voyage of the Tai-Mo-Shan.* London, UK: Geoffrey Bles, 1935.

Stewart, Hilary. *Cedar: Tree of Life to the Northwest Coast Indians.* Madeira Park, BC: Douglas and McIntyre, 1995.

Tompkins, John B., ed. *A Voyage of Pleasure: The Log of Bernard Gilboy's Transpacific Cruise in the Boat "Pacific," 1882–1883.* Cambridge, MD: Cornell Maritime Press, 1956.

Voss, J.C. *The Canoe Tilikum.* BCARS #91-32222, Call# E D V93. This is a copy of Captain Voss's narrative from his original manuscript written in a number of school notebooks, now lost. Before their loss they were typed for Harry T. Barnes, manager of the Victoria Publicity Bureau and one of the Victoria officials responsible for bringing the *Tilikum* back to Victoria from England. BC Archives transcript copied verbatim from Mr. Barnes's transcript, January 1944.

----- *The Venturesome Voyages of Captain Voss: Around the World in the Tilikum, 1901*. Sidney, BC: Gray's Publishing Ltd., 1976. With an introduction by Frederick E. Grubb.

----- *The Voyage of the Indian War Canoe, Tilikum, Across the Pacific from Canada to Australia: Being the First Portion of the Voyage Round the World, by Captain Voss, in the Smallest Boat that has Ever Crossed the Pacific Ocean, Travelling a Distance of 12,300 Miles*.[304] Invercargill, New Zealand: McConechy and Joyce, 1903. In the collection of the library of the University of British Columbia, G530 V786.

MAGAZINE AND JOURNAL ARTICLES

Anon. "Tilikum." *The Graphic* magazine (September 10, 1904).

Begent, Simon. "Lost at Sea: Walter Louis Begent." *The Resolution: The Journal of the Maritime Museum of British Columbia* (Spring 2001).

Champion, George. "The Fascinating Voyage of the *Tilikum*." *Journal of the Royal Australian Historical Society* 91, no. 1 (June 1, 2005): S11.

Chandler, Graham. "Around the World by Canoe." *The Beaver* 81, no. 2 (April/May 2001).

Clark, Stanley. "He Sailed a Canoe Round the World." *The Star Weekly Magazine* (May 17, 1958).

Das, Robbert. "*Tilikum's* Amazing Voyage." *Sail* 39, no. 1 (January 1, 2008): 66.

Dickie, Francis. "The Truth about Voss." *Seacraft Magazine* 23, no. 3 (October 1959).

Drent, Jan. "*Tilikum's* 34,759 Nautical Mile Voyage in Waterlines." *Newsletter of the Maritime Museum of British Columbia* (undated).

Fisher, John. "Tillicum [sic] Tale." John Fisher Reports, transcript from the Canadian Broadcasting Corp. (January 17, 1953).

Gillard, W.S. "Round the World in a Canoe: The Voyage of Captain Voss." *World Wide Magazine* 1904.

Howard, Sidney. "The Adventures of Captain Voss." *Shipping Wonders of the World*, Pt. 35 (September 29, 1936): 1092.

"John Voss et *Tilikum*: Une Pirogue Autour du Monde." *Le Chasse-Maree Histoire at Ethnologie Maritime*, no. 70 (February 1993), Paris, France.

Locke, Ralphine. "*Tilikum's* First Mate." *The Resolution: The Journal of the Maritime Museum of British Columbia* (Spring 2001).

Luxton Fonds. Luxton/II/ B.1.a/11. Oversize clippings. Archives of the Canadian Rockies, Banff, AB.

MacFarlane, John. "A Venturesome Voyage." *The Resolution: The Journal of the Maritime Museum of British Columbia* (Spring 2001).

Malherbe, V. C. "Forty Thousand Miles in a Canoe: The *Tilikum*." *Quarterly*

Bulletin of the South African Library (June 1, 1995): 198.

Palinurus. "Two Men in a Boat: The *Tilikum* in New Zealand Waters." *New Zealand Marine News: Journal of the New Zealand Ship and Marine Society* 36, no. 3 (1986).

Ross, W. Gillies. "The Travels of *Tilikum*." *The American Neptune* (January 1968).

"Tilikum." *Ripley's Believe It or Not!*, internationally syndicated newspaper column (April 28, 1942).

Warn, Nicol. "*Tilikum*—the Dugout Canoe." *The Resolution: The Journal of the Maritime Museum of British Columbia* (Spring 2001).

Warrender, Susan. "Mutiny!" *The Resolution: The Journal of the Maritime Museum of British Columbia* (Spring 2001).

INTERNET ARTICLES

Begent Family Website. Simon Begent biography: "The Voyage of the *Tilikum*: Walter L. Begent is Drowned; Captain Accused of Throwing Him Overboard." http://www.begent.org/voss.htm. Accessed June 16, 2018.

Bilyk, Brett, Montanna Mills, and Alex Weller. "The Crowd of Crazy Fools: The Gold Rush in British Columbia and the Yukon." Canadian Museum of Immigration at Pier 21. http://www.pier21.ca/research/immigration-history/the-gold-rush-in-british-columbia-and-the-yukon. Accessed July 8, 2018.

Captain Voss. http://www.telusplanet.net/public/albear1/voss2.html. Accessed June 16, 2018.

Cool Antarctica. "Horace Edgar Buckridge (1877–1961) Biographical notes." http://www.coolantarctica.com/Antarctica%20fact%20file/History/biography/Buckridge-Horace-Edgar.php. Accessed June 16, 2018.

Holm, Don. Chapter 2, "The Venturesome Viking." In *The Circumnavigators: Small Boat Voyagers of Modern Times*. New York: Prentice-Hall, 1974. http://www.stexboat.com/books/circumnav/ci_02.htm Accessed July 8, 2018.

Püttger-Conradt, Armin. "Johannes Claus Voss: Mit dem Einbaum übers Meer." August 28, 2007. https://www.shz.de/459256. Accessed June 17, 2018.

Thres, Mark. "Captain Voss and Tilikum: The circumnavigation of the world in a 38-foot long first nation dug-out canoe." Canvey Island. org: Canvey Community Archive. http://www.canveyisland.org/page/captain_voss_and_tilikum. Accessed June 16, 2018.

Tilikum (Boat). https://en.wikipedia.org/wiki/Tilikum_(boat).

INDEX